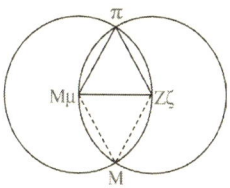

Ames | Berlin | Gainesville | Tokyo

Resonance in the Intersection of Music and Architecture

Volume 1

Mikesch W. Muecke
Miriam S. Zach
            Editors

First published by Culicidae Architectural Press
918 5th Street
Ames, IA 50010
USA

Distributed in North America by Lulu.com

RESONANCE: ESSAYS ON THE INTERSECTION OF MUSIC AND ARCHITECTURE. Copyright © 2007 Selection, introduction, and editorial matter: Mikesch Muecke and Miriam Zach; for their respective individual chapters: the contributors Garth Ancher, Kim Chow-Morris, Jim Lutz, Kourosh Mahvash, Galia Roe, John Sands, Sven Sterken, and Yu Zhang. All rights reserved. No part of this book may be reproduced in any form by any electronic or mechanized means (including photocopying, recording, or information storage and retrieval) without written permission except in the case of brief quotations embodied in critical articles and reviews. For information address Culicidae Architectural Press, 918 5th Street, Ames, IA 50010, USA.

Every effort has been made to seek permission to reproduce those images whose copyright does not reside with Culicidae Architectural Press, and we are grateful to the individuals and institutions who have assisted in this task. Any omissions are entirely unintentional, and the details should be addressed to Culicidae Architectural Press.

Library of Congress Control Number: 2007901542

ISBN-10: 1-84728-337-3
ISBN-13: 978-1-84728-337-5

Design and layout by 918studio.com © 2007
Cover design by polytekton.com © 2007

Table of Contents

Mikesch Muecke and Miriam Zach
    Introduction   5

Sven Sterken
    Music as an Art of Space: Interactions between Music and Architecture in the Work of Iannis Xenakis   21

Kourosh Mahvash
    Site + Sound : Space   53

Galia Hanoch-Roe
    Scoring the Path: Linear Sequences in Music and Space   77

Kim Chow-Morris
    Rhythm of the Streets: Sounding the Structures of the City   145

Jim Lutz
    Transpositions: Architecture as Instrument/ Instrument as Architecture   169

Yu Zhang
    Altar and Studio: Musical Design in 18th-century Chinese Architecture   191

John Sands
    Transgressing Boundaries: Considering a Societal Function of Music and Architecture Through Markus Pernthaler's Helmut-List-Halle   213

Garth Ancher
    Translating the Intangible Qualities of Miles Davis' Jazz Rock Fusion into Architecture   231

Mikesch Muecke and Miriam Zach
    Resonance: Music and Architecture   251

Author Biographies   273

Index   283

...to the daffodils, rabbits, and clouds...

Mikesch Muecke and Miriam Zach

Introduction

The origin of the word 'resonance' goes back to the Latin *resonantia*, meaning 'echo', which derives from the Greek ēkhō, related to ēkhē, 'a sound' that, to be heard, requires a resonating space. This book is based on a particular resonance—perhaps the one with the rather romantic definition of the figurative meaning in astronomy (see Figure 1)—that made us look with our complementary expert knowledge beyond the proper horizon of both music and architecture to find that single primary body around which both fields might revolve. Let

res•o•nance |'rezənəns|
noun
the quality in a sound of being deep, full, and reverberating : *the resonance of his voice.*
- figurative the ability to evoke or suggest images, memories, and emotions : *the concepts lose their emotional resonance.*
- Physics the reinforcement or prolongation of sound by reflection from a surface or by the synchronous vibration of a neighboring object.
- Mechanics the condition in which an object or system is subjected to an oscillating force having a frequency close to its own natural frequency.
- Physics the condition in which an electric circuit or device produces the largest possible response to an applied oscillating signal, esp. when its inductive and its capacitative reactances are balanced.
- Physics a short-lived subatomic particle that is an excited state of a more stable particle.
- Astronomy the occurrence of a simple ratio between the periods of revolution of two bodies about a single primary.
- Chemistry the state attributed to certain molecules of having a structure that cannot adequately be represented by a single structural formula but is a composite of two or more structures of higher energy.

ORIGIN late Middle English : from Old French, from Latin ***resonantia*** *'echo,'* from ***resonare*** *'resound'* (see RESONANT).

Figure 1: Definition of 'resonance'. From *Dictionary*, version 1.0.1, Apple Computer, 2005.

us speculate then, for a moment, on the genesis of this work and its content, keeping in mind that vision and hearing, even into the past, are just like its projection into the future, never perfect.

Borrowing from Arthur Koestler (1905-1983) who suggests that "creativity arises as a result of the intersection of two quite different frames of reference"[1]—in this case ways of consciously viewing and hearing our environment—the genealogy of this creative project can be traced back to 1980 when we, the editors, first met at a Sitar concert in the appropriately named venue *Crossroads*—a private residence operated by two elderly ladies as a salon for intercultural events—located on Blackstone Avenue in Hyde Park near the University of Chicago (Figure 2). It was a cold January night when we met at this creative intersection of music and architecture, and we both seemed to need the company of the other, not realizing perhaps in this early stage of our relationship that there would be much more to this intersection of sound in a space than we could imagine.

Preparation:[2] 1980-1991

Music and architecture tend to work in slow-motion for us. After that first fortuitous intersection in Chicago we moved to Germany and after several fits and starts found ourselves living in a rural commune. Our spatial relations in this place of sharing and privacy describe perhaps best how our understanding

Figure 2: Photograph of *Crossroads* house in 1980. The proprietors have now retired, and the building has been converted into a private residence. Photo by Mikesch Muecke.

of music and architecture related at that time to each other. By 1985, just before we moved back to the United States, we shared a single circus trailer named Da Capo (Figure 3) for our residence but our professional spaces were clearly divided. Music Miriam found her home in a renovated construction trailer named Al Fine (Figure 4) while Architecture Mikesch worked—together with Painting—in the untitled 'studio,' just like Al Fine this was a properly chopped construction trailer (Figure 5). It took us another six years to focus our mind on the problem at hand while we both finished advanced degrees in our respective fields—working adjacent to each other—intersecting at lunch time for a quick repast under the palm trees on the University of Florida campus where the music and architecture buildings sit next to each other in polite proximity.

Figure 3: View of circus trailer Da Capo on the grounds of the commune in 1982. Photo by Mikesch Muecke.

Figure 4: View of the music trailer Al Fine, which contains a piano for giving music lessons, in 1982. Photo by Mikesch Muecke.

Figure 5: View of studio trailer in the winter of 1982. The trailer contains the basics of visual creation: a table for drawing, an easel for painting, and a stove to keep things toasty. Photo by Mikesch Muecke.

Incubation: 1991-2003

During the next twelve years we marinated in our individual disciplines while internalizing what we knew then about music and architecture into our respective unconscious, and nothing appeared to be happening for the duration. However, we also advanced in our specific professional fields, earning Ph.D.s while teaching and practicing full time at different universities.

Intimation: 2003-2004

In 2003 necessity became the mother of our intersection. We needed to renovate our apartment in Florida to make it more accessible for Miriam's mother who had had a stroke in 1994, requiring a walker to get around. We had a feeling that the renovation might turn into an opportunity to explore the adjacent boundaries of music and architecture.³ During the modernization of the foyer and kitchen we also replaced the carpet in the living room-*cum*-music studio with solid pecan flooring, discovering in the process that the room had gained a voice. The wood floor in combination with the newly exposed concrete ceiling of the kitchen created a continuous and sonorous environment for house music, giving the piano and harpsichord in the space a liveliness we had not experienced before.

Illumination: 2005-2006

We took this creative symbiosis to the academy in 2005 when we combined two courses— an architecture option studio at Iowa State University and an honors seminar at the University of Florida—for a few weeks in the Spring semester. Our respective students collaborated on three projects. The first was a Sensory Garden (initially a Garden for the Blind) to be located behind Hume Hall, the honors residence at the University of Florida. The second project was a sound space for a hearing-impaired person at Crescent Beach on the Atlantic coast, and for the third studio project we asked our students to design a Music and Architecture Research Institute (M.A.R.I.) located on a barge that would travel between Davenport, Iowa and Cedar Key, Florida.[4] Out of this academic collaboration grew our session proposal for the international conference Architecture | Music | Acoustics in Toronto, and in the Fall of 2005 Colin Ripley from the Department of Architectural Sciences at Ryerson University invited us to be session chairs for the topic Intersections of Music and Architecture at the conference that he and several other colleagues had organized for the Summer of 2006.[5]

Verification: 2006-2007

The conference then led to the final phase of this creative process where we verified, elaborated, and applied the ideas about the intersection of music and architecture to this larger project. While participating in the amazing range of papers and discussions at the conference in Toronto, we wondered aloud about making some of the essays—from our group of fifteen presenters— available to a wider audience, and the idea for this book was born. Eight of the essays presented originally at the Ryerson conference are available in this first volume (plus a new essay by the editors), and we plan a second volume to be published with additional authors in 2008.

Contents

The book can be conceptually divided into a four-part composition:

1 In the first section three authors—Sven Sterken, Kourosh Mahvash, and Galia Hanoch-Roe—lay the historical and theoretical groundwork for issues related to the intersection of music and architecture. Sven Sterken explores the intellectual and phenomenological resonance in the work of the architect, engineer, and composer Iannis Xenakis who, according to Benoît Gibson was one of the "first modern composers to foresee the need for a broader approach to music, one that would not limit itself to musical tradition."[6] In the process Sterken discovers how Xenakis' diverse skill sets in each field can advance the creative work at the intersection of sound and space, aural expression and architectural form through an approach that combines the arts with the sciences without losing the identities of either.

Kourosh Mahvash follows Sterken with a paper in which he emphasizes pedagogy, eschewing the visual at the expense of the sonic while he elaborates on the theory and practice of the soundscape maven R. Murray Schafer, and the sound artist and architect Bernhard Leitner. Mahvash develops in his investigation a pedagogical approach to teaching architecture and design that uses collaborative techniques promoted by both Schafer and Leitner in order to create a qualitative sense of sound awareness in his students.

The next essay by Galia Hanoch-Roe advances through her research the idea that the linearity of perception in music and space can be harnessed to develop a new notation system for representing and developing designs that bridge the arts from music via architecture and landscape architecture to urban design. She borrows from such diverse sources as Kevin Lynch, Walter J. Ong, Philip Thiel, Edward Hall, Claudia Mausner, Karlheinz Stockhausen, John Cage, Lawrence Halprin, Earl Brown, Rudolph and Joan Benesh, and others to create an instrumental tapestry of ideas that lead to a holistic scoring/notation system for designers.

2 Kim Chow-Morris and Jim Lutz follow this three-part introduction with a duet of essays. Chow-Morris describes the interdisciplinary translation of an architectural environment into music, using the city of Toronto, and here more specifically Queen Street, as a sounding board for her work. In collaboration with Ryerson architecture professor Ian MacBurnie and several other students she chronicles the transformation of the design/composition process during which the visual reading of the city yields to measured soundscape that considers the diverse migration and population patterns of Toronto, and codes these into the instrumentation of the musical performance piece. Meanwhile, in the second essay, Jim Lutz explores the dialectics of instrument and architecture, uncovering

in his research the limits of good instrument design by such big-name architects as Hans Hollein, Richard Meier, and Daniel Libeskind. He also expands the reading of architecture-as-instrument by examining the Experience Music Project and the Disney Concert Hall by Frank Gehry, and ends his essay by sounding the historical and musical narratives of Santiago Calatrava's bridge designs in the Netherlands.

3 Another three-part section of case studies continues the composition with papers by Yu Zhang, John Sands, and Garth Ancher. Yu Zhang investigates the intersection of musical designs with eighteenth-century Chinese architecture, specifically the Altar of Heaven (1749) and the Zither Rhythm Studio (1757) both of which were built under the direction of Emperor Qianlong. Zhang connects these spatial projects with a larger system of tonal measurement, *huangzhong*, and the 'sage-king' notion of the emperor, showing how architecture can be a representational tool for the aesthetic and political aspirations of a dynasty. Musician and composer John Sands, meanwhile, finds a new metaphor of the concert hall-as-factory embodied in Markus Pernthaler's *Helmut-List-Halle* which was recently built in Graz, Austria. Sands reads the building against the works of two early twentieth-century figures—the architect Frank Lloyd Wright and his design for the suburban utopia of *Broadacre*, and the musicologist Heinrich Besseler and his theory of *Gebrauchsmusik*—arguing that both projects

converge through a reconceptualization of functionalism in Pernthaler's design of the experimental music performance space in Graz. Finally the Australian architect Garth Ancher chronicles his design for the Launceston School of Contemporary music in Tasmania by adopting the tools of Miles Davis' jazz fusion—reinvention, resourcefulness, and adaptation—as design generators, and creating a contemporary space for music experimentation using high-tech materials and communicative projection technology.

4 In the finale section Mikesch Muecke and Miriam Zach complete the composition with a musing on resonance, tracing the reverberation between music and architecture through the centuries, including the Paleolithic rock paintings in Lascaux, the physical and spiritual experience of Peter Zumthor's Thermal Baths in Vals, Switzerland, and ending with a number of contemporary case studies that create new venues for a collaborative practice between music and architecture.

In retrospect we realized that a book like this requires a divergent thought mode—the creative generation of multiple answers to a set problem—a kind of thinking outside the box rather than convergent thinking whose aim is a single, correct solution to a problem. In 1994 Marcos Novak conceded that architecture, with respect to music, had not yet gone beyond its own boundaries when he wrote his essay *Breaking the Cage* in Elizabeth Martin's book *Architecture as a Translation of Music*. However, we hope that the essays in *this* book, taken as a whole, transform the one-way street from music to architecture—implied in that earlier publication title—into a two-way boulevard of open communication and creation.

Mikesch Muecke and Miriam Zach, editors
Gainesville, Florida, February 2007

Endnotes

[1] Koestler, Arthur. *The Act of Creation*. (New York: Macmillan, 1964).

[2] In a convergence of the private and the professional we will borrow from Graham Wallas (1858-1932) who in *Art of Thought* (1926) discusses a model of creative process with five stages: Preparation, Incubation, Intimation, Illumination, and Verification.

[3] See misumiwaDesign. *Accessible Design: Kitchen*. (Ames: Culicidae Architectural Press, 2005). In 2004 we renovated the bath suite in the same apartment [see misumiwaDesign. *Accessible Design: Bathroom*. (Ames: Culicidae Architectural Press, 2006)] without linking both fields explicitly.

[4] See http://www.mikeschdesign.com

[5] The conference coincided with the larger two-week-long event named soundaXis that was organized by the New Music Arts Projects in Toronto. As we found out during the conference, Colin is also a member of the soundaXis Advisory Board, along with Murray Schafer and several other famous composers, researchers, and musicians. We were lucky enough to attend some of the superb soundaXis performances, lectures, and installations that seemed to be taking place everywhere in the city at that time.

[6] See http://www.uoguelph.ca/~jharley/Gibson/Gibson.html, accessed January 15, 2007.

List of Figures

All figures courtesy of polytekton.

Sven Sterken

Music as an Art of Space: Interactions between Music and Architecture in the Work of Iannis Xenakis*

Introduction

The speculations about the relation between music and architecture are probably as old as both arts themselves. Generally speaking, they occur on two levels: the intellectual and the phenomenological. The first interpretation dates back to ancient Greek thought and is linked with the problems of form and structure. The most elaborate paradigm here is the theory of 'harmonic proportions'. This synthesis of rationalism and metaphysics knew its peak in the Renaissance when numerous architects and composers tried to shape architectural and musical form according to the same numerical principles. In the second interpretation, originating from 18th-century aesthetic relativism, the expressive quality of art is central. Here, beauty does not arise from the intricate structure of the work of art, but from its aesthetic effect and its immersive power. As Paul Valéry states in *Eupalinos ou l'architecte*, in this context, music and architecture differ from the other arts in their capacity to surround man entirely.[1] This immersive quality derives from the fact that both arts deal with space.

In both interpretations the link between music and architecture has less to do with common features than with the existence of a third element that acts as an intermediate between both fields: mathematical proportions in the first case; the concept of space in the second. Both aspects of the music-architecture relationship have found a contemporary assimilation in the work of Iannis Xenakis (1922–2001). Throughout his career, Xenakis was active as an architect and a composer, building a substantial record of research and production in both fields.[2] Nevertheless, despite one of his books being entitled *Musique Architecture*, he has hardly conceptualized the relation between both arts on the theoretical level, nor has he clearly pointed out a common method in his dealing with musical and architectural form.[3] This paper discusses precisely these aspects of Xenakis' work. Situated within the theoretical perspective mentioned above, the analysis will be carried out on the basis of a number of Xenakis' works in both fields, supported by fragments of interviews and writings. It is our contention that in his early work, Xenakis approached both music and architecture from a scientific and mathematical perspective. As a consequence, his musical compositions and built work from this period stem from similar formal concepts and methods. In his later work, Xenakis' approach has become more pragmatic, using space as a means to articulate the complexity of the musical language and enhance the sensuous experience of sound. His elaborate proposal for a 'City of Music' in Paris can be considered the climax of this evolution. Thus, a shift will be revealed from an abstract, conceptual relation between music and architecture, to a more sensual and practical approach to sound and space.

From Numerical Proportions to the 'Transfer of Models'

While becoming acquainted with architecture in Le Corbusier's studio (1947–1959), Xenakis studied musical composition with the French composer Olivier Messiaen (1908–1992). Rather than teaching his pupil the traditional techniques of the art, the latter advised Xenakis to seek musical inspiration in his Greek roots, his engineering background and his work as an architect.[4] The young composer took this advice almost literally: his first pieces rely to a great extent on two central elements of his then daily routine, namely the *Modulor* and the use of graph paper. While he used the first tool to organize time in a rational way, he recurred to the second to shape pitch envelopes and musical form. Based on the Fibonacci series (1,2 3, 5, 8, 13, ...) and the Golden Section, the *Modulor* is a metric system introduced by Le Corbusier in 1950 at the height of an important neo-Pythagorean wave in Western European culture.[5] It was hailed as a means to settle any problem of form not only in architecture, but in art in general. Familiar with the Golden Section from classical Greek architecture and encouraged by Messiaen's comments as well as Le Corbusier's many references to music in the *Modulor*, Xenakis must have thought it a quite logical step to experiment with similar numerical proportions in musical composition. Indeed, in 1952, he created an 'aural picture' of the series of Fibonacci by means of a magnetic tape with blips at intervals defined by the Golden Section. He assimilated this experience in his orchestra piece *Le Sacrifice* (1953), constructing the entire musical edifice on the basis of a melodic series of 8 pitches, associated with a scale of 8 durations whose values (in 16ths) were determined by the first 8 numbers of the Fibonacci series (Figure 1).[6] The musical development in this piece derives from the constant permutation of both sets of values. Contrary to traditional Western music, where the pulse of time is an externally determined, fixed element, in this work, it varies throughout the piece, and thus becomes intimately linked with the development of the musical material. On the auditory level however, this rigid algorithmic approach was not really successful, the simple permutation of two sets of values being too simple a system to keep the ear's attention.

Xenakis' research into rhythmic patterns proved very useful for the design of the famous 'undulating glass panes' that cover the façade of the Monastery of La Tourette. Paradoxically, this celebrated feature originated as an economical answer to a practical problem. In order to take advantage of the magnificent view over the valley, Le Corbusier considered the Western façade of the

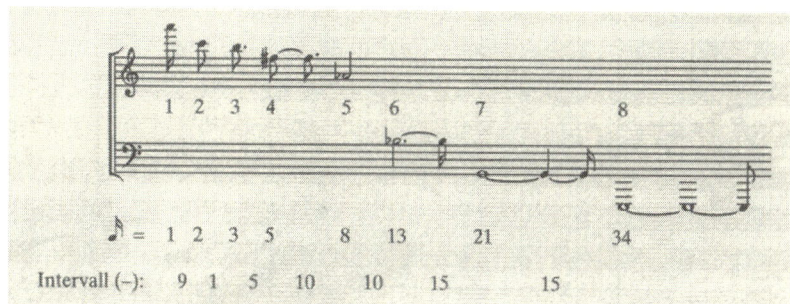

Figure 1: Iannis Xenakis, *Le Sacrifice* (1953). Source: André Baltensperger, *Iannis Xenakis und die Stochastische Musik. Komposition im Spannungsfeld von Architektur und Mathematik* (Bern: Haupt Verlag, 1996): 231.

convent as a "windowed outer skin." The restricted budget however did not allow for expensive large glass panes. The solution for the problem came from Chandigarh: there, Indian masons realized large glass partitions by piling up smaller glass panes of varying height one on top of the other between regularly spaced vertical casings. Realizing that an endless repetition of identical glass panes would result in a dull façade, Le Corbusier asked Xenakis to play with the distances between the concrete casings so as to give the façade an asymmetrical appearance. Similar to the way he organized the temporal development in *Le Sacrifice*, Xenakis first experimented with permutations of a set of window panes of different widths to obtain certain rhythmical motifs. Soon however, he was again confronted with the limits of the permutation technique: whereas too limited a number of elements results in an arid and predictable composition, too many elements make it impossible to aesthetically control the resulting configurations.

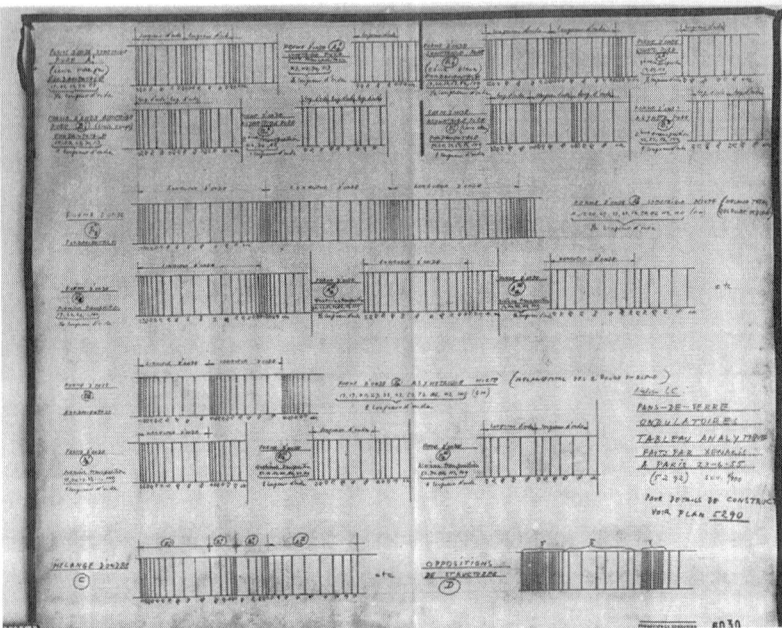

Figure 2: Iannis Xenakis, table with progressions of rectangles with increasing widths drawn from the Modulor. Source: Fondation Le Corbusier, Paris.

Here Xenakis had an intuition that would prove to be of major significance for his further compositional approach: he considered the problem on a more general level, above the individual elements, by replacing the concept of rhythm by that of *density* (in the sense of 'number of events per time or length unit'). Rather than considering the individual distances between the upright casings, he now demarcated zones in the façade where a higher or lower number of casings per length unit would be required and then decided how the transition between these two states would occur: fluently or abruptly. To this aim Xenakis drew up a table with progressions of rectangles with increasing widths in golden sections drawn from the *Modulor* (Figure 2). All he had to do now was to juxtapose

Figure 3: Le Corbusier, Monastery of La Tourette (1953-1956). View of the West façade with the undulating glass panes designed by Xenakis. Source: Le Corbusier, *Oeuvres complètes 1957-1965* (Zurich: Boesiger, 1966): 45.

patches containing dense, upright casings and patches containing rarefied ones in the façade so as to obtain the desired undulating effect. Thus Xenakis created a vertical polyphony in a triple-layered arrangement, resulting in a detailed polyrhythmic study of light and shade (Figure 3). Although each layer in the façade—corresponding to a story—has in itself a fairly simple structure, the resulting visual composition is of great complexity. While trying to follow the development of the façade, the eye quickly starts to travel from story to story and gets lost. This principle—the stacking of several independent layers of duration whose proportional relationships may vary throughout the piece—would become the cornerstone of the complex rhythmical polyphony in many pieces by Xenakis.[7]

Xenakis also recurred to numerical proportions in his first major composition, *Metastasis* (1954), to determine the temporal macro- and microstructures. Whereas the number of bars of the melodic subdivisions in the first part is determined by the Fibonacci series, in the second part, the *Modulor* principle intervenes on the 'microscopic' level to articulate both pitch and time. Consequently, just as in *Le Sacrifice*, duration is treated in a relativist manner. The notoriety of *Metastasis* derives however from the massive glissandi at the beginning and the end of the piece: moments of unison, where all the musicians play the same tone, fold out to form gigantic clusters where all 46 strings play at a different pitch. This transition occurs without interruption. The idea of continuity – in the sense of the continuous but (almost) imperceptible transformation between two discrete sonic states (loud-soft, high-low, fast-slow) – was central in Xenakis' theoretical preoccupations at that time. More specifically, he wondered how a fluent transition between two sets of notes could be obtained. Xenakis' answer to this question may have been inspired by his daily use of graph paper. Before the advent of the computer, engineers used graphical methods to calculate the resistance of a beam or determine the numeric value of shear forces and bending stress in construction elements. For Xenakis, the analogy between the orthogonal co-ordinate system and the musical notation system must have been too obvious to pass unnoticed.

Although the graphical method somehow became Xenakis' trademark as a composer, his use of it has always been pragmatic. Drawing was primarily a tool to fix his ideas, enabling a constant feedback between the hand and the ear. This did not preclude the definition of the work in musical terms however, since drawing music on graph paper along two orthogonal axes is in fact no more than a generalization of the traditional musical notation system: the vertical axis represents pitch, while the horizontal axis represents the flow of time. Nevertheless, musically speaking, it engendered a major conceptual step: whereas traditionally, the composer only considers discrete intervals between the twelve tones of the tempered scale, in the mind of Xenakis, drawing straight lines between dots on graph paper raised the question of what could happen *between* these twelve tones. The graphical method also had another important implication for Xenakis' compositional approach: it engendered a global conception of musical form, clearly inspired by his work as an architect. Contrary to the traditional organic composition technique, where one starts out from a cell (a theme or base row) and out of it creates the 'building' of a composition, Xenakis dealt with the overall form and the tiniest details simultaneously, doing away with the notion of form as a result of development. As an alternative to the organic model, Xenakis adopted the principle of collage and juxtaposition, which explains why many of his compositions consist of sections with no apparent connection. His collaboration on the Monastery of la Tourette might have been crucial in this respect. Rather than a homogenous unity, the forcefulness of this building derives from the expressive contrast between its parts. Nonetheless, the entire edifice is governed by one single formal principle, the *Modulor*. Xenakis has adopted a similar approach in *Metastasis*: although the four parts are clearly distinct on both the macro and micro level, the edifice is tied together by the Golden Section.

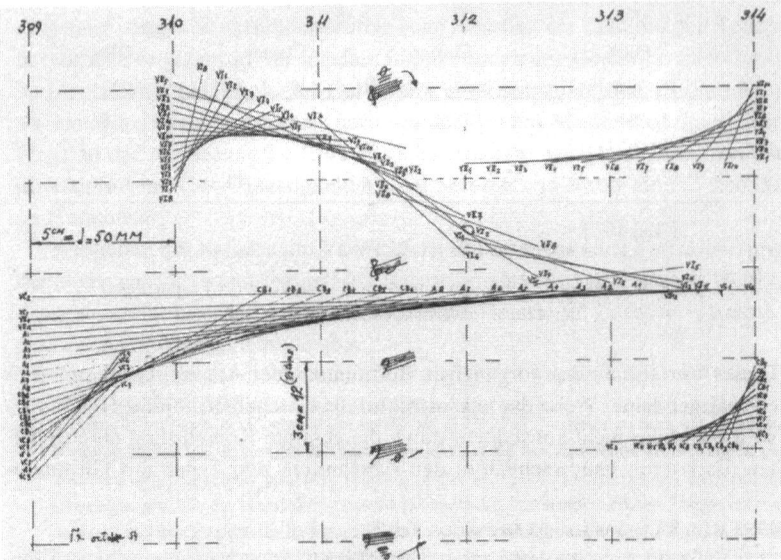

Figure 4: Iannis Xenakis, *Metastasis* (1954). Graphic score of bars Nr. 309 - 314. Source: Baltensperger: 55.

The famous drawing of the Coda part of *Metastasis* (bars 309-314) features the projection, in a plane, of a hyperbolic paraboloid (Figure 4). Despite its complex volumetric aspect, this type of warped surface can be defined by only two families of straight lines (hence the name 'ruled surfaces'); as a consequence, it can be calculated relatively easily. This paradigm was very popular in the visual arts and architecture in the 1950s. It was considered a rational alternative for the arid formal aesthetics of the International Style and a means to introduce the idea of space-time—a critical ingredient in the formulation of modern architecture—in the visual arts and architecture. The spatial sculptures by Naum Gabo are a clear example of this. The beauty of such mathematical form has to do with its fluid development from a two-dimensional shape to a three-dimensional volume, thereby implying a movement or unfolding over

Figure 5: Le Corbusier and Iannis Xenakis, Philips Pavilion (1956-1958). Wire model of the first scheme with suggestion of the straight lines that compose the ruled surfaces. Source: Fondation Le Corbusier, Paris.

time. *Metastasis* is a literal sonic interpretation of this idea: here, 'sound volumes' are created on the basis of simple straight lines (glissandi). The ruled surfaces in the graphic score of *Metastasis* can thus be interpreted as a musical interpretation of an avant-garde emblem. Nevertheless, on the auditory level, there is little notable difference from the glissandi in the first part, organized numerically and not geometrically.[8] In this respect, the graphical notation of bars 309-314 is to be considered in the first place as a formal exercise. It reveals however Xenakis' experimental attitude towards musical composition—experimental because the sonic result of what is being written down is hardly imaginable beforehand.[9]

Soon after completing *Metastasis*, Xenakis would create a powerful architectural icon within the paradigm of the ruled surfaces: the Philips Pavilion at the 1958 World Fair in Brussels (Figure 5). For this project Xenakis was given almost free hand by Le Corbusier, who concentrated mainly on the *Poème Electronique*, the multimedia show that was projected inside the pavilion. Whereas ruled surfaces were generally used only for roofs, the Philips Pavilion was probably the first building in architectural history to be designed with this type of surfaces exclusively. Walls and ceilings merged fluently into each other, resulting in a fluid interior space with a seemingly endless character. The similarity between the plans of the Philips Pavilion and the graphical score of *Metastasis* goes however beyond the formal level. Both creations can be considered as two different hypostases of the same idea, namely the continuous transition between two discrete states. In acoustic space this condition is articulated in the development from unison to clustered sounds while in architectural space it is expressed by merging the horizontal level surface and the vertical wall plane.

Apart from designing the pavilion's architecture Xenakis also contributed to the Philips project as a composer: his interlude *Concret PH* was broadcast over 300 loudspeakers between two representations of the *Poème Electronique*. Although the idea of using glissandi in a building composed with hyperbolic paraboloids must have been tantalizing, Xenakis chose a 'pointillist' approach: he mixed fragments of the sound of smoldering coals—the single sound source of the piece—to produce an evocative world of constantly varying and infinitesimally detailed clouds of sound. We can derive from this that Xenakis was not really interested in musical 'translations' of architecture or vice versa. Indeed, as he stated: "we are capable of speaking two languages at the same time. One is addressed to the eyes, the other to the ears."[10] In this view, addressing the same message to the different senses would result in a pleonasm. The opposite idea, a total dissociation between visual and aural perception, would become the key concept in the later *Polytopes*, large abstract sound and light installations in which Xenakis delivered his own interpretation of the total work of art.[11]

Another element allows us to grasp Xenakis' understanding of the relation between music and architecture even better: whereas Le Corbusier spoke about the 'musical glass panes', Xenakis preferred the denomination 'undulating glass panes'. This difference is significant: it illustrates the divergent viewpoints of Le Corbusier and Xenakis concerning the 'musical' aspect of architecture. According to Le Corbusier, architecture is linked to music by the concept of movement and the successive perception of volumes and spaces.[12] In other words, the 'musicality' of the façade at La Tourette resides in the diachronical perception it imposes upon the eye. Stressing the 'undulating' aspect of the façade, Xenakis, on the contrary, was not so much interested in the perception of this dynamic aspect, but in its underlying structure. Rather than in the effect, he was interested in the cause, namely the variation in densities.

As a conclusion, we can say that Xenakis has lifted the ancient Pythagorean idea of numerical proportions as a structural bond between architecture and music to a more general level by applying mathematical and scientific 'models' in both arts. The *Modulor* and the paradigm of the ruled surfaces are but two examples amongst many, and in fact the only models of an architectural nature.[13] Although such a method might appear exotic, mystifying or mannerist, Xenakis' application of scientific paradigms has always been pragmatic. His interest was not in the technically 'correct' translation of such models into music or architecture but in their expressive potential. The introduction of mathematical concepts and scientific formulas in music and art served in the first place as a generator of creativity and a means to discover new sonorities or architectural forms. Further, Xenakis was not so much interested in the phenomenological correspondences between a musical composition and a building, but in the similarity of their underlying structuring principles.[14] Given the fact that Xenakis referred to architecture and urbanism as 'sciences' and to music as 'the most abstract of the arts', it becomes clear now that his approach to architecture and music should not be dealt with in isolation but in connection with the ideas developed in *Arts/Sciences Alliages*, the account of his thesis defense in 1976.[15] In this book Xenakis breaks a lance for a 'general morphology', a classification of fundamental shapes along with their applications and expressions in different fields of observation and production. Consequently, the parallels that occur between the music and architecture of Xenakis are but specific examples of a more general formal research.

Space as a Compositional Parameter

As stated in the introduction, architecture and music can not only be related via mathematical principles; both arts also have to do with space. It is through the spatial experience that the abstract plan or the score is transformed into phenomenological realities. We will consider now how Xenakis deals with this idea both as a composer and architect. Given the predominance of his musical activity, we will concentrate on the role he attributes to the concept of space in musical composition and the diffusion of sound.[16]

At first sight, Xenakis seems to adopt a pragmatic attitude towards space. For example, in an interview with Andras Balint Varga, he states:

> Space first and foremost has the task of allowing sound to be heard properly. If, for instance, we seat four, five, six musicians performing a chamber piece close to one another the sound coming from one point is too thick, the instruments can't be differentiated from one another. [...] The sound will be much purer if we seat the musicians well apart.[17]

Space is thus called upon to 'clarify' the musical discourse and serves the purpose of efficiency. Xenakis is not the only composer to express such a view. In the piece *Gruppen* (1955–57) by the German composer Karlheinz Stockhausen for instance, the musicians are grouped in three separate

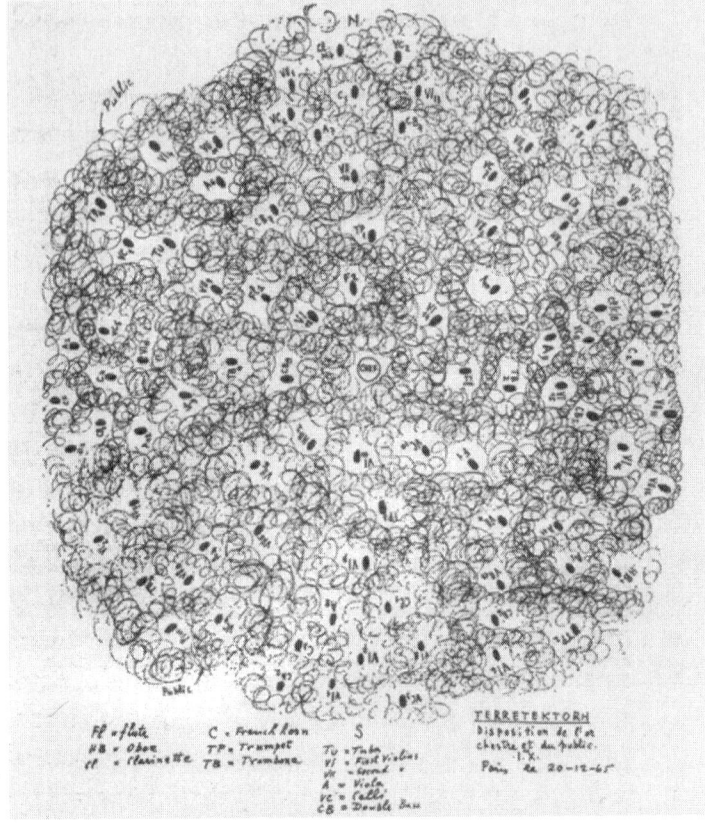

Figure 6: Iannis Xenakis, *Terretektorh* (1965). Diagram suggesting the distribution of the musicians amongst the audience. Source: Mario Bios, Xenakis. *Der Mensch und Sein Werk* (London: Boosey & Hawkes, 1966).

orchestras in an attempt to articulate the different temporal strata of the composition in acoustic space. In this case, the sound sources are spatially distributed in order to make the polytemporal structure of the composition perceptible. Given Xenakis' principle of stacking independent time layers, as explained in the context of the undulating glass panes, one would expect to find a similar approach in his dealing with space.

Xenakis introduced the idea of dispersing the orchestra in the performance space in several pieces of the 1960s such as *Terretektorh* (1965) and *Nomos Gamma* (1967–68), where the musicians are seated amongst the listeners (Figure 6), and *Persephassa* (1969), where the six percussionists form a hexagon around the audience. Although Xenakis was not the first to introduce such an idea, his conception of it is far more complex than the discrete and dialectical play of sound sources in most historical examples, such as the polychorality of the Venetian School and the *Fernorchester* in the Finale of Mahler's *Symphony Nr. 2*. To obtain an effect of spatial relief and perspective, he introduced (apparent) continuous sound movement. The clearest instance of this can be found in *Persephassa*: throughout the piece, several layers of sound are simultaneously superimposed, each rotating in different directions and in its own tempo. The result is a multifaceted spatial polyphony, as if several independent space-time systems collide in the performance space. The spatial placement of sound here has less to do with extravaganza or efficiency than with compositional technique: space is given compositional significance and becomes a fully fledged expressive parameter. Thus, rather than using space as a means to tame complexity, Xenakis seizes it to achieve an even greater compositional sophistication.[18] Inversely, sound becomes a means to create a spatial effect and to explore the acoustic qualities of a space.

The emergence of electro-acoustic music in the 1950s must be taken into account here: new sound technologies allowed the composer no longer to decide solely when a sound should be produced, but also where. Similar techniques soon found their way in acoustic music, often in a far more complex fashion than electronically realizable. It was as if the composers wanted to prove that the traditional orchestra was not dead yet. The same is true for Xenakis: he applied spatial distribution of sound sources first and foremost as a means to create new aural experiences with traditional instruments. His collaboration on the Philips Pavilion has been decisive in this respect. Xenakis theorized this experience in an essay entitled 'Notes sur un geste Electronique'.[19] In this seminal text—it forms the blueprint for the later *Polytopes*—Xenakis describes his vision of a dynamic and spatial visual art that would consist of colored light and electronic music. A crucial aspect of such an abstract total work of art would be a three-dimensional acoustic grid. Featuring loudspeakers in its 'knots', it would form an acoustically homogenous space with sound emanating from numerous points dispersed in the floor, the walls and the ceiling. Assuming that the ear can provide us with spatial orientation just as much as the eye, Xenakis argues that these manifold loudspeakers should be considered as geometric points, and that by consequence "all that is true for Euclidian space can be transposed into acoustic space."[20] Consequently, abstract morphological sound patterns such as geometric shapes and surfaces can be articulated in space and recognized by the ear. Sound is here no longer only a carrier of musical expression, but a means to expand the boundaries of architecture through the creation of immaterial and dynamic spaces. In other words, in Xenakis' vision, the acoustic grid was not only a highly sophisticated sound projection system but a device to generate ephemeral architectures and virtual spaces. Apart from the Philips Pavilion, Xenakis had the opportunity to put this idea into practice only once, at the EXPO '70 in Osaka. In the Pavilion of the Japanese Steel Federation, his electro-acoustic piece *Hibiki Hana Ma* was broadcast via 800 loudspeakers following all sorts of geometrical configurations.

Besides being a means to explore or create spaces, the dispersion of musicians and sound sources also has to do with Xenakis' philosophical views on music. One of the implications of this technique is that the audience no longer hears one single, homogenous sound; everyone literally hears the music from a different angle. As Xenakis has suggested, this mode of listening somehow resembles the way one perceives a building.[21] By consequence, one has to listen like a recording engineer, who, screening the individual parts separately on his mixing table, mentally reconstructs the musical edifice. This appeal for an analytical and active mode of listening derives from Xenakis' interpretation of music as "a matrix of ideas", or, in other words, "human intelligence in a particular state of crystallization."[22] In his view, music is not made to please but ought to serve as "a catalyst for reflection and a means of self-realization."[23] In such a view, rather than to be passively consumed, music must be actively explored and discovered. This doesn't mean however that Xenakis' music only addresses the intellect. On the contrary, one of the most striking aspects of his pieces—both acoustic and electro-acoustic—is precisely the almost physical presence of the sound textures. *Concret PH* is undoubtedly the clearest instance of this; it appeals to all the senses at once. Its scintillating texture must have made the audience feel as if the thin concrete shell of the pavilion was going to burst.[24]

It becomes clear now that Xenakis used the distribution of sound sources as a means to augment spatial awareness and aural attention. Consequently, space no longer constitutes a passive link between music and architecture but becomes an active element that gives rise to new auditory experiences and enhances the musical expressiveness. The idea of surrounding the listener with music brings us to a fundamental element in Xenakis' approach to sound, namely the concept of immersion. His desire to immerse the audience in sound should not be understood in terms of 'domination' however. It has rather to do with a situation of proximity that enables the listener to grasp the manifold details of the musical edifice and fully experience the sensuous impact of the sound. This leads us to the following question: according to Xenakis, how can architecture contribute to the realization of a mentally and corporally immersive experience?[25]

Xenakis once stated that concert hall designers should seek inspiration in the fine art of instrument building.[26] The form of an acoustical instrument not only has a fundamental impact on the quality of the sound, it also determines its timbre and thus its identity. Xenakis believes that architectural form affects the experience of a space in a similar way. Moreover, in his view, architecture has a conditioning capacity. Buildings have an influence on the mental state and corporeal behavior of the visitor just as spaces have an impact on the events they host. As a consequence, a concert hall has not only to do with acoustics and functionality, it can also become a catalyst or an obstacle in the development of new auditory experiences. In this respect, the architect bears as much responsibility as the composer: his failure can put a hypothesis on the progress of music. In this context it is interesting to note that almost all of Xenakis' architectural projects have to do with the diffusion of music. Apart from the Philips Pavilion he also designed a concert hall for the famous conductor Herman Scherchen in Gravesano (project, 1959), a mobile pavilion (called 'Diatope') to host his light and sound show *La Légende d'Eer* (1978), and a proposal for the international architectural competition for a new City of Music in Paris, in collaboration with the French architect Jean-Louis Véret (1984) (Figure 7). A brief analysis of this last project will shed more light on Xenakis' viewpoint on space as a composer.

Although he experimented with music in open air, Xenakis accepts that sound can only exist within confined spaces.[27] Rather than material enclosures however, his proposals are to be considered as 'spatial envelopes' shaped according to the paradigm of the ruled surfaces. Apart from their structural characteristics and aesthetic/symbolic appeal, such surfaces have good acoustic qualities. Their constantly varying curvature makes for a non-polarized reflection of the sound waves, resulting in a homogenous diffusion of sound. In the City of Music proposal, Xenakis carried this idea further

Figure 7: Iannis Xenakis, Experimental concert hall (competition project, 1984). View of the hall and the concrete shell. Source: Archives d'Architecture du XXIème Siècle, Fund Jean-Louis Véret.

in the asymmetrical plan and sections of the concert hall: it is conceived as a bucket with a 'potatoid' plan, placed as an independent element under the large concrete shell. While the floor of the hall is made out of one-meter-wide cubes so as to allow all sorts of seating topographies, a spiral gangway encircles the perimeter of the hall several times. Both architectural features enable a truly three-dimensional distribution of the audience, the musicians and the technical apparatus. Finally, the empty space under the shell is connected with the hall through large openings, serving as a resonating chamber. In this respect, Xenakis has not only taken inspiration from the organic geometry of musical instruments, his building is simply designed to function as one. He never had the opportunity to test the validity of this hypothesis however: although the jury praised the conceptual richness and the acoustic qualities of the scheme, Xenakis' highly experimental proposal was rejected in the final round of the competition.

Conclusion

As we have seen, Xenakis evolved from an abstract, conceptual relation between music and architecture based on the transfer of models from the mathematical and scientific world, to a more sensual and practical approach to sound and space where space is called upon to achieve a greater compositional sophistication, and sound becomes a means to create immaterial and dynamic spaces. Xenakis' goal though has always remained the same, namely to propose new auditory experiences and explore alternative modes of listening.

Towards the end of his career, Xenakis' developed an increasingly abstract viewpoint on this matter, doing away with the aspect of collectivity, physical proximity and bodily presence. In an interview in 1994, he stated for example:

> I have practiced architecture and conceived spectacles, but what really counts for me is music. It passes through the ears and not through the eyes. That's why the concert is a manifestation that is in fact very hostile to

music: you are surrounded by many people, some cough, sometimes they even smell bad! They prevent the sound from coming: at the concert, one should close his eyes and listen.[28]

This purist point of view must be understood in the light of a growing tendency towards asceticism and abstraction in Xenakis' later work of the mid-1980s and 1990s. At first sight, it seems to contradict Xenakis' search for an immersive experience and his attention to the visual and architectural aspect of the listening environment. Yet if one looks closer into the matter, one finds that this statement does not contradict Xenakis' earlier ideas. In *Notes sur un geste électronique*, published 40 years earlier, he described for instance an isotropic acoustic space paved with speakers. His aim was to disconnect the aural experience from the physical presence of the architecture, the audience, instruments and the musicians. Consequently, this text already announces Xenakis' abstract approach to listening. Thus, the statement above is only a radical reformulation of his vision of a proto-virtual listening situation, providing a context for the listener to become only ears.

Endnotes

* I wish to thank Katleen Craenen for the revision of the English manuscript of this paper.

[1] Paul Valéry, *Eupalinos ou l'architecte* (Paris: Gallimard, 1924): 131.

[2] The present article resumes some of the arguments developed in my Ph.D. Dissertation on the architectural and multimedia work of Xenakis: Sven Sterken, *Iannis Xenakis, architecte. Analyse thématique de l'œuvre, suivie d'un inventaire critique de la collaboration avec Le Corbusier, les projets réalisés en tant qu'architecte indépendant et les Polytopes* (University of Ghent, 2004, 549p.).

[3] Iannis Xenakis, *Musique Architecture* (Tournai: Casterman, 1971).

[4] Nouritza Matossian, *Xenakis* (London: Kahn & Averill, 1992): 48. Xenakis was born to Greek parents in Brailla (Roumania). He studied civil engineering in Athens and fled to Paris during the Greek civil war. Via Georges Candilis, Xenakis was offered a job in Le Corbusier's studio, that initially consisted in the computation of concrete elements for the Unité d'habitation de Marseille. Later Xenakis became more and more involved in the architectural aspects of the projects. In the second half of the 1950s, he became one of Le Corbusier's principal project architects. In this position he was responsible for the Monastery of La Tourette (1954–1956), the Youth House in Firminy (1956–1958), the Philips Pavilion (1956–1958), and a

huge sports complex in Bagdad (1955–1973, only partially realized). Xenakis also intervened in almost all the projects realized by Le Corbusier in Chandigarh in the 1950s. For a general overview of Xenakis' activity in architecture, see Sven Sterken, "Une invitation à jouer l'espace" in *Portrait(s) de Iannis Xenakis*, ed. François-Bernard Mâche, (Paris: Bibliothèque nationale de France, 2001): 185-195.

[5] The *Modulor* consists of two sets of harmonic numbers, that is to say that the ratio of two following values in the set corresponds to the Golden Section while each value is the sum of the two preceding ones. One set is based on the number 226 (the length in cm of an average man, arm raised), the other on the number 113 (the distance between the ground and his navel). Le Corbusier summarized the theoretical background of his invention in his book *Le Modulor* (1950), adding a second volume in 1955 with a portfolio of applications. I refer here to the facsimile edition: Le Corbusier, *Modulor* (Basel: Birkhäuser, 2000).

[6] For an analysis of *Le Sacrifice*, see André Baltensperger, *Iannis Xenakis und die Stochastische Musik. Komposition im Spannungsfeld von Architektur und Mathematik* (Bern: Haupt Verlag, 1996): 231-234, and Makis Solomos, "Du projet bartokien au son. L'évolution du jeune Xenakis", in *Présences de Iannis Xenakis*, ed. Makis Solomos, (Paris: Centre de documentation de la musique contemporaine, 2001): 15-29.

[7] On this aspect see Anne-Sylvie Barthel-Calvet, "Temps et rythme chez Xenakis: le paradoxe de l'architecte", in *Portrait(s) de Iannis Xenakis*, ed. François-Bernard Mâche, (Paris: Bibliothèque nationale de France, 2001): 159-171.

⁸ For a detailed analysis of Xenakis' use of glissandi in *Metastasis*, see Baltensperger: 295-311.

⁹ On this aspect, see Makis Solomos, *Iannis Xenakis* (Mercuès: PO Editions, 1996): 25.

¹⁰ Xenakis, in Balint Andras Varga, *Conversations with Iannis Xenakis* (London: Faber and Faber, 1996): 114.

¹¹ On the *Polytopes* see the beautifully illustrated book by Oliver Revault D'Allones, *Les Polytopes* (Paris: Baland, 1975). For an interpretation of these spectacles in the context of new media art, see Sven Sterken, "Towards a Space-Time Art: Iannis Xenakis's Polytopes", *Perspectives of New Music*, 39, Nr. 2 (2001): 262-273.

¹² In the first volume of the *Modulor*, Le Corbusier writes about this aspect: "Architecture is judged by eyes that see, by the head that turns, and the legs that walk. Architecture is not a synchronic phenomenon but a successive one, made up of pictures adding themselves one to the other, following each other in time and space, like music." (Le Corbusier, *Modulor*: 74).

¹³ Amongst the other 'models' Xenakis has introduced in musical composition are, for example, the Brownian motion resulting from the movement of gas molecules, the mathematical theory of probability (stochastic calculations), and the theory of groups and chaos. On the concept of transfer of models with Xenakis, see also Elisabeth Sikiaridi, "'Morphologies' or the Architecture of Xenakis", in *Présences de Iannis Xenakis*: 201-211, and Makis Solomos, "Du projet bartokien au son. L'évolution du jeune Xenakis", in *Présences de Iannis Xenakis*: 15-29.

[14] In *Modulor II*, Xenakis states: "Goethe said that 'architecture was music become stone'. From the composer's point of view the proposition could be reversed by saying that 'music is architecture in movement'. On the theoretical level the two statements may be beautiful and true, but they do not truly enter into the intimate structures of the two arts." (Le Corbusier, *Modulor II*, 326).

[15] Iannis Xenakis, *Arts/Sciences. Alliages* (Tournai: Casterman, 1979).

[16] As Xenakis admits (in Varga: 208), he did not extensively theorize the spatial dimension of music. He deals however with the question in his conversations with Varga (97-100) in an unpublished interview with Maria Ana Harley (1992), as well as in François Delalande, *Il faut être constamment un immigré* (Paris: INA/Buchastel, 1997): 101-104.

[17] Xenakis, in Varga: 97.

[18] On the concept of sound movement in Xenakis' music, see Maria Ana Harley, "Spatial Sound Movement in the Instrumental Music of Iannis Xenakis" *Journal of New Music Research* 23, Nr. 3 (1994): 291-314.

[19] Iannis Xenakis, "Notes sur un geste électronique" in *Le Poème electronique*, ed. Le Corbusier (Paris: Editions de Minuit, 1958). The text was reprinted in Xenakis, *Musique Architecture*: 143-151.

[20] Author's translation. Original text: "Ces points sonores *[the speakers, ss]* définissent l'espace au meme titre que les points géométriques de la stéréométrie. Tout ce qui peut être énoncé pour l'espace euclidien pourrait être

transposé dans l'espace acoustique." (Xenakis, *Musique Architecture*): 148.

[21] Xenakis, in Varga: 98.

[22] Xenakis, *Musique Architecture*: 16.

[23] Xenakis elaborates on this issue in his conversations with Delalande: 138.

[24] As suggested by Bart Lootsma in "En Route to a New Tectonics" *Daidalos*, Nr. 68 (1998): 35-47.

[25] In two of his writings, Xenakis theorizes the link between (musical) performance and architectural space. The first one is an unpublished text, entitled 'Lieu' (8 pages, probably early '70s, Xenakis Archives, Bibliothèque nationale de France, Paris) where Xenakis develops some general ideas concerning the architecture of musical performance spaces. He presents two opposites: the anechoic chamber and the acoustic concert hall, and pleads for a compromise of both. The second text is 'Espaces et sources d'auditions et de spectacles', originally a speech delivered at a conference in Greece in 1980, reprinted (in French translation) in Makis Solomos, *Présences de Iannis Xenakis*, 197-200. Here, Xenakis develops a general theory concerning the interrelation between 'sources' and 'audiences'. The different categories are illustrated with examples from his own oeuvre.

[26] Cf. Xenakis, 'Espaces et sources d'auditions': 197 and 199.

[27] See Xenakis in 'Lieu': 3.

[28] Xenakis, in Peter Szendy, *Espaces* (Paris: IRCAM/Centre Pompidou, 1994): 110, translated from the French by the author. Original text: "[...] J'ai fait de l'architecture,

des spectacles, mais ce qui compte vraiment pour moi, c'est la musique. Elle passe par les oreilles et non pas par les yeux. C'est pourquoi le concert est une manifestation qui lui est très défavorable: il y a beaucoup de monde autour de vous, les gens toussent, font du bruit, parfois ils sentent mauvais! Ils empêchent le son de venir: au concert, il faudrait fermer les yeux et écouter."

List of Figures

Figure 1: Iannis Xenakis, *Le Sacrifice* (1953). Source: André Baltensperger, *Iannis Xenakis und die Stochastische Musik. Komposition im Spannungsfeld von Architektur und Mathematik* (Bern: Haupt Verlag, 1996): 231.

Figure 2: Iannis Xenakis, table with progressions of rectangles with increasing widths drawn from the Modulor. Source: Fondation Le Corbusier, Paris.

Figure 3: Le Corbusier, Monastery of La Tourette (1953-1956). View of the West façade with the undulating glass panes designed by Xenakis. Source: Le Corbusier, *Oeuvres complètes 1957-1965* (Zurich: Boesiger, 1966): 45.

Figure 4: Iannis Xenakis, *Metastasis* (1954). Graphic score of bars Nr. 309 - 314. Source: Baltensperger: 125.

Figure 5: Le Corbusier and Iannis Xenakis, Philips Pavilion (1956-1958). Wire model of the first scheme with suggestion of the straight lines that compose the ruled surfaces. Source: Fondation Le Corbusier, Paris.

Figure 6: Iannis Xenakis, *Terretektorh* (1965). Diagram suggesting the distribution of the musicians amongst the audience. Source: Mario Bios, *Xenakis. Der Mensch und Sein Werk* (London: Boosey & Kawks, 1966).

Figure 7: Iannis Xenakis, Experimental concert hall (competition project, 1984). View of the hall and the concrete shell. Source: Archives d'Architecture du XXIème Siècle, Fund Jean-Louis Véret.

Kourosh Mahvash

Site + Sound : Space

As ironic as it may sound, it was my interest in light that led to the following piece on sound and the creative process of design. Immersing myself into two years of intense and focused study of the notion of light and space resulted in what one may call a kind of 'sensory awakening.' Hence, what I am similarly proposing here is a rather radical approach: a method of design based purely on sounds of site. The ultimate goal is that sensitizing the designer to the contextual soundscape[1] culminates in an awareness of all the sensory and supra-sensory perceptual aspects of the site not only as a source of inspiration and tool for design but also as a means of creating spaces that in turn fully engage the perceptual capacities of the user. The antagonist in this process is the visual. But I must emphasize that it is the unjustified dominance of the visual in today's culture—or in Juhani Pallasmaa's words, the "strictly hierarchisized"[2] status of our senses—that is being criticized, and not the sense of vision per se.

After all, the fundamental premise of this paper calls for a total sensory experience of architectural space; an experience in which all our senses, including vision, are involved. The essay begins with offering its broad definition of the concept of site and multi-sensory perception, and goes on to explain sound and hearing in such a context. Directly inspired and influenced by R. Murray Schafer and Bernhard Leitner, I propose next a method of observation, documentation, and representation that uses sound as its sole material. I conclude with a discussion of how, in the final step, a design based on the outcome of the previous purely sound-based stages might be developed. The roots of this text can be traced back to a one-week design exercise[3] that I developed in 2003. However, just as I avoided using any visual materials during the original presentation of this paper in Architecture | Music | Acoustic Conference[4], there are no images of the one-week exercise accompanying the following text. It is partly because of my own conviction that a representation must reflect and be consistent with the very principles it is to communicate—in this case an essay representing a purely non-visual approach to design. But it is also because of the fact that any images I include would inevitably be no more than an individual's interpretation of a concept, and might potentially narrow the realm of imagination. So, let me hope this ensures my wish that the imagination of the readers expands the scope of this paper, both in depth and breadth.

Thierry de Duve has been quoted as suggesting that "SITE—a concept he theorizes as a harmony of place, space and scale—can be recuperated only by linking two of these factors at the expense of a third, which at a later moment is paradoxically redefined and re-inscribed as if in recognition of its failure."[5] De Duve defines "place as the cultural tie to ground, territory and identity, space as the cultural consensus on the perceptive grid of references, and scale as the human body as measure of all things."[6]

The concept of site as outlined by de Duve embodies three fundamental elements in the design of the built environment.[7] Indeed, under the title of site it addresses the notion of context that is considered by the author to be the point of conception for an idea and the main platform for the process of architectural design. Embedded in the definition are the very elemental and indispensable concepts of culture, identity, history, human scale as well as perceived physical aspects of the locale.

This paper focuses on the sounds of a site and as such is mainly concerned with the perceptual aspects. However, by definition (as outlined above), it pursues a notion of site that transcends the physicality of locale and context; an assumption that, in turn, results in the expansion of the realm of perception.

STEVEN HOLL: PHYSICAL PHENOMENA ACTIVATE OUTER PERCEPTION WHILE MENTAL PHENOMENA ACTIVATE INNER PERCEPTION.[8]

The first necessary step in a contextual design process is the ability to *read* the site. Given the multifaceted nature of site which comprises both physical and non-physical—or as Steven Holl puts it, mental—phenomena, it is vital that the perceiver be open to a range of diverse experiences. What is almost readily perceivable, in Yi-Fu Tuan's words, is the "abstract knowledge *about* a place."[9] However, "the feel of a place takes longer to acquire…. It is a unique blend of sights, sounds, and smells, a unique harmony of natural and artificial rhythms such as times of sunrise and sunset, of work and play. The feel of a place is registered in one's muscles and bones."[10]

Once a full perception of a site is achieved, the next crucial task is to reflect the feel and identity of the place through the artifact in a manner that those qualities could be effectively communicated. The more comprehensive and inclusive the perceptual immersion in the conceived architectural space, the more successful and engaging the design would be. In fact, "an object or place achieves concrete reality when our experience of it is total, that is, through all the senses as well as with the active and reflective mind,"[11] says Yi-Fu Tuan. One of the reasons that historical buildings and structures are so moving and impressive to us is based on the same principle. For instance, the Persian garden with its patterns of light and shadow, reflecting pools, gurgling fountains, scents of flowers and fruits, and gentle cool breezes "offers an amazing richness and variety of sensory experiences which all serve to reinforce the pervasive sense of coolness."[12] The medieval cathedral is another example of such a multi-sensory spatial experience where the acoustic quality of the material and space, together with the massiveness of the structure, dramatic play of light and shadow, and the feel and touch of materials provide a very powerful sense of spirituality through a harmonic manipulation of our sensory experiences.

Be it sacred or profane, it seems that our ancestors were much more in *touch* with their senses and more skillful in applying them to the process of building the principles of a perceptual way of design. Of course, there are also contemporary projects like the House Near New York by Charles Moore or TOM Gallery of Touch-me Art in Japan which are specifically designed to cater to the senses of hearing, touch, and even smell. But it should be noted that these buildings were so designed because the needs of the client—in both cases visually impaired or blind—forced the architect to think of creative means to use non-visual sensory experiences as way-finding and orientation tools. Otherwise, most, if not all of today's architecture is under the influence of a culture dominated by visual stimuli.

We perceive the world through the simultaneous use of all senses but in modern societies the visual perception has been heavily and disproportionately favored, and this has been at the expense of depriving ourselves from the potential capacity of other senses. Meanwhile, responding to the world through sight differs from responding to it through the other senses in several important respects. For instance, seeing is objective, seeing – as the expression goes – is believing.... Seeing does not involve our emotions deeply.... The person who just 'sees' is an onlooker, a sightseer, someone not otherwise involved with the scene. The world perceived through eyes is more abstract than that known to us through the senses.[13]

The objectivity and precision of visual data has another drawback for the process of design, that is, it loses a very inspiring source of creativity. The ambiguity and vagueness associated with other sensory experiences allows the imaginative mind to dream and create its own version of reality that, in addition to being liberating, is inspiring and generative as well.

If we are to expand our perceptual horizon, if we are to *feel* space and if we are to enjoy a sense of delight in architecture, not only should we appreciate the capacity of all our senses and learn to experience space in a holistic way, but also our almost exclusive reliance on visual perception in the process of design must be replaced by a recognition of the full spectrum of perceptual capacities. In other words, it is not adequate, although necessary, to educate ourselves to be better receivers of sensory stimuli; we should also learn to design with and for all senses. Among our senses and next to seeing, hearing stands as the most prominent. It would then be fair to start our quest for the perceptual way of design by examining our perceptual response to sound.

R. MURRAY SCHAFER: WE ARE CONDEMNED TO LISTEN.[14]

Biologically we are not capable of closing our ears. In fact, even in absolute silence, as we think, we speak voicelessly to ourselves. But paradoxically, this constant exposure to voices and sounds of the inside and outside has desensitized our sense of hearing. This is quite remarkable especially given the fact that, as Murray Schafer observes, the creation of the world began through speech.[15]

On another level, studies have shown that sound has enormous psychological impacts on our life. **SOUND** has a dramatizing effect.

> We are usually more touched by what we hear than what we see. The sound of rain pelting against leaves, the roll of thunder, the whistling of wind in tall grass, and the anguished cry excite us to a degree that visual imagery can seldom match. Music is for most people a stronger emotional experience than looking at pictures or scenery.... Partly, perhaps, because we cannot close our ears as we can our eyes. We feel more vulnerable to sound.[16]

Without sound space feels lifeless. It is also known that the effect of loss of hearing could be as traumatic as the loss of sight. "With deafness, life seems frozen and time lacks progression. Space itself contracts, for our experience of space is greatly extended by the auditory sense which provides information of the world beyond the visual field."[17] And to the designer and architect, this latter point should be of particular interest.

There could hardly be anyone who could deny the more spatial, enriching and exciting experience of watching movies with surround sound systems. "Sound enlarges one's spatial awareness to include areas behind the head that cannot be seen."[18] Murray Schafer has similarly elaborated on the concept when he explains: "Auditory space is very different from visual space. We are always at the edge of visual space, looking in with the eye. But we are always at the centre of auditory space, listening out with ears.... Visual awareness faces forward. Aural awareness is centered."[19]

It is also a very well-known fact about the effect of rhythmic sound and music on the sense of space and time. This has been historically used for rituals and religious purposes. For instance, Sufism's whirling dervishes experience a sense of timelessness, placelessness and spiritual awakening due to the mystical music and the endless cycle of invocations accompanying their dance. In another context, Tuan explains the negating effect of music on the directionality of time and space as follows:

> Walking purposefully from A to B is felt as leaving so many steps behind and as having so

much more ground ahead to cover. Change the environment by introducing band music and, objectively, one still marches from A to B with seeming deliberation. Subjectively, however, space and time have lost their directional thrust under the influence of rhythmic sound. Each step is no longer just another move along the narrow path to a destination; rather it is striding into open and undifferentiated space. The idea of a precisely located goal loses relevance.[20]

Sound can also evoke other sensory associations or conjure up a sense of volume or distance. Lisa Heschong quotes Yoshida as reporting that in the "hot and humid Japanese summer people like to hang a lantern or a wind chime under the roof of the veranda. The lightly swaying lantern or the ringing of the bell gives a suggestion of refreshing wind and coolness."[21] In addition, the reverberation of sound in space and the quality of reflected sound, both affected by geometry, proportion and material—in other words, by architecture—could considerably enrich the sense of volume and space.

> MURRAY SCHAFER:
> THE MODERN ARCHITECT IS
> DESIGNING FOR THE DEAF....THE
> STUDY OF SOUND ENTERS MODERN
> ARCHITECTURE SCHOOLS ONLY AS
> SOUND REDUCTION, ISOLATION AND
> ABSORPTION.[22]

Almost thirty years ago, Murray Schafer criticized the culture of architecture schools for having a negative approach to acoustic design. Unfortunately, to this day things have not changed much. Acknowledging the problem, I am proposing a series of sound-based exercises that would constitute the foundation of a sensory-based design. The exercises and ideas have been inspired and directly influenced by Murray Schafer's *The Tuning of the World and World Soundscape Project* as well as the spatial sound installations of Bernhard Leitner.

It is worth reiterating that the adopted methodology is based on an approach to architectural design that lends itself to site-specificity. As the first step in such a process, a total sensory immersion and experience of the site that is informed by cultural undertones of place is needed. This requires a diverse set of perceptual *tools* by means of which one could do a full survey of site in its broad sense of the word. Site studies would be followed by the creative/interpretive representation of the unique blend of perceptual characteristics of the site. The third and last stage in the process would consist of translating the previously conceived representations of place into architectural

SPACE, combined with individual interpretation of cultural characteristics.

The dominance of visual culture has taken its toll on architecture as well. As a result, even a site-specific approach with a focus on the sensory experiences and perceptual design could fall victim to fascination with form, visual composition, and aesthetics. In response, the methodology offered here takes an aggressive and rather radical stance on the basis of which sound would be the theme and the only material to document and to design with.

> BERNHARD LEITNER:
> JUST LIKE THE EYE, THE EAR IS
> A FINELY TUNED INSTRUMENT
> FOR MEASURING SPACE.[23]

Sites, whether natural or manmade, have their own idiosyncrasies. Soundscape, one of those peculiarities, is a unique and rich data bank of history, culture and nature of the site. In his analysis—somewhat parallel to Kevin Lynch's well-known elements of site—Murray Schafer introduces "keynote sounds", "signals", and "soundmarks" as the elements of soundscape.[24] On the other hand, he also offers different systems of sound classification. The one that this essay is based on is called "classification according to referential aspects,"[25] which is a comprehensive taxonomy of sounds from those of nature and human to sounds of society and industry to "Mythological Sounds," "Sounds of Utopia", and of course quiet and silence.

The following design process is founded upon an exercise in measuring with ears and constructing with sound. It uses the intrinsic diversity and richness of soundscape to provide the raw *material* that is to be identified and collected in observation[26] and documentation stages of the process. It would be followed by interpretive representation of the site through spatial means. The resulting interpretive sound pieces would then be translated into a design concept or *parti* model.

From this stage on, the process basically consists of the development of concept in a *perceptual way* that is also informed by programme and site—again in its broad sense of the word and considering place, space, scale, and all cultural, physical and mental phenomena.

Observation: The focus of the design process proposed in this text is sound, and as such it takes any opportunity to make full use of sound as its medium. At the observation stage this would mean focusing on what could be heard or listened to on-site, or whatever form of sound that could be associated with physical, perceptual or cultural characteristics of the site. Moreover, just as darkness makes light visible, and shadow gives it depth, silence makes sound perceivable, and hearing an enjoyable experience. Thus, it is as important to listen to the silence of the site.

We should learn to listen more attentively and appreciate sound in all forms and ways of utterance.

> In a sense one could consider the whole sounding universe as a composition in which we are simultaneously the audience, the

composer and the performers. The task then would be how to improve the orchestration. But just as [a] composer subjects himself [or herself] to intensive training before writing [...] symphonies, we too must train ourselves before setting out to beautify the world.[27]

What follows is a tentative catalogue of sounds that could represent the characteristics of a site. The list, far from being exhaustive, has been compiled to include sounds that could reflect one or more social, economic, ethnic, cultural, historical, traditional, natural, and aesthetic characteristics of a site. It should also be noted that scale has a decisive role in determining which categories would be of greater relevance and more resourceful. For instance, designing a community building means much bigger inventory of social and human sounds at hand while a small group, a family, or an individual client might limit the use of such a category.

CULTURAL AND MUSICAL SOUNDS: Religious, ritual or folklore music / Popular or locally made musical instruments / The dominant type(s) or piece(s) of music that is best enjoyed by client or people / A piece of music that has been composed for or inspired by the place and people, or one that is about the place, its history and people / Stories, music, songs or other aural cultural and artistic pieces created by people from the place.

SOUNDS OF PEOPLE: Voices of individuals or crowds, such as those of routine and recurring activities of an individual, a family, or a community (markets, festivals, parades, and sports events) / Spoken word in the form of linguistic features such as dialects or linguistic constructs such as expressions and idioms / Words uttered to give an account of an important social issue, to describe a scene or simply talking about daily needs / Oral tradition of the place, which is reflected in specific stories and narratives about the place and its people / Sounds of streets and open spaces such as joyful cries of kids playing in a playground, the cry of street vendors or murmuring voice of a panhandler.

NATURAL SOUNDS: Sounds of weather (windy environment, rainy climate, icy surface, etc.) / Sounds of animals / Sounds of geographic features such as a river flow or ocean waves / Sounds of vegetation, trees and plants / Sounds of earth and materials.

SOUNDS OF MOVEMENT: Transportation sounds such as those of cars, vehicles, boats, planes and other means of transportation (train, sled, or horse-drawn carriage) / Pedestrian sounds of walking or running.

SOUNDS OF BUILDINGS and structures from the squeaking sound of a wood door to the silence of an abandoned warehouse.

SOUNDS OF dominant TRADES OR INDUSTRIES such as blacksmiths, glassblowers or shipyards, sawmills and power plants.

SOUNDS OF AWARENESS from alarming sirens of police cars or fire engines or soothing sounds of church bells to abrupt roar of a cannon to declare noon.

Documentation: It was previously noted that in response to the dominance of visual culture, this text takes a radical methodological stance. This would particularly be manifested in this stage of the process where, unlike what is the norm, no visual documentation of the site will be completed. In other words, documentation of the site should be accomplished by recording its soundscape, which is purely aural. Other than sound recording, the only other ways of documentation could be written words and memory (each of which could indeed be considered a mode of *silent speech*.) On the other hand, it is encouraged to aurally document visual, tactile and other sensory features of the site. Therefore, a tape-recorder, for example, could register sounds that by association would remind us of some other perceptual aspect of site. Here are some methods of documenting site features:

DIRECT SOUND RECORDING for registering aural features, be it natural, social, cultural or human sound.

ASSOCIATIVE SOUND RECORDING that represents another sensory feature of the site. For instance by recording the sound of wind-rattled leaves of a tree, one would become aware of the existence of both wind and a tree on the site. Another example is walking and recording the sound of footsteps that would represent the material quality and texture of the ground surface.

GEOMETRIC SOUND RECORDING, where the recorded sound represents geometric entities relative to the site. One example is *point recordings*, that is, recordings at defined points on-site such as four corners of a rectangular lot. Another example is *linear recording* that could be the result of moving along a line, such as a site boundary. *Sectional or planar recording*, where multiple recordings would be done at different elevations on site, is another way of geometric sound recording. For instance, using a unidirectional microphone and pointing it to the sky or ground, sounds at the higher and lower planes could be recorded. Using an omnidirectional microphone, however, ambient sound recording at the ear-level could be done. Also in urban contexts, it may be possible to do ambient sound recordings at multiple levels using neighbouring buildings.

WRITING, which is a visual medium, but, architecturally speaking, a non-conventional method.

MEMORY, as a mental recording device.

FOUND OBJECTS, peculiar to the site, would later be used to aurally represent the site.

Representation: If creativity and imagination were assets in the previous two stages of observation and documentation, they are indispensable parts of the representation stage. Here, indeed, the process of design that started with the observation stage reaches its pinnacle; sound is both the material and medium, and listening and perceptual tool. In composing the pieces, one should once again be reminded of Murray Schafer's elements of soundscape, namely, "keynote sounds," "signals," and "soundmarks" that would represent—to use a pictorial analogy—ground, figure, and distinct elements of the piece. Below is a list of some pieces that could be conceived using the collected *materials*:

CONTEXTUAL SOUND PIECE would be an assemblage of one or any number of the documented materials. A wide variety of composition of diverse or congruent materials would be possible. The key is that the piece must be spatial; an installation in a room. The technical aspects of sound playback would also have a tremendous impact on how the piece would be perceived. For instance, using multiple speakers or players and their location in the room would be crucial. The purity of aural experience—for instance, with eyes closed—and its association with other sensory experiences would be some of the other factors to consider.

SPATIAL SOUND INSTRUMENT would be an environmental/walk-through instrument that would generate sounds that are replicas of site sounds or that by association revoke peculiar sensory site experiences. One of the ways to make the piece more site-specific is to construct the instrument using only objects found on site.

SOUND COLLAGE would be an assemblage of sounds, songs, words, music and all other forms of aural material that were collected in the previous stages. This piece is meant to be listened to and its spatiality would be in musical and acoustic terms. However, decisions should be made as to how the listener would be engaged. For example, using headphones, or being blindfolded could substantially impact the experience of listening.

INTERPRETIVE SOUND PIECE would be a free interpretation of site features through sound and/or music. It could be an intuitive composition based on the total perceptual experience of the site or it could represent some specific features of the site. An example of the latter is how some Australian aboriginals used songs to affirm territorial boundaries and determine the limits of a particular area. The contour of the melody of the song describes the contour of the land with which it is associated. In any case, off-site recorded sounds, tones and even pieces of music would be used to create a direct, associative or geometric representation of site feature(s). Once again, the goal here is to create an aural piece that is meant to be mainly experienced through listening alone.

ASSOCIATIVE SOUND PIECE: Bernhard Leitner uses vibration—one of the forms of inaudible sound—as a way of expanding the sense of hearing through its association with the sense of touch. There is no reason why one cannot use the same technique to design objects and pieces that represent the sounds of a site by tactile means.

Developing a Design Concept or *Parti*: The next crucial step in the process is to develop an architectural design concept or *parti*, which is essentially not as complicated as it may sound. In fact, translating sound pieces into three-dimensional compositions has been successfully done before, both in academic and professional contexts. It is actually a historical practice that has led to describing architecture as frozen music. The method is essentially based on the use of numbers and the proportional aspects of music, which correspond in architecture to geometry and such aesthetic aspects of visual composition as the golden ratio. Even contemporary examples of such practices are available; Steven Holl's Stretto House being one of them.

Two of the four representation exercises would produce musical or sound pieces (*the interpretive piece* and *sound collage*) that, in a similar manner, could generate three-dimensional conceptual models that are the nexus of architectural design. But, more importantly, completing any of the suggested exercises will create a qualitative sense of sound awareness that could inspire any imaginative mind. In fact, the main reason for the shortage of aurally pleasing and delightful buildings is not the lack of design talent in the creative use of sound as a phenomenon. On the contrary, whenever and wherever there has been a need or will for creative uses of sound, remarkable achievements have been made. Why, then, do we not see buildings and spaces that are as perceptually stunning, moving and full of feeling as those that employ light? The answer is simple: we, as designers, do not educate and train ourselves to be as sensitive to sound as we are to light.

Some thirty years ago, Murray Schafer voiced his concern about architect's attitude towards sound. We ignored what he said then and we have not progressed from where we were. It is time to sincerely appreciate his words and follow his path.

> MURRAY SCHAFER:
> THUS THERE CAN BE NO SCIENCE
> OF SOUND, ONLY SENSATIONS…
> INTUITIONS… MYSTERIES…"[28]

Endnotes

[1] It should be noted that the word "soundscape" is a borrowed term originally coined by R. Murray Schafer.

[2] Quoted from Juhani Pallasmaa's keynote speech titled "Dwelling in the World: Vision, Hearing and Hapticity in Existential Space" delivered at Architecture | Music | Acoustics International Cross-Disciplinary Conference; Toronto, Canada; June 2006.

[3] In the summer of 2003, I was involved in teaching a design studio at the School of Architecture, Dalhousie University (Nova Scotia, Canada), where acoustics happened to be the underlying theme for almost all courses in that term. The students' task was to design the North Preston Gospel Technology Centre with a performance hall as its centerpiece. The studio included a set of exercises for the different stages of the design process and each instructor was individually responsible to devise and develop one of the exercises. With phenomenology, site and experiential aspects as the recurring focus of my design studios, I took on the responsibility of 'designing' an exercise that I dubbed 'Mapping the Soundscape.' My colleagues in the studio were: Professor Christine Macy (coordinator), Sarah Bonnemaison, Peter Henry and Catherine Venart. Bill Gastmeier taught the Acoustic Module and Steven Mannell the Structures course.

[4] Architecture | Music | Acoustics International Cross-Disciplinary Conference; Ryerson University, Toronto, Canada; 8-10 June, 2006.

⁵ J. Fiona Ragheb *Dan Flavin: The Architecture of Light* (New York, NY, Guggenheim Museum publications, 1999): 14.

⁶ Ibid.: 18.

⁷ Although it may be self-evident, it should be noted that the idea of space as discussed throughout this paper is the architectural space, which is to be overlaid on top of the existing grid of places and objects. This space is different from the one defined by de Duve since it would be an addition to the existing grid or matrix of spaces and places of the site and informed by intuition, feelings, human scale and perception. De Duve's place and space could be expressed in the same manner that Yi-Fu Tuan in *Space and Place: The perspective of Experience* (Minneapolis, University of Minnesota Press, 1977): 12, defined them: "Place is a special kind of object. It is a concretion of value, though not a valued thing that can be handled or carried about easily; it is an object in which one can dwell. Space ... is given by the ability to move. Movements are often directed toward, or repulsed by, objects and places. Hence, space can be variously experienced as the relative location of objects or places, as the distances and expanses that separate or link places, and – more abstractly – as the area defined by a network of places." Tuan later (page 17) elaborates on the notion of architectural space: "Human beings not only discern geometric patterns in nature and created abstract spaces in the mind, they also try to embody their feelings, images, and thoughts in tangible material. The result is sculptural and architectural space, and on a large scale, the planned city...."

[8] Steven Holl, *Kiasma - Steven Holl: Museum of Contemporary Art* (Helsinki: Museum of Contemporary Art and the Finnish Building Center Ltd, 1998).

[9] Yi-Fu Tuan, *Space and Place, The Perspective of Experience* (Minneapolis, University of Minnesota Press, 1977): 183.

[10] Ibid.: 183.

[11] Ibid.: 18.

[12] Lisa Heschong, *Thermal Delight In Architecture* (Cambridge, Massachusetts, MIT Press, 1979): 28.

[13] Yi-Fu Tuan, *Topophilia: A Study of Environmental Perception, Attitudes, and Values* (Englewood Cliffs, New Jersey, Prentice-Hall, 1974): 10.

[14] R. Murray Schafer, *Voices of Tyranny Temples of Silence* (Indian River, Ontario: Arcana Editions, 1993): 163.

[15] Murray Schafer in his book *Voices of Tyranny Temples of Silence* beautifully and in detail argues for the idea of primacy of sound to light. For example he says, "… Everything in the world was created by sound and analyzed by vision. God spoke first, and saw that it was good second.": 163.

[16] Yi-Fu Tuan, *Topophilia: A Study of Environmental Perception, Attitudes, and Values* (Englewood Cliffs, New Jersey, Prentice-Hall, 1974): 8.

[17] Ibid.: 9.

[18] Ibid.: 16.

[19] R. Murray Schafer, *Voices of Tyranny Temples of Silence* (Indian River, Ontario: Arcana Editions, 1993): 164.

[20] Yi-Fu Tuan, *Space and Place, The Perspective of Experience* (Minneapolis, University of Minnesota Press, 1977): 128.

²¹ Lisa Heschong, *Thermal Delight In Architecture* (Cambridge, Massachusetts, MIT Press, 1979): 25.

²² R. Murray Schafer, *The Tuning of the World,* (Toronto: McClelland and Stewart Limited, 1977): 222.

²³ Bernhard Leitner, *Sound: Space* (Ostfildern, Germany: Hatje Cantz Publishers, 1999): 297.

²⁴ In both of his books mentioned and referred to in this paper, "*The Tuning of the World*" and "*Voices of Tyranny Temples of Silence*," Murray Schafer explains the terms as follows: Keynote Sounds are background sounds both natural and man-made; Signals are foreground sounds which would be the "figure" if one considers the keynote sounds as "ground," and Soundmarks, corresponding to what is called landmark in landscape and urban studies, is a community sound which is unique or possesses qualities which make it specially regarded or noticed by the people in that community.

²⁵ R. Murray Schafer, *The Tuning of the World* (Toronto: McClelland and Stewart Limited, 1977): 137-144.

²⁶ Although essentially representing a visual concept, the word observation has been used in the text for its connotation that encompasses the passive reception of what is seen, heard or noticed in the data collecting stage of site survey.

²⁷ R. Murray Schafer, *Voices of Tyranny Temples of Silence* (Indian River, Ontario: Arcana Editions, 1993): 105.

²⁸ Ibid.: 162.

Galia Hanoch-Roe

Scoring the Path: Linear Sequences in Music and Space

The following essay focuses on the linear sequence as a primary factor in the experience of certain spaces. Linear sequences incorporate notions of movement, motile perception and rhythm, which make their experience akin to that of other arts such as music, dance and film. The conventional design representations, which rely on static visual depictions such as plans, sections and perspectives, have demonstrated limitations in expressing the temporal and motile dimension of the linear sequence and path experience. This essay explores the evolution of representational techniques of scoring in an attempt to emulate temporal theories of music and related arts into the scoring of a path. It examines the evolution of musical scores from the traditional to the open and graphic scores of the mid-twentieth century, which are more directly related to the spatial realm, and proceeds to evaluate past efforts in dance notation and environmental scores, in an attempt to understand their values and limitations in regard to scoring the linear sequence.

Finally, this essay presents an original scoring system for paths in the landscape, which integrates the valuable elements of existing scoring systems into a tool that could be used by designers to analyze existing 'successful' paths and to design future paths. This system incoporates elements of motion and rhythm with multisensory, physical, ocular and subjective experiences into a simultaneous score representing the polyphony of concurrent experiences, which is visibly appealing and readily understood.

Paths and Linear Sequences in Space

Linear sequences are a vehicle by which architects and landscape architects lead and manipulate the perception of the person experiencing a space. Any sequence is built of movements and creates a succession of events. Each event is relative to the preceding one—for example moving from a closed to an open space or from light into the dark—and might affect future responses and choices. The observer weaves his or her path by combining choice with restrictions. He may choose to stop, walk faster or slower, look around, reverse the position in space, but the freedom is confined by certain designed obstacles on the way such as walls, slopes, water, staircases, and points of view that affect her perception.

Spatial sequences may vary considerably between being directed and controlling or open and offering choices. Clearly, in a spatial setting one cannot be totally free to construct sequences. Yet, different spatial designs lend varying amounts of choice to the person experiencing them. A classic example of a controlled sequence, manipulating the experience of the sequence in a way similar to a traditional musical score, is Frank Lloyd Wright's *Taliesin West*, as described by the late Philip Johnson:

> I think the essence of his house is the procession through the building. I once counted the turns that you [make] since you approach[ed] the buildings until you get to into what he calls the cove, the holy of holies where you finally sit down with the high priest, and the number of turns I think was 45. He is playing with you as you walk through that space…then when he opens this flap under this little secret garden you say there can't be more surprises, there can't be any more unfolding of space, but there are, and you get into this private courtyard with this green grass and the falling water…then you finally get into the cove, and just when you are used to his six foot ceiling it has fourteen-foot ceilings, and the fireplace runs the full length of the building, there are no windows all of a sudden, and no canvas, you are entirely enclosed in the middle of this experience, and by the time you get there you realize that you have been handled and padded and twisted much as a symphony will caress you, or an opera, until you get to the crisis.[1]

The experience of moving within a space is very personal, yet it is confined to a certain slice of time which is inherently culturally, historically, and individually bounded. A person experiences a space not only in a slightly different sequence every time, but also under different lighting and climatic conditions. She is confined to certain clothing of certain eras that allow him or her to move at a certain pace; he hears different sounds and echoes from the surrounding environment, from birds to cellular phones and traffic. The person's subjective feeling of space will change throughout the day, week or years he or she experience the place. Each experience respresents a highly individual path that can never truly be repeated in quite the same way. James Corners describes this as an accumulation of meaningful events:

> There is duration of experience, a serialistic and unfolding flow of befores and afters. Just as a landscape cannot spatially be reduced to a single point of view, it cannot be frozen as a single moment in time. The geography of a place becomes known to us through an accumulation of fragments, detours and incidents that sediment meaning, 'adding up' over time. Where, when and how one experiences a landscape precipitates any meaning that is derived from it.[2]

Many of these ideas apply to any experience of a work of art, but architecture and even more so, landscape architecture, are more extreme in their requirement of body movement and a total enveloping of the person experiencing them. This process is similar to the one experienced by a performer of a musical work in the sense that it can not be replicated twice in the same manner and temporality; body movements and the enveloping quality of sound perform in a similar manner to the all-encompassing qualities of space.

The linear structures of roads, paths and streams become ordering devices for an experience as well as a place from which to view the space. In his book *The Image of the City* Kevin Lynch notes that for most people, paths are the predominant city elements. Lynch emphasizes that the city and its paths are sensed in motion and provoke a need for motion awareness, defined by him as "the qualities which make sensible to the observer, through the visual and the kinesthetic senses, his own actual or potential motion."[3] He emphasizes that since a city is sensed in motion, these qualities are fundamental, and they are used to structure and even identify, wherever they are coherent enough to make this possible. Appleyard, Lynch and Myer, in an analysis of highway sequences, point out that "the road itself furnishes an essential thread of continuity, but it must be supported by successions of space, motion, orientation and meaning which seem to be parts of a connected whole."[4] They conclude that "a basic sense of rhythm of attention will strengthen the sense of continuity, whereas too sudden a change in the tempo will snap the thread."[5]

Limitations of Conventional Design Representations

When interpreting a design of a linear sequence, it is traditionally understood in terms of vision, emphasizing the construction of three dimensional visual images in space. The conventional tools used for analysis and design of paths are plan views, diagrams and perspectives that focus on forms and functions of the visual elements. These spatial representations of communication do not directly relate to the elements of time and movement inherent in the real life experience of a space and therefore do not communicate these aspects. They do not convey other components of the sensual exploration of the space as well, such as smells, sounds, feelings of enclosure and openness, and subjective feelings of excitement, boredom, contemplation and such, which may be enhanced by design.

Man has not always been dominated by vision. Robert Mandrou stated that "the hierarchy of the senses was not the same as in the twentieth century because the eye, which rules today, found itself in third place, behind hearing and touch and far after them. The eye that organizes, classifies and orders was not the favored organ of time that preferred hearing."[6] Walter J. Ong in his book *Orality & Literacy* points out that "the shift from oral to written speech was essentially a shift from sound to visual space," and that "print replaced the lingering fearing dominance in the world of thought and expression with the sight dominance which had its beginning in writing."[7]

The dominance of the sense of vision in architectural design was reinforced by writings of modernist architects such as Walter Gropius, who stated that the designer "has to adapt knowledge of the scientific facts of optics and thus obtain a theoretical ground that will guide the hand giving shape, and create an objective basis,"[8] and Le Corbusier, who wrote "I exist in life only if I can see," supporting the notion that vision is the crux of everything by stating "I am and I remain an impenitent visual—everything is in the visual," and "one needs to see clearly in order to understand."[9]

However, it has been demonstrated that man cannot make sense of the visual world unless the other senses are involved.[10] The anthropologist Edward Hall has gone so far as to say "this two-dimensional visual bias has exerted an unanticipated and pervasive influence on our lives causing us to intellectualize what is almost entirely a sensual experience. This has certainly been one factor among many that are responsible for man's estrangement from himself."[11]

Therefore, acknowledging the importance of other senses, and mostly incorporating temporal elements such as rhythm and motion which interact and fuse into each other in a spatial design, cannot be overestimated. We close our eyes when we want to envision (in-vision) or engage in activities such as imagining, listening to music, dreaming or embracing. Yet, instead of incorporating these sensorial media positively into our thought process, we acknowledge more readily our other senses in negative terms of "sound pollution", disturbing smells or elements causing physical discomfort. The consideration of them is rarely incorporated into the initial thought of design, in trying to create beautiful, pleasing and intriguing environments integrated by the senses.

Mark Treib in his essay "Must Landscape Mean?" asserted that "today might be a good time to once more examine the garden in relation to the senses."[12] A growing number of architects, landscape architects and planners acknowledge the importance of constructing a multi-sensorial holistic experience in the design process. Kevin Lynch designates an important element of site design to center on "what we see, hear, smell and feel and what that means to us." He explains that the designer is concerned with what it is like to act in a place, to move through it and to experience it...She must make a set of simultaneous decisions which seem at first too numerous to grasp, which all depend on each other, like linked dancers in a ring."[13] Steven Krog states that "composed of ephemeral, temporal, and spatial qualities, the landscape is difficult to describe, evaluate, or interpret. Yet landscape architecture cannot afford to overlook or neglect the very necessary, though admittedly unsettling, and confrontation with the interactive, non-mappable, non-quantifiable and difficult-to-predict components."[14]

The subject in space is a fully enveloped and integral part of spatial, temporal and material relations, and nothing can reproduce the meaning that comes from this lived experience, no matter how accurate or skillful the representation is in other media. James Corners argues in his intriguing article *Representation and the Landscape* for a new form of drawing of landscape design that will incorporate the landscape spatially, temporally and materially.[15]

Kevin Lynch suggested in a number of instances that the design of a space, especially a linear construction such as a path or a road could draw inspiration from related artistic fields:

> One is drawn toward another kind of organization: that of sequence, or temporal pattern. This is a familiar idea in music, drama, literature, or dance. Therefore it is relatively easy to conceive of, and study, the form of a sequence of events along a line, such as the succession of elements that might greet a traveler on an urban highway. With some attention, and proper tools, this experience could be made meaningful and well shaped.[16]

Since linear sequences in architecture assume a mode of art which resides in between space and time, mediating between its dichotomies, they can be designated as a fluid, spatio-temporal art form that integrate, mediate and provide opportunities to incorporate the diverse aspects into its experience. Taking Johann Wolfgang von Goethe's famous quote "architecture is frozen music" as a starting point, in the experience of linear sequences one can determine that they represent architecture's melting into regained fluidity. Thus, developing a new form of drawing of spatial linearity in general, and the path experience in particular, must capture elements of movements and time inherent in design. The fields of architecture and landscape architecture could benefit from looking into related arts such as music and dance that inherently have to deal with temporal and movement aspects, to derive a new and more complete understanding of the process of conveying these elements into the design of space.

The Evolution of Scoring in Music

Performed, 'real-time' music never exists as a whole at any given moment, but rather unfolds in a linear manner over time, and assumes an entity only in retrospect, in the memory of the listener or the performer. However, reading a compositional music score is a process closer to perceiving a space, as it exists as a whole at any given moment but may be retained by the observer only by a process of observation over time, walking around, through, and above it.

Music, as it is perceived by the listener, is linear in essence. The linearity is reflected in the traditional compositional score, though the score is composed in 'frozen time' (rather than 'real' time of a performance) and allows a deliberate suspension of time. In that sense, the silent reading of a score is similar to experiencing a sequence in a space. The person chooses the tempo, accentuation, and the linearity of the process, and may stop, turn back, return, and do as he pleases. When the silent reading of a score is performed the interpreter must choose one possibility among the numerous ones inherent in the score, as does the person in the space, constructing a particular sequence of experiences from the certain choices she is offered.

Scores can record events from the past or notate what is happening in the present, but the real importance of a score is its relationship to the future, conveying the ideas that exist in the creator's imagination as a set of instructions to the performers who will create the sound of the music. The essential quality of scores is that it is a system of symbols which can convey, guide, or control the interactions between elements such as space, time, rhythm, people, and their activities and the combinations which result from them.

Using the traditional stave, musical notation specifies to the performer an array of dimensions using a variety of scoring symbols such as circles, lines, dots, arches, numbers, letter abbreviations, words and other specific symbols. The stave depends upon the conventions of 'high' and 'low' in the vertical plane, and duration—moving from left to right—on the horizontal plane.

Stave notation indicates the following dimensions:[17]

> 1. Pitch and pitch relationships: this includes harmony (chords and simultaneous soundings), and melody (consecutive sounding).
> 2. Pace, duration and duration relationships: rhythm, tempo (the frequency of stress) and meter (the shape of stress patterns).

3. Dynamics: loudness degrees and change.
4. Attack and touch.
5. Expression: the deliberate variation of any of the above elements for expresive purposes.

The notational system captures concurrently many of the musical elements, but also leaves much open to interpretation. Many of the elements remain relative. For example, when a specific pitch is noted it can still vary in the tuning of that pitch on the instrument in different time periods (as the A' was tuned differently in different eras); there are specified duration and dynamics but they are relative to the performer's pulse and touch chosen at the beginning, and change throughout the work. Beyond that, elements that communicate form and structure are not always explicit, and rely on the musical interpretive ability of the performer, such as continuity of phrasing, breathing, imbuing the piece with a sense of spontaneity and movement, and bringing out musical voicings and motifs.

In classical music one can obey all the rules of the interpretation of the notation, and still not give a moving performance, as even the most explicit score remains symbolic, and therefore cannot fully convey the intentions of the composer. It is possible to criticize a performance as being played correctly but failing to express the intention, or on the other hand not playing all the notes but conveying the composer's intention. Fidelity to the intention of the composer thus appears to be separate from fidelity to the notation. The composer Karlheinz

Stockhausen had once joked: "A perfect notation? Would that be one where you can immediately imagine 'how it sounds'? Then order me one right away...when you read music, it's better to imagine music than to think all the time what the signs mean."[18]

Open Scores

In the second half of the twentieth century musical notation still guided performers 'what to do', but reflected a shift in creative priorities and hierarchies. As discussed earlier, the visual codes of the notational language have traditionally left the score open to interpretation regarding different aspects such as tempo, dynamics, touches, and atmosphere. Yet until 1950 the musical score was based on the idea that the performer reads it in a linear manner, and does not intervene in the formal construction of the notation. During the second half of the twentieth century, composers such as Ligeti, Boulez, Stockhausen, and others began to challenge the linearity of the musical score and offered the performer a choice in the construction of the musical work. These works are composed in terms of individual sections or fragments, and yet they are flexible in the order of appearance, creating a certain unpredictability during the performance. The conventions underlying the intelligibility of a traditional musical work as casual logic, linearity, continuity and predictability no longer endure, since in open compositions each unit is predominantly

Figure 1: Earl Brown *Available Forms I* (1961). The image shows page six of a score made up of six loose plates, all of which are in view of the eighteen performers. The conductor indicates the sections to be played by moving an arrow on a large board which contains the numbers 1 to 6.

important in itself, and the initial order of these units has become less significant. An open-structured composition could be implemented in many different ways. The significance of the work lies not in any one of its realizations but in their very multiplicity, in the range of interpretations the model allows.[19]

Earl Brown's *Available Forms* (1961) is a good example of such an open form (see Figure 1). It was the first of the orchestral open forms in which the conductor determines the inclusion, omission, repetition, and order of materials to be performed. The open form encourages the performer thereby to achieve a newly won spontaneity.[20]

The unraveling of an open composition lends a choice of movement to the performer and allows her to move freely about the musical work. In such constructions, the function of the musical score changes from an object to be read by the performer into a process to be constructed. The choice of movement ruptures the linearity of the score inherent in the performance of a musical composition up to that time, and resembles a silent reading of a score in which the reader may stop, turn back, and return. The process of performance becomes similar to that of a movement within a structural space, where the observer chooses his way about it. In a comparable manner, both the performer in the open composition and the observer in the structural space gather several of the infinitely existing possibilities inherent in the art-work to an artistic entity which is but one of its many 'realizations'. However, there is obviously a difference in the ability of the performer to connect any two sequences in the music and the observer of a space who is usually confined to a limited choice at different points.

The composer György Ligeti compared the various interpretations of open compositions to flash-photos of a Calder mobile, in which changes are manifested only indirectly, since each performance is merely a momentary incarnation of the manifold possibilities of the form. In a Calder mobile, the shape, color, and design of each part is fixed, while the order and angles constantly change. In Earl Brown's *Calder Piece* (1966) for four percussionists, Brown used a Calder mobile, produced by Calder especially for this piece, as a 'conductor'. These ideas imply art as a process; no longer will 'objects' of music exist in that sense, but each new performance, each new circumstance will create a continually variable process of ideas.

Graphic Notation

In the 1950's several composers such as John Cage, Earl Brown, Hauberstock-Ramati, and Paul Ignace took the advancement of scores and their underlying structures even further and developed the idea of graphic notation (see Figure 2). Extending the idea of indeterminacy of forms existing in open scores, graphic scores use a simple picture without instructions instead of conventional notation. Here the semantic communication between composer and performer is narrow, and the visual communication has more weight. It is no longer possible to infer the composition from the interpretation, and therefore the criteria of a musical drawing are to be sought exclusively in the visual field.

The composers let go of the control they have over the details of the composition, revert to approximations—that indicate the general idea and atmosphere—and give the performers a meaningful role in the construction of the work. Composers who work with such notation, where the distinction between symbol and drawing is ambiguous, hope that it may excite the performer's imagination. "One cannot determine exactly what effect the notation causes" wrote John Cage in 1960, and, he continues, "the observer-listener is able to stop saying I do not understand,

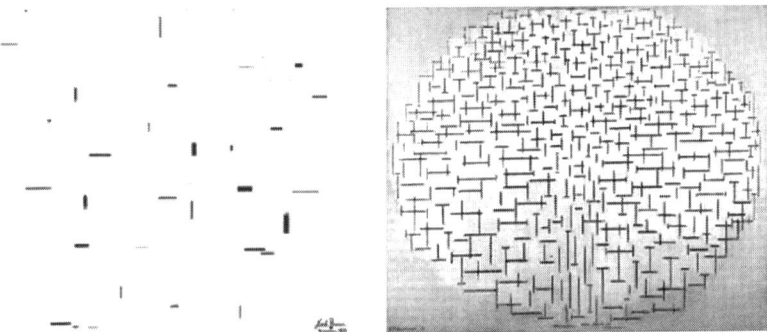

Figure 2: Earl Brown *December 1952* (left), and Piet Mondrian *Composition 10 Pier + Ocean* (right). *December 1952* is the first wholly graphic score. It suppresses all familiar notational devices and places black rectangles of various sizes in a pleasing but irregular pattern on the page. The result resembles Piet Mondrian's painting *Pier + Ocean* from 1915.

Figure 3: John Cage *Aria* (1958).

since no point-to-point linear communication has been attempted. He is at his own center (impermanent) of total space-time."[21] The suggestive visual power of the graphic score offers multiple possibilities of interpretation, by which a second performance of a work by the same graphic notation and even the same performers will yield a completely new rendition. This rendition is not only a different interpretation, but taken to different degrees, could be a new form altogether, with different structures, sequences and sometimes even notes. In such works the relationship between composition and interpretation becomes ambiguous.

John Cage's *Aria* from 1958 (see Figure 3) contains no specific pitches, although each vocal phase is notated as a general contour, which functions as an "ideaogram," visualizing an entire concept rather than an alphabetic construction of component parts. Cage uses colors throughout the printed score to denote change in singing style and has given suggestions (but does not specify) for some stylistic possibilities: blue for jazz, green for folk, and brown for nasal.

John Cage compared the process of reading graphic notation to that of a traveler trying to catch trains and departures, which have not been announced but are in the process of being announced. The performer here takes the role of the observer. By deciphering the graphical aspect of the score and the affinity with the atmosphere it evokes, it offers a purely aesthetic-associative manner of translation into music. Here, the process of "catching trains" is similar to an exploration of a spatial work of art. Observing a work of spatial art calls for movement, and movement in turn requires the use of time. A two-dimensional work of art requires movement of the eye, and a three-dimensional work requires the actual movement around or within the work. The actual movements of the eye or the observer around a work are in themselves limited, as are the musical sections of an open score, but their combinations create an infinite range of variation. The architect cannot predetermine all movements and thus must leave the observation of the building to chance, as does the composer of an open score. The movement of the observer, in turn, is also subject to chance, as his attention may drift to many different angles and views, focusing for long on one area, skipping another, et cetera.

The new open attitude towards performance of temporal art was not limited to music but could also be observed in concrete poetry, in dance, in design as well as in other media.[22] For example, the score for the dance *Parades and Changes* by Ann Halprin employs 'cell blocks'—resembling the musical blocks of Earl Brown—as a scoring device. Each collaborating artist, musician, dancer-choreographer, lighting designer, sculptor, and coordinator developed a series of sound actions, movement actions, light actions, environmental or sculptural actions in discrete thematic ideas called cell blocks.[23]

In music and dance the composer or choreographer uses the score to direct the performer (not the listener). In spatial design, in contrast, there is no mediating performer. The score is meant as a design tool to enhance communication between a team of designers. It can also be used later to validate notions of the designers in the newly built environment by letting the inhabitants experience the space and score it according to the same system.

As architecture and landscape architecture can be described as spatio-temporal arts—incorporating strong elements of motion and rhythm—it seems appropriate to derive inspiration from the notion of linear open and graphic scoring systems in music and dance to better understand the idea of linear sequences, their meanings and construction in space. It is potentially useful to rethink the idea of systemizing a scoring technique which can capture the linearity of the path with its ever changing 'interpretations', those of nature, the stimulus itself, and of the person perceiving and experiencing it. The innovations of scoring techniques in music and their relation to spatial arts can be emulated to develop a more coherent scoring system for linear paths in space.

Scores and Past Efforts of Scoring in Dance and Body Movement

There have been many attempts in the past to notate different aspects of spatial design and movement. These include dance notational systems such as Rudolph von Laban's "Labanotation", Joan and Rudolph Benesh's "Visual System", Valerie Sutton's "Dance Writing system," and others, which try to capture body movement in space by developing different stave systems representing a time line which incorporates movement of body parts.[24]

The Labanotation system, invented by Rudolph Laban in the 1920's, uses a vertical stave to represent the body. It is interesting to note that Laban initially studied architecture at the École-des-Beaux-Arts in Paris, and became interested in the relationship between the moving human form and the space surrounding it. The stave he invented is read from the bottom up and combines the vertical physical image with continuity in movement. It is the only system in which four factors are combined into one symbol: direction of the action (shown by the shape of the symbol), level (shown by shading), timing (shown by length of symbol) and the part of the body moving (shown by placement on the stave; see Figure 4).

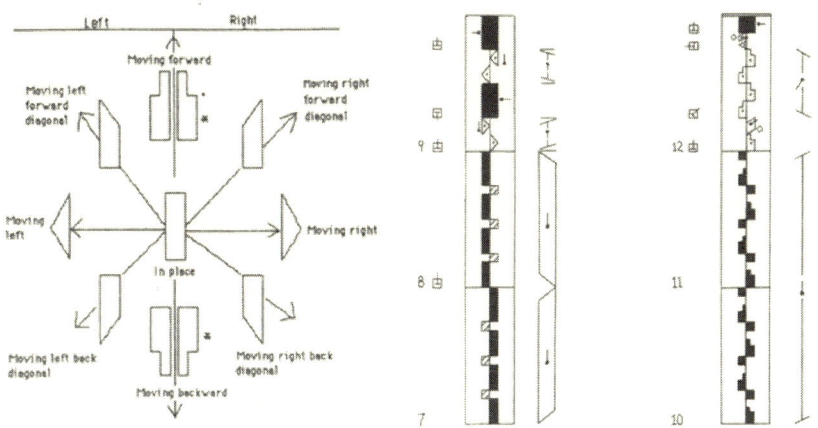

Labanotation diagram and vertical score.

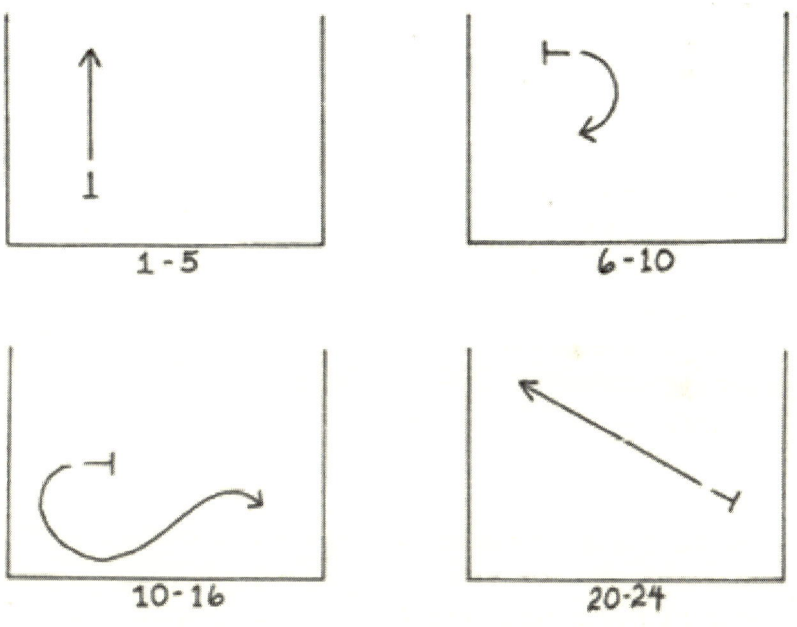

Floor diagrams

Figure 4: The stave is accompanied by a notation of movement in side diagrams and stage plans.

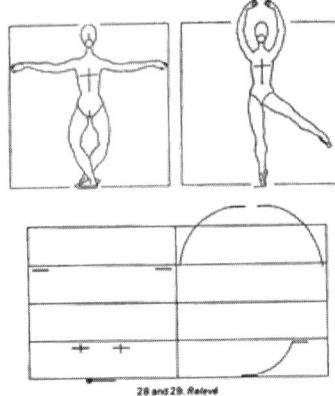

Figure 5: The Benesh score includes movement lines, drawn as the actual paths taken by the limbs, and rhythms notated with bar lines as in music.

The Benesh system, invented by Joan and Rudolph Benesh in the late 1940's, is based on abstracting the stick figure into marks of the stave while the person is recorded from a backstage or performer's view (see Figure 5). It notates the exact spots occupied by the hands and feet. Additional bends are indicated in three dimensional space (level, in back or in front of the body, etc.; see Figure 6).

Figure 6: Benesh Dance Notation. The score is accompanied by floor plans with movement paths.

The Sutton system, developed in 1972 by Valerie Sutton, is part of a greater body of work called Movement-Writing or the International Movement-Writing Alphabet. The system uses the five-line musical stave providing an audience's view of a stick figure representing the dancer. This figure changes in perspective as the performer faces into different room directions. Additional signs underneath the staves called 'position symbols' indicate the direction the figure is facing, and the relation of one limb to the other (see Figure 7). The top circle shows a head view and arm postions, the bottom circle shows a plan view and leg position (see Figure 8).

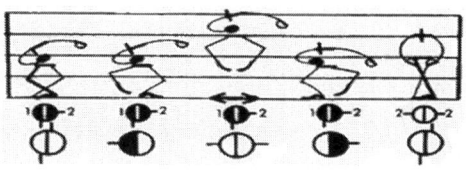

Figure 7: Sutton Dance Notation. The stave, stick figure and 'position symbols'.

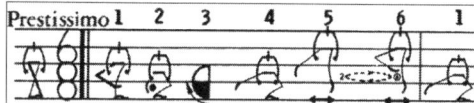

Figure 8: Within the stave signs of musical pulse and meter are added as well as signs to show travelling, walking, jumping, et cetera.

Dance notation systems can provide a useful model to think about paths in terms of continuous body movement, rhythms, pacing and space, but they do not incorporate the environment (other than stage plans) into their systems. Furthermore, other notions important to spatial scoring such as sounds, smells, textures, views, enclosure, and subjective experiences are not recognized in these systems either.

The anthropologists Birdwhistell and Hall developed notation to represent body movements in relation to interpersonal communication. Birdwhistell concentrated on an annotation system for the recording of body motion

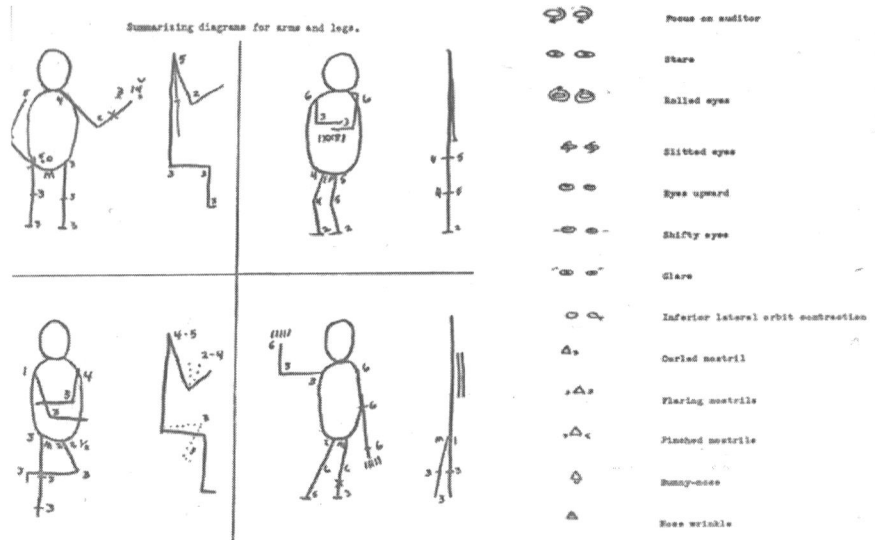

Figure 9: Birdwhistell *Body Notation*. An example of movement diagrams and coding for arms and legs (left), and diagrams for the face showing eye expressions (right).

which was designed specifically for the recording and analysis of cross-cultural data. He provided symbols to record movement for each body section concentrating on human interaction (see Figure 9).

Hall regarded the entire body as a single unit, and he developed numerical codes for scoring types of touch, types of viewing behavior, detection of body heat, body odor, and voice loudness. These two systems concentrated on interpersonal relationships and the use of movement in a social context but still, as in the dance notation systems, they do not capture the body movement through the environment.[25]

Scores and Past Efforts of Scoring in Spatial Design

A few efforts of scoring urban design have been attempted. Kevin Lynch, who together with Appleyard and Myer studied the aesthetics of highways, developed in 1964 a detailed notation system to represent visual sequences seen from an automobile. They used this system to analyze existing highways, concentrating heavily on the Northeast Expressway in Boston. They viewed highway design as a potentially artistic endeavor and stated that "the sense of spatial sequence is like that of large scale architecture; the continuity and insistent temporal flow are akin to music and the cinema. The kinesthetic sensations are like those of the dance or the amusement park, although rarely so violent. These are all arts and situations from which the highway designer may begin to learn his technique."[26] They focused on the view as seen from the driver's perspective rather than as seen from the outside (see Figure 10).

Their scoring system includes ideas of near versus distant focus of attention, awareness of moving versus static features, reactions to texture, color and width of road, tempo of attention, impact of driving speed on what people notice, and reactions to the quality of natural and artificial light. They used the scoring system to analyze highways in order to develop recommendations for improving road design (see Figures 11 and 12). They collected momentary impressions from drivers and passengers using tape recorders, cameras, sketch pads and motion pictures.[27]

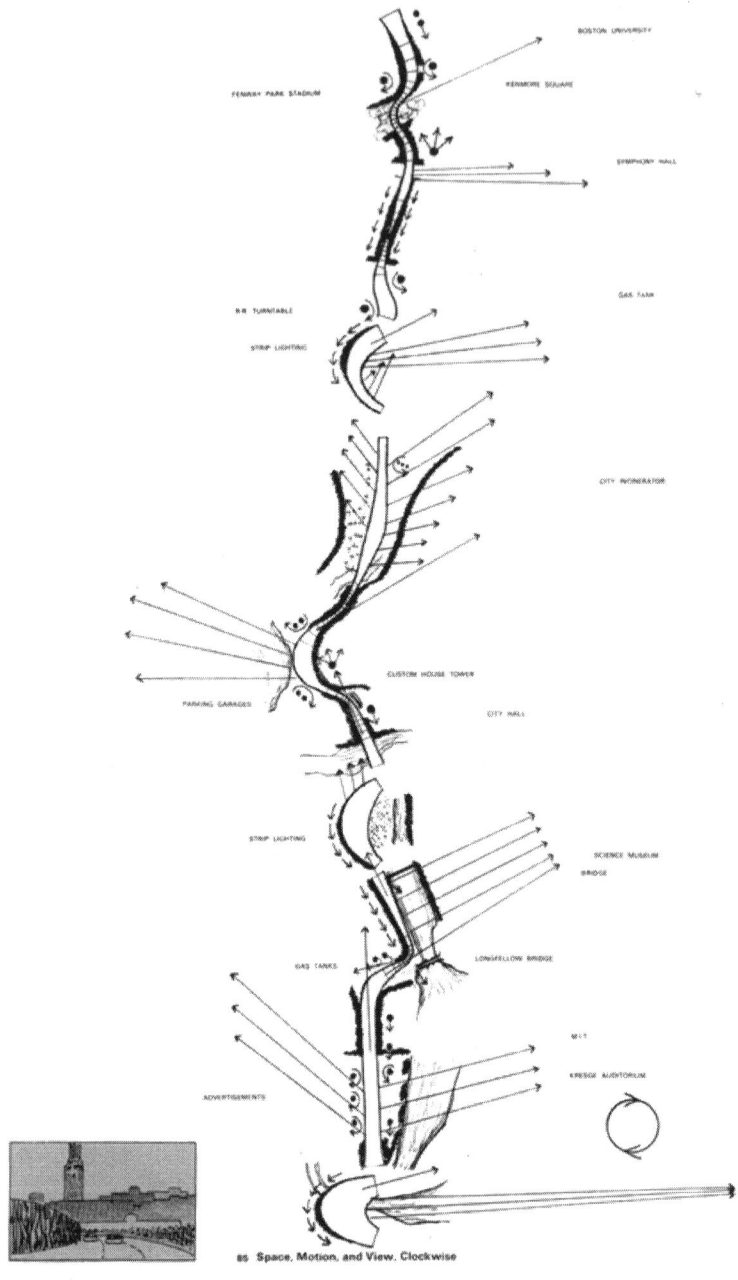

Figure 10: Lynch, Appleyard and Myer *Highway Score* (1964). In this score the speed is indicated by the number of horizontal lines within the road, the width of the roads indicates slope, narrowing as it goes downhill. Views of landmarks, edges, confining walls and turns of the road are all indicated in this score.

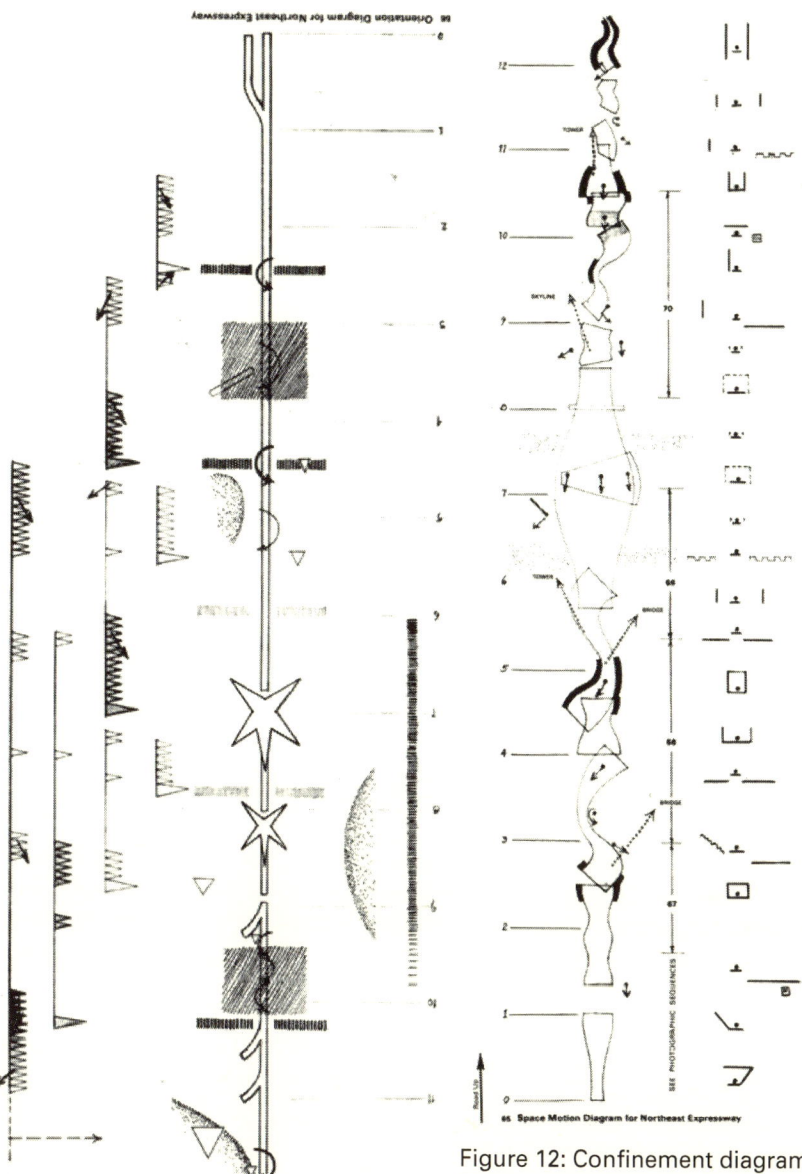

Figure 11: Orientation Diagram. This diagram shows landmarks and edges—indicating their degree of visibility—as well as marking intersecting roads.

Figure 12: Confinement diagrams. These diagrams show confinement through miniature cross section diagrams (on the right) and presumed tempo of attention connecting speed, slopes and curves. Speed is indicated by the density of horizontal lines and slopes are indicated by width of line, widening as it goes uphill.

Their system can provide an excellent model for recording ideas of designing visual sequences for the observer in motion, near/far focus of attention, and reaction to texture, color and width of road. The highway experience is similar to the path experience in that it is usually reversible, and people may enter and leave it at intermediate points. The sequence must therefore be interruptible. Yet, when attempting to emulate this system to describe the path experience, it would need to adapt to the view and the rhythms of the much slower pedestrian pace. Lynch, Appleyard, and Myer state that "the sensation of driving a car is primarily one of motion and space, felt in a continuous sequence. Vision, rather than sound or smell, is the principal sense. Touch is a secondary contributor to the experience, via the response of the car to hands and feet…Sounds, smells, sensations of touch and weather are all diluted in comparison with what the pedestrian experiences. Vision is framed and limited; the driver is relatively inactive. He has less opportunity to stop, explore, or choose his path than does the man on foot."[28] These elements all need to be addressed when attempting to apply this system or expand it to pedestrian or bicycle paths.

Philip Thiel, an urban planner and architect, developed a notational system designed to facilitate 'participatory envirotecture' in which the 'user participant's' experience of the landscape would guide professionals in landscape design (1997). His scoring system scored variables such as distance, field of view, position, and elevation in a time line measurements,[29] providing numerous diagrams for different elements of the environment. Two examples

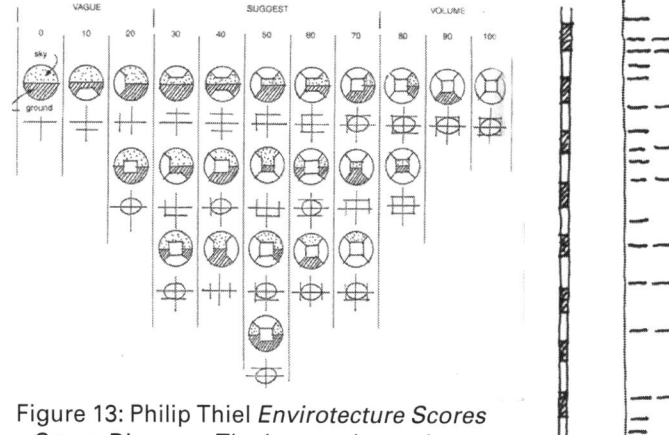

Figure 13: Philip Thiel *Envirotecture Scores* – Space Diagram. The image above shows the degree of explicitness in space from the empty terrestrial void on the upper left to the completely established and explicit space on the upper right.

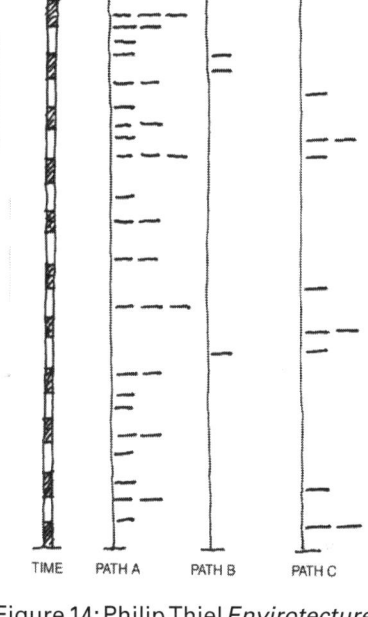

Figure 14: Philip Thiel *Envirotecture Scores* – Path Event Diagrams. A comparative time notation of path events per minute analyzing three different paths in Tokyo: an elevated freeway, a city street, and a garden path. Although the average rates of path events per foot were different, the average rates of path events per time, when traveled at the normal speeds appropriate to each, were almost identical.

are the explicitness of the space diagram and the path event diagram (see Figures 13 and 14).

Thiel's preliminary idea of developing a system which would guide professionals in analyzing and designing new places is intriguing, but his notational system scores vast amounts of data in which he abstracts each variable independently. He provides a compilation of snapshots viewed in sequence rather than a time-space continuum, more in accordance with the great film master Sergei Eisenstein's montage technique, in which Eisenstein managed to combine spatial and temporal dimensions with movement in the medium of cinema.[30]

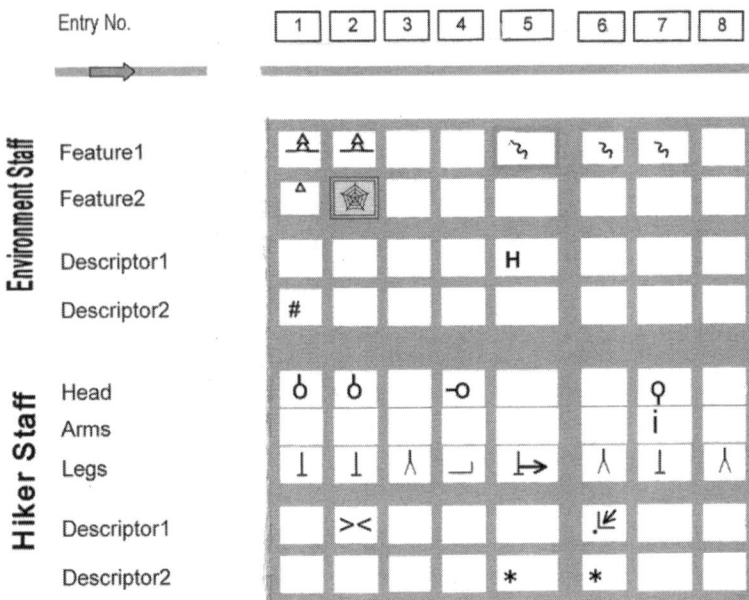

Figure 15: Claudia Mausner's HIKEN™ Trail Notation. This system of dual staves records the experience of the hiker in the environment. The notational system scores emotions, thoughts and perceptions, incorporating the environmental features of terrain, significant changes in hikers' perceptions, multi-sensory information, body action and emotional responses (Note: Many HIKEN™ symbols for the environment were borrowed or adapted from International Orienteering Federation symbols, using the O Symbol font © 1990-1994 by Martin Minow).

A recent attempt in scoring hiking trails (2001), which incorporates objective and subjective experiences of the hikers, was made in a Ph.D. thesis by the environmental psychologist Claudia Mausner. She provided a system of dual staves, one for the hiker and one for the environment, in which she developed a notational system that scores emotions, thoughts and perceptions. It incorporates the environmental features of terrain, significant changes in hikers' perceptions, multisensory information, body action and emotional responses (see Figure 15). Providing hikers with a forehead-mounted microvideo camera to make

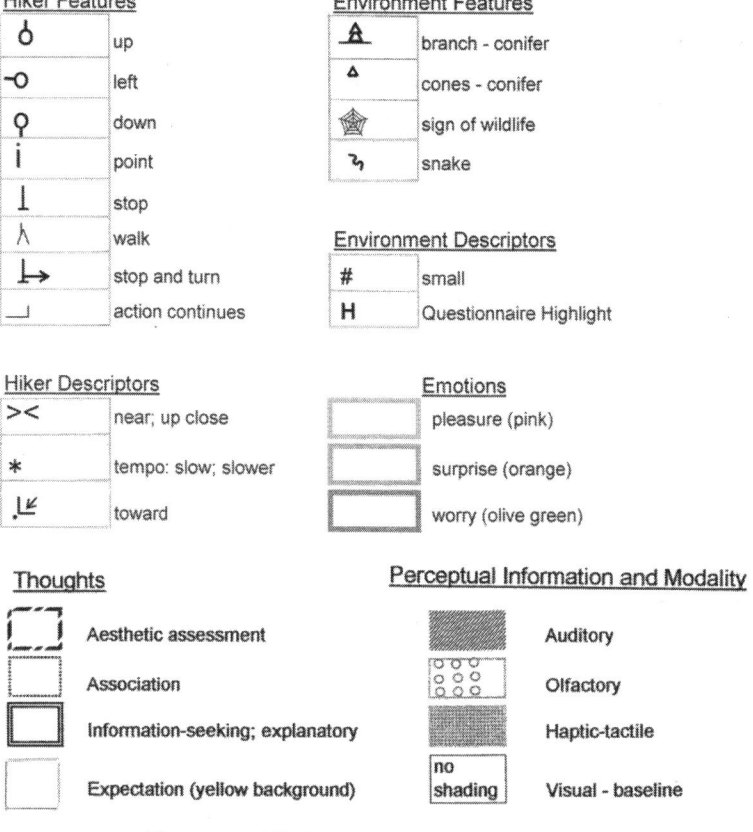

Figure 16: HIKEN™ Trail Notation Legend

continuous recordings, she later used the scoring system to analyze their experience of the hike.

Mausner concludes that when analyzing each videotaped hike as a sequence of events, there is so much data that it needs to be condensed in the form of a graphic representation (see Figure 16). She further claims that "in spite of the difficulties inherent in this task, there" is also "a real need for composite notation, for without such notation any large-scale, cross-hike visual analysis cannot be effectively accomplished." Her system is not designated

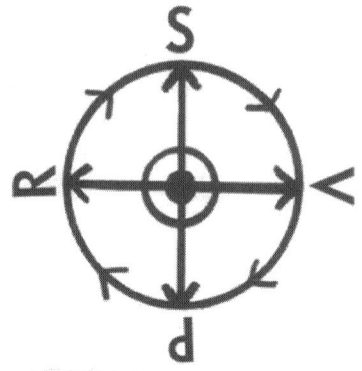

Figure 17: Lawrence Halprin *RSVP Cycle* Diagram (1969). The diagrams shows the interrelated parts of the design process: *R*esources, *S*cores, *V*aluaction and *P*erformance.

for design purposes as much as for recording subjective experiences.[31]

One cannot discuss scoring techniques without mentioning the work of Landscape Architect Lawrence Halprin, who saw the score mainly as a device of conveying the *process* of design. Halprin's basic concept diagram of the RSVP Cycle—the basic structure of the design process—notates the reciprocal relationship between *Resources* (inventoried resources, established motivations, enun-ciated purposes, determined requirements), *Score* (describes processes leading to performance), *Valuaction* (incorporates change based on feedback and selectivity, including decisions) and *Performance* (establishes "style" of the accomplishment of the process (see Figure 17).[32]

In his book, *RSVP Cycles*, Halprin maintains that the score is a device that can help a participatory process in design. He claims that the scoring process is the *crux* of creativity for any artist, be it musician, dancer, or architect. The scores focus on the transformation of the role of the "performer," which lends him or her a new control over the events, and points out the far-reaching consequences of their new role when concerning artistic processes in the realm of architecture and urban design in the community.

Scores are symbolizations of processes, which extend over time. The most familiar kind of score is a musical one but I have extended this meaning to include scores in all fields of human endeavor...I saw scores as a way of describing all such processes in all the arts, of making process visible and thereby designing with process through scores. I saw scores also as a way of communicating these processes over time and space to other people in other places at other moments and as a vehicle to allow many people to enter into the act of creation together, allowing for participation, feedback and communications.[33]

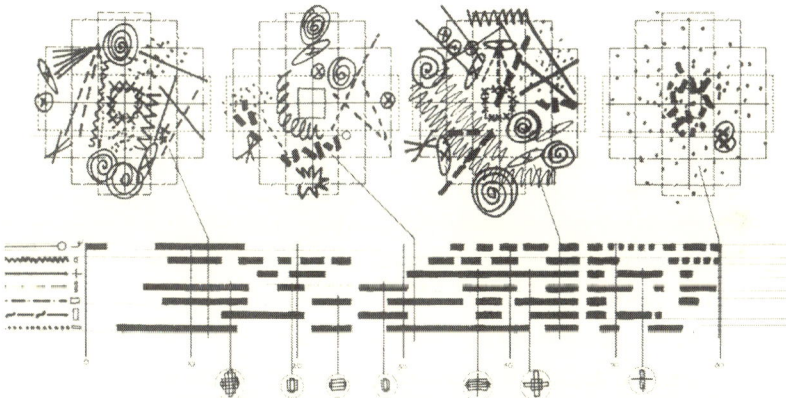

Figure 18: Lawrence Halprin's score for the *Overhoff-Halprin Fountain*, Seattle, WA. The score for the fountain notates motion over time as a physical element, without the interaction of people. It scores the process of water effects over a period of time based on the piping, water pressures, wind, timing, gallons per minute, and special types of heads.

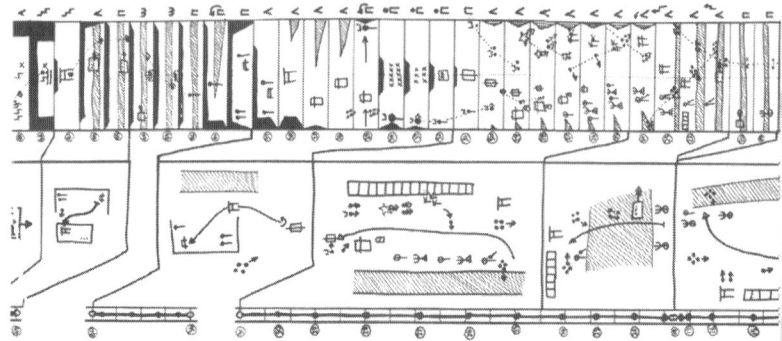

Figure 19: Lawrence Halprin, *Motation study – Nicolett Mall Between 6th and 7th Streets,* Minneapolis, MN. This study attempts to score actual people-motion through space. Halprin's basic conception is that environments and people can be scored together in a choreography of motion.

Halprin suggests different approaches to scoring the environment. A few examples are his scores of motion over time in physical elements, without the interaction of people, such as the score for the Overhoff-Halprin fountain at the Seattle Center (see Figure 18) and scores of actual people-motion through space for analysis purposes called *Motation Studies* (see Figure 19).

Halprin's notion of the score as a means of communication is very appealing, as this aspect is traditionally neglected in the process of recording a design. The score as a means of interaction between designers and people experiencing the landscape should be incorporated in any attempt to create an environmental scoring technique, though the focus need not necessarily be applied only to the communal process.

From the previous review of noticeable efforts to score linear sequences, movement and the environment, it is evident that these diverse attempts to date have not offered a comprehensive, systematic way of scoring the spatial linear experience. The limitations of each system calls for a need to integrate the succesful elements of each and provide the missing components, in an effort to create a systematic scoring approach that is well adapted to the pedestrian experience of linear sequences in space. This system should incorporate the strong elements of each system to better capture the holistic experience of the landscape path and the multisensorial experience it offers, and provide a system with which designers could conceive future spaces.

In the following section I propose a new scoring system for linear paths that, following Philip Thiel's notion, could be used as a tool for the designer to analyze existing 'successful' paths as well as to design future ones. This system incorporates elements of motion and rhythm with multi-sensory, physical, ocular and subjective experiences into a simultaneous score representing the polyphony of concurrent experiences, which should be visibly appealing and readily understood. It attempts to bring together the many elements which the score can communicate as considerations of design.

I chose to begin by developing a scoring system which is most applicable to landscape settings, since the landscape envelops us totally and controls our experience extensively, and the linear sequences of paths within the landscape settings are more extensive. In the future, the system could be applied and further developed to capture the linear sequences within architectural settings as well as sequences of much larger contexts such as roads and city networks.

A New System of Scoring the Path

The scoring system for paths is to be used by the designer of linear sequences and space to analyze the experiences that his or her path will capture, and convey it to others involved in the process. It is therefore a tool of analysis, process and design. It should assist the architect or landscape architect to reach his or her design goals of shaping the path experience to provide a rich and multi-sensorial sequence with continuity, rhythm and development; an experience that provides contrasts, well-joined transitions, and a moving balance. Its objective is to lend the person experiencing the landscape an orientation where he or she can locate him or her self and the major features of the landscape, sense their movement throughout it and deepen the grasp of the meaning of their environment. The system could help to provide an understanding of the use, history, nature or symbolism of the landscape.

Rudolph and Joan Benesh, while developing their dance notation system, stated that "the key to the break-through is simplicity." They go on to explain that a work of art is complex but it must appear simple. "Simplicity does not necessarily mean omitting and reducing the value of things; it means embracing everything that is needed into a simple unified theory or concept."[34] Their conclusion is that a scoring system must be extremely flexible if it is to be alive and continue to grow.

Lynch and Appleyard have identified that without a technique of recording, analyzing and communicating visual sequences they were unable to express or refine design alternatives..."this would be analogous to music without a notation, or architecture without drawing, both are possible and have occurred but the growth of the art is thereby restricted."[35] A plan view presents the material as a static overall pattern rather than a dynamic sequence and misses much of the information. In order to design a moving and meaningful path, with multi-sensorial effects and experiences, the designer has to notate the components he or she tries to incorporate as well as the ones they strive to avoid. The scoring system rises upon these notions.

The scoring system is to accompany the traditional plan view, therefore it should not repeat the elements obvious from the plan, such as the exact planting, lighting, water fountains, paving and such, but should concentrate on notating the effect they have on the experience. For instance, not every tree will be notated on the score but a tree of special significance (being a landmark) or a grouping which gives a certain rhythm will be indicated as such in the score.

In developing this notational system I have identified ten preliminary components, though the scoring system should be open and flexible enough to incorporate an array of additional ones. The designer must decide on the details of the following:

1. Environment, general "feel" and intended ambiance.
2. Season or time of day to which the score applies
3. Linear pattern of path
4. Crossroads

5. Enclosure, sense of enclosure or openness
6. Direction of movement, curves and diversions
7. Rhythm
8. Pace
9. Slopes and their relation to tempo and views
10. Sensual stimuli symbols :
    - Smell: the specifics of positive smells (eliminate bad smells)
    - Sound: the specifics of positive sounds (eliminate bad sounds)
    - Views: distant or near focal points

The Stave

The elements will be displayed as an array of graphic symbols and words, arranged vertically and horizontally on a linear stave moving from left to right, in a manner similar to traditional music and dance scores. The first measure displays the time of year or day it was scored or meant to be experienced. It defines at what distance intervals the path was scored according to the intensity of

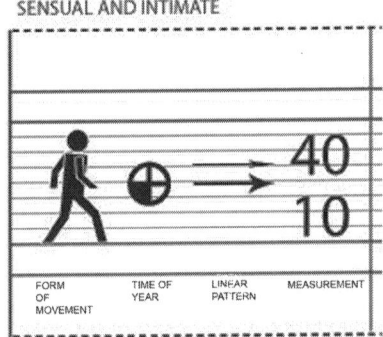

Figure 20: The Opening Measure of the Stave. The first measure of the stave indicates a general environment of "sensual and intimate" path for pedestrian experience during the spring, which is part of a parallel path pattern with a pace of 10' per note and 40' per measure.

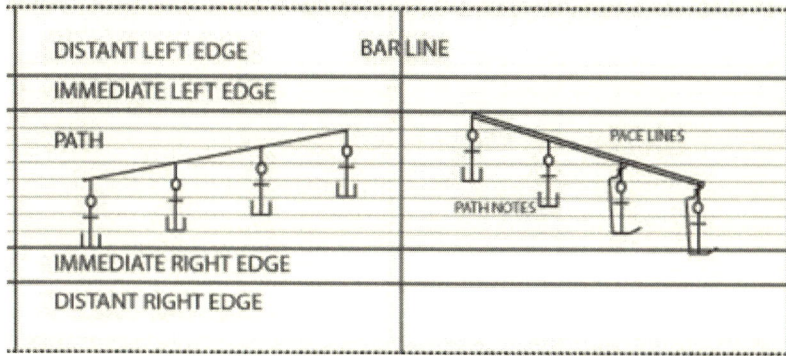

Figure 21: The Path Stave. In this example the three parts of the stave are seen: path, immediate and distant edge.

events along the path. For instance, a very straight direct and monotonous path can be scored with path-notes indicating change every 20' as compared to a very winding path with constantly changing views and enclosures which would be better scored at the distance of 5' for each path-note. The first measure of the stave indicates this path-note distance and how the path-notes are grouped into measures (see Figure 20).

The Stave is a translation of information found in plans and section that highlights, amplifies and isolates important aspects of the path experience. It is a combination of the path in plan and section viewed simultaneously; the height of the path-notes on the stave follows the slope of the path as a continuous cross section, while the bottom and top lines of the stave correspond to the right and left sides of the path in that order, as seen from the plan view (see Figure 21). These are aligned with graphic symbols of events, and stimuli along the path's sides. As in the Benesh and Sutton dance staves and the Appleyard et al. highway score, the proposed stave has several different sections. The middle represents the actual area of the path and contains the path notes and experiences on the path itself, such as odors and plaques. The adjacent narrow sections represent the immediate edges of the path, containing rhythmical indications and symbols of edges and experiences such as nodes, rest areas, and aural experiences. They represent the left (upper part) and right (lower part) sides of the path. The outer sections represent the distant edges of the path, and are more symbolic as they include views of landmarks which are miles away but shape the experience of the path itself.

Path Notes

The path-notes are a combination of musical notes, indicating height of pitch and duration, with Appleyard, Lynch and Myer's symbols of road enclosure. The placement of the path-notes on the stave indicates the relative height of the path, in a manner similar to a cross section as displayed in Figure 21. The graphic symbols themselves indicate the path's immediate enclosure and confinement representing the height of a person's head and arms, and the changing states of confinement in which he or she is at certain moments of their movement.

Figure 22: Path-Note symbols indicating enclosure (images courtesy of the author).

1. Environment, General "Feel" and Ambiance Intended

As in many artistic mediums, a title or indication of ambiance can provide an idea of the overall interpretation. Musical scores will often begin with indication of tempo and ambiance such as "Andante Religioso" (at a walking religious pace) of "Allegro Vivace" (fast and full of life). In some cases the designer may choose to indicate such an ambiance to a certain path or segment of a path. Words such as "mysterious", "intimate", "royal", "passionate", "energetic", "contemplative" and others can reveal much about the intention of the design in order to later test its degree of success in providing that environment. The descriptive words should be indicated at the beginning of the score.

2. Time of Year or Day or Any Specific Information About the Scoring Implications

Certain rhythmic elements, landmarks, a sense of enclosure and other factors are strongly affected and transformed by the change of seasons. A graphic symbol of a circle divided into the four seasons of the year should show to which specific time of year the score corresponds (see Figure 23). It is important to remember that the scoring can include an additional stave or staves to indicate important changes throughout time, be it time of day or time of year, or stage of development over a few years. If a landscape is meant to be experienced differently night and day, it must be scored twice. Most landscapes might

Figure 23: Season Symbols

need a multiple scoring of effects for changing seasons, as bare trees or certain flowering trees can be landmarks or rhythmic indicators in themselves.

3. Linear Pattern of Path

Paths are commonly parts of larger networks that have various degrees and directions of linearity and choice. Adapting notions of musical open scores that allow degrees of choice in constructing a linear sequence, the designer needs to take into consideration the degree of openness of his or her proposed path. When scoring a path or a segment of a path one must indicate in a symbolic manner at the beginning (see Figure 24) to which of ten general patterns this specific path belongs.

- **Linear: A Sequence of Events Along a Line**
    - Infinite linear – circulating paths, such as the ones at Olmsted's Mount Desert Island and Valkenburgh's Mill Race Park
    - Linear directional – a one-direction, often narrative sequence, such as Ross's landing designed by EDAW, and Lawrence Halprin's design of the FDR Memorial in Washington D.C..
    - Linear reversible – sequences which are interruptible such as Frank Lloyd Wright's Taliesin West.

- **Forking Paths of Limited Choice:**
    - Hierarchic forking paths such as the *Forbidden City* in Beijing, China.
    - Non-hierarchic forking paths such as the main path system designed by Olmstead in *Central Park*, New York City, NY.
    - Layered polyphonic paths such as the path systems of Bernard Tschumi's *Parc de la Villette* in Paris.
    - Parallel paths such as the *Shakespeare Garden* in Central Park, NY, offering parallel alternatives to the same destinations.

- **Open Paths:**
    - Grids and Scribbled paths, such as the Manhattan grid.
    - No paths, diverse focuses of attention, such as Isamu Noguchi's *Moerenuma Park* in Japan.
    - No paths, the meadow experience.

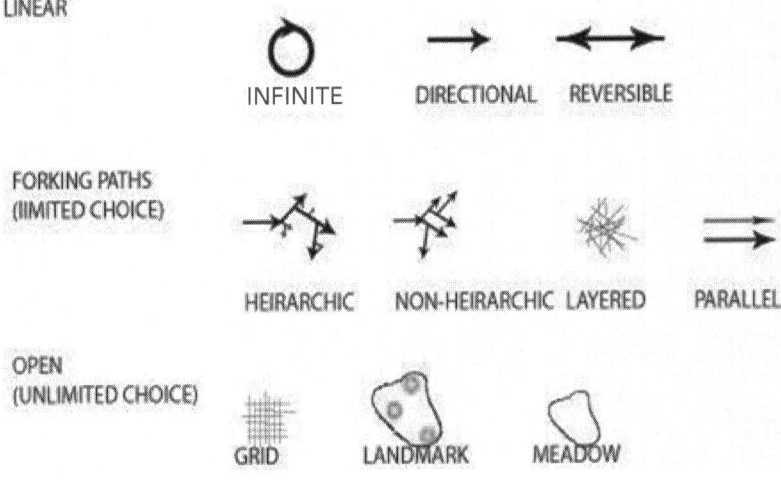

Figure 24: Linearity patterns

4. Crossroads

Since the path is part of a larger system of possibilities, a certain path taken by the scorer must indicate the meeting points and crossroads of this path with others in the system (see Figure 25).

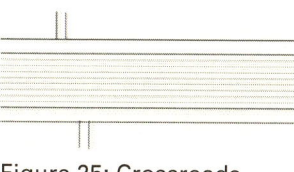

Figure 25: Crossroads

5. Sense of Enclosure

The sequences of enclosed or open spaces are a dominant factor in the experience of a path. They can be very dramatic and provide a strong sense of rhythm and pace as well as indicate change versus monotony vis-à-vis the path sequence. They also affect other physical elements such as wind, temperature, and light and shade. Spatial contrast, coming in or out of enclosures, makes a strong visual impact. Confinement is always notable: walls, tunnels or sides of hills, overhead enclosures, bridges and trellises are especially significant, as are the moments of spatial freedom. Immediate enclosure is indicated by the path-notes as explained before, and these are expanded by the edge symbols shown in Figure 26. These symbols are

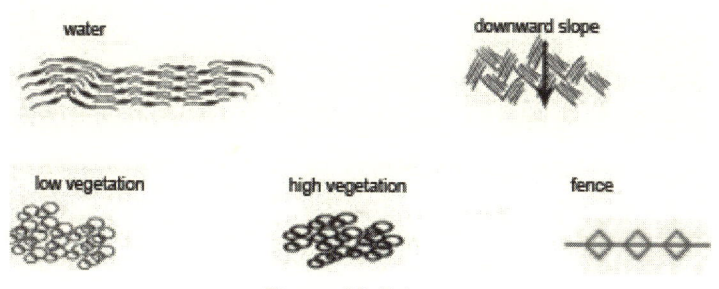

Figure 26: Edges.

derived from Appleyard, Lynch, and Myer's edge notation adapted to the pedestrian experience.

The ambiance of the enclosure and its degree of light are added as an optional layer of color and shape, going from dark (representing high enclosure) to light (representing open space, see Figure 27). This idea relates to the representation of musical graphic scores such as John Cage's *Aria* which incorporated colors in the score to denote ambiance and style.

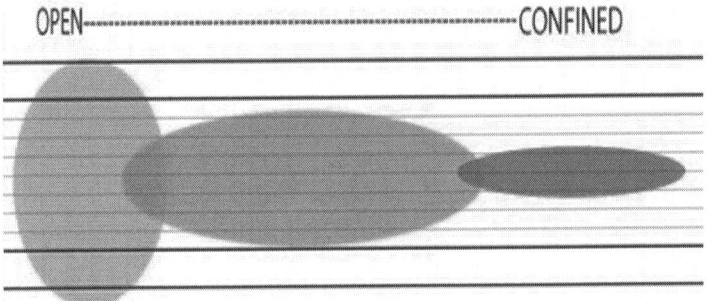

Figure 27: Enclosure and confinement

6. Direction of Movement, Curves and Diversions

Sharp changes in direction provide a sense of drama on the path and affect the change of views. They function as part of the concealing and revealing effects of a path. Graphic symbols of arrows underneath the stave will indicate curves and sharp turns (see Figure 28).

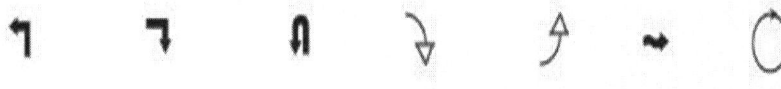

Figure 28: Symbols indicating directions and turns.

7. Rhythm

Rhythm and pace can be controlled and designed to a certain degree. The decisions should be made according to questions such as: How fast would the designer like people to go, to which places, and with what degree of change along the way; what are the indicators of resting points and the elements of visual rhythm; should they be constant or changing; should they relay a strict or flowing rhythm; should they be homophonic or polyphonic (one- or multi-layered)?

Lynch, Appleyard, and Myer conclude that "it may be that there is an optimum range for the time interval between strong impressions: that longer intervals cause boredom and shorter ones bring on strain and confusion." They conclude that it would mean that a "road-scape should have a basic beat, a regular frequency with which decisions and interesting visual impressions are presented,…the rhythm itself could differentiate and clarify the transport hierarchy."[36]

In the score, the rhythmic events on each side of the path will be indicated by dots or symbols representing the grouping and pacing of vertical elements along the path, together with a verbal description of the element (fence, poles, trees etc.; see Figure 29).

Figure 29: Rhythm as an example of different rhythmical groupings on each side of the path.

8. Pace

The pace of movement, effected by slope, views, width of path, points of interest, and such will be indicated by a system of lines connecting the path notes, similar to that of musical notes. One line indicates a relatively slow pace, growing faster as the number of lines added, increases (see Figure 30).

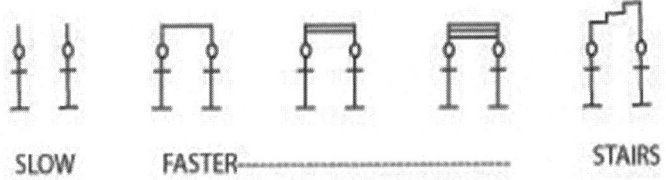

Figure 30: Speed of Pace.

9. Slopes

Slopes correspond to a change of pace. One usually slows down going up and speeds up going down. The direction of the head and the views change with strong slopes, as one's view ahead is usually restricted going up on a strong slope and going down, though the view is open, people tend to look at their feet. Slopes are indicated in the score by the height of the path notes on the staff from bottom to top, emulating a diagrammatic cross section (see Figure 31).

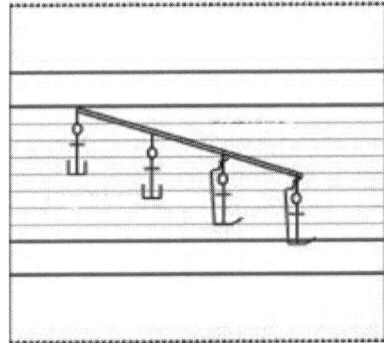

Figure 31: Slope lines – this examples shows a downward slope.

10. Sensual Stimuli Symbols:

The multi-sensorial experience must be taken into account by the designer and incorporated into the design (see Figure 32). The symbols of sensual stimuli can be placed in different places on the stave from the path itself to the near and distant edges, and can be accompanied by a verbal indication.

> Odor and Auditory Stimuli
>> Graphic symbols showing the placement of positive disturbing smells show up in the corresponding placement along the path by a symbol of dots accompanied by a verbal description of the specifics of positive or negative odors.
>
> Auditory Stimuli
>> The auditory stimuli can be very strong and effective in the path experience. Areas with strong echoes, sound-producing ground covers, auditory landmarks along the way such as amphitheaters, bells, concentration of birds as well as sound pollution of roads or factories, would be noted in corresponding placement on the path. These are scored with the symbol of a megaphone and a verbal description of the specifics of positive or negative sounds.
>
> Views and Landmarks
>> The near and distant landmarks can play

a remarkable role in the unfolding of the path. They provide the path a sense of direction, destination, and a pacing of events. Landmarks are experienced in motion and have an ever changing quality, being revealed and concealed, changing in size and point of view from which they are seen. The designer can decide what he wants to emphasize—a total skyline, a distinct character, or a single landmark—and adjust his viewing distance accordingly. As in the cinema, contrasting distances will keep his sequences legible and eventful.[37] Landmark symbols with a verbal description are scored on the sides of the stave and connected with lines to points where they are revealed. Since the stave does not curve and the paths themselves do, the same landmark may show up several times on the score, sometimes on different sides of the path and in different distances, even though it is the same single landmark in reality.

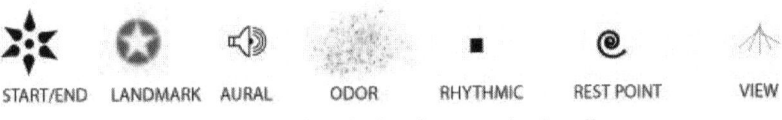

START/END LANDMARK AURAL ODOR RHYTHMIC REST POINT VIEW

Figure 32: Symbols of sensual stimuli.

A Score of Two Paths

The proposed scoring system was used to notate the experience of two very different paths. The first is the *Shakespeare Garden* path in Central park, NYC (see Figure 33). It is described by a tourist brochure in the following manner:

> The main garden path, which initiates a steep climb from the Cottage grounds, meanders through the central garden area and continues east until it reaches the summit of the rock... Bronze plaques with the quotations from the bard's great masterpieces line the winding paths adding a true bit of poetry to any romantic stroll through this spiritual space.[38]

In the Shakespeare Garden there are two alternatives to this path, a broad direct path and a narrow winding path. The latter was chosen as the subject of this score.

The second is the path on the north-eastern side of the Cherry Esplanade in the Brooklyn Botanical Gardens, NY (see Figure 34). The path accompanies a broad green field planted with 76 specimens of the dazzling Prunus 'Kanzan'. It is a straight direct path lined with Cherry trees on both sides in a very rhythmical manner.

It is my assumption that the comparison of the two scores, even at first glance, can convey a great deal of information on the experience of each path and express their very diverse characters. An alternative method to

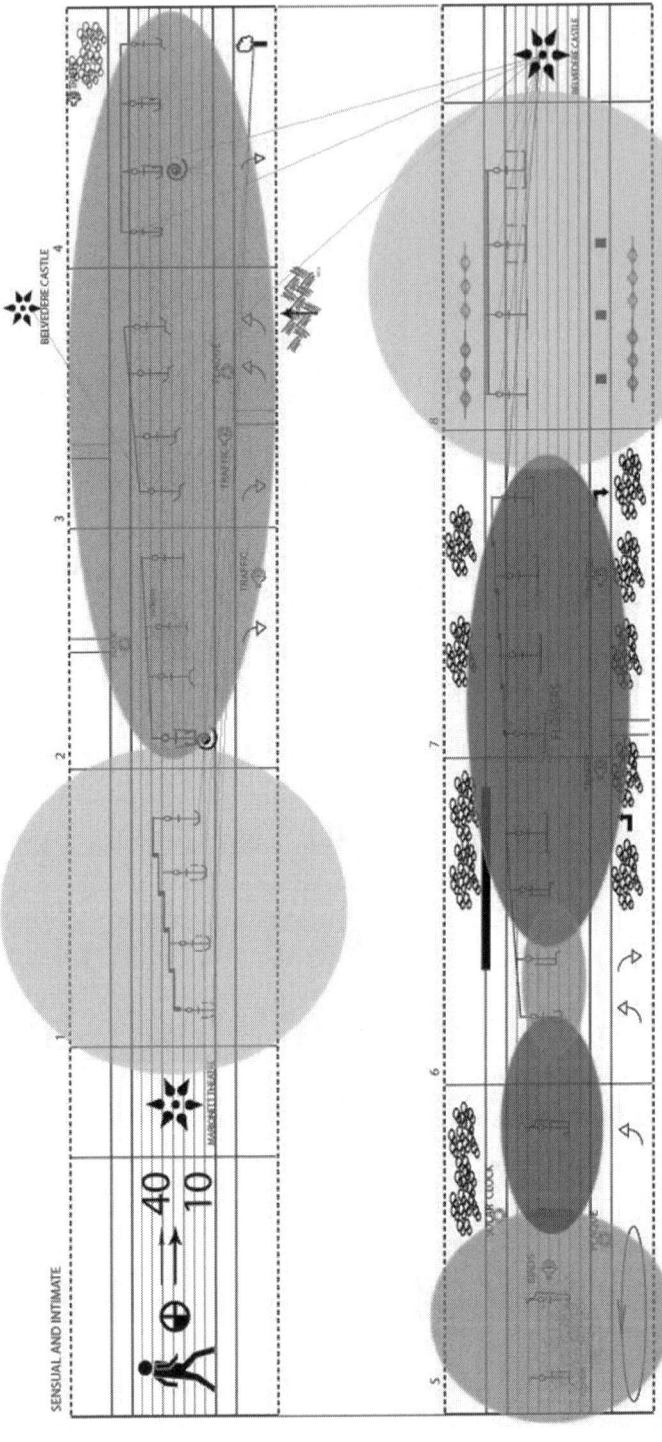

Figure 33: Score of the Shakespeare Garden

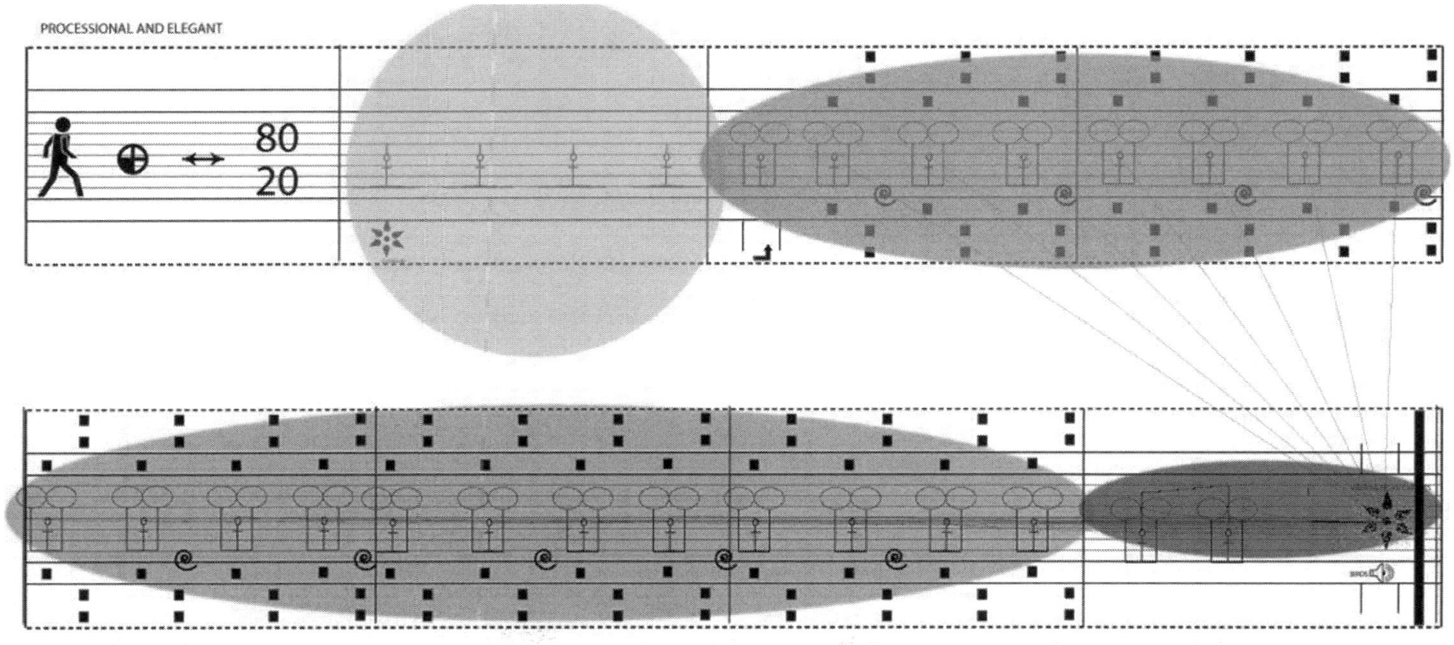

PROCESSIONAL AND ELEGANT

80
20

Figure 34: Cherry Esplanade Path

express the paths would be a detailed verbal description of the path experience. In an attempt to compare the effort of the score to that of the verbal description I shall describe the Shakespeare Garden path verbally aligned with the measure numbers of the score.

Alternative Verbal Description Method

The Shakespeare Garden path was experienced at walking pace during the spring. It is a part of a parallel path network. The chosen path stayed within the intimate and sensual path and did not choose the wider more direct path parallel to the beginning and ending landmarks. It was scored such that each path note represents 10', and each measure 40'. The starting landmark was the Marionette theatre and the ending landmark was Belvedere Castle. The path chosen went uphill continuously with steps and curves.

Measure 1: One climbs up a staircase limited by a wooden handrail and reaches a fence-confined rest area with benches on both sides. Throughout this sequence a landmark oak tree can be seen to the front right. The space is relatively unconfined and open.

Measure 2: A resting space with benches is reached. The path becomes elevated, then ground-level and curves to the right. An option to divert to a path returning to the Marionette theatre is passed on the left. A plaque of a Shakespeare quote is passed on the left, traffic is heard to the right and a strong flower aroma arises from the flower beds of the spring. The space becomes more confined by trees at a distance of a few feet from the path.

Measure 3: At the beginning of the third measure a glimpse of Belvedere castle is experienced. Two cross paths are passed on the left hand side and later on the right. Traffic is heard on the right. The path curbs almost every few steps and the castle can be seen to the right on the third path note. On the fourth note the elevated path is now confined by the slope to the right.

Measure 4: The Marionette theater can be viewed in the first two notes. The path turns to the right and a resting area with benches providing a view is reached. The path begins low, and on the third note a slope edge confining the space to the left is present, and traffic is still heard beyond it. On the fourth note the landmark oak is passed on the left.

Measure 5: This section is mostly circular with points of interest. It is confined by trees with strong flower aroma and bird chirps. There are plaques and a solar clock. On the fourth note a strong tree edge is present to the left and the path curves to the left. The sense of enclosure and intimacy is strong in this measure.

Measure 6: The path here curves to the left, then to the right and the fourth note is a sharp left turn, joining into the parallel path. The path starts out sunken and is then confined with a wall to the left. On the third and fourth note a strong tree edge confining the person is present.

Measure 7: The path passes a bed of flowers with strong aroma. It climbs a set of stairs confined by low walls with a strong edge of trees on both sides. The space feels confined and dark. Traffic noise is present to the right. On the fourth note the path turns right and Belvedere Castle is seen clearly for the first time, leading the path to approach it now very directly.

Measure 8: A faster pace is apparent as the elevation stabilizes. The final landmark is clearly seen ahead. There is a rhythm of trees to the right. The path becomes confined by a fence on the third and fourth notes as one reaches the endpoint of the wall surrounding Belvedere Castle and the steps leading up to it. For the first time there is a sense of open space beyond the immediate trees and a clear progression towards the ending landmark.

Language represents meaning successionally while notation can represent meanings simultaneously. A comparison of utilization of the verbal description versus the score to analyze and understand an existing path demonstrates that different notions such as of the sense of space, degree of curviness, diversion versus monotony, rhythmical aspects, and an understanding of views, directions and landmarks are more readily available to the observer of the score than to the reader of the verbal description. Understanding the verbal description would require more imagination on the behalf of the reader and not necessarily relate to the spatial and visual aspect of the discipline. It is therefore evident that the detailed description provides a very laborious alternative to the reading of the score. A second alternative to the score would be a linear vertical filmstrip of still photos taken at a measured distance emulating the experience of motion through the path (see Figure 35). The limitation of this alternative is the camera, its focal range, and its focus on the ocular perspectives. If it is focused on the path itself one misses the edges and enclosures, and the ability to observe views and distant landmarks. It does not incorporate the other senses, nor does it indicate odors and aural stimuli, and it does not relate to changes over time.

The traditional plan view, sections and perspectives, as discussed earlier, lack the ability to incorporate a sense of motion, rhythm and pace as well as multi-sensorial information, and the possibility of change over time.

Figure 35: A linear vertical filmstrip of still photos (images courtesy of the author).

Conclusions

The idea of perceiving space as a stream of voices, each representing a different aspect of the experiential quality of a linear sequence, could broaden the visual approach to design into a means for a richer experience. When scoring the multi-dimensional space it should be regarded as polyphony, incorporating voices that are independently layered but converge to create harmony at certain points. The term, being musical in essence, refers to a texture consisting of two or more independent melodic voices, as opposed to music with just one voice (monophony) or music with one dominant melodic voice accompanied by chords (homophony). A musical polyphony traditionally involves the idea of harmony or points where independent voices join into a single harmony along the way. The polyphony of a landscape or an architectural space will incorporate the use of all senses, and focus on ideas that are readily available to the person experiencing it, observing, touching, and smelling, moving or listening within it. It could offer a new form of drawing integrating Corners' vision of spatiality, temporality and materiality.[39]

Capturing the holistic experience of the path and the multi-sensorial experience it offers, proposes a challenge to the fields of architecture and landscape architecture. The limitations of the plan view, filmstrips and verbal descriptions provided above are evident and have demonstrated a need for a new notational system as observed in other arts such as music and dance. While many related scoring systems in music and dance have made efforts to incorperate linear aspects of sequence, form and movement, and many spatial designers have argued its importance and have made some efforts of developing new scoring systems, to date there is no comprehensive, systematic way of scoring the landscape path experience.

The proposed notation system for linear sequences in space could assist the design goals of shaping the path experience to provide a rich and multi-sensorial sequence with continuity, rhythm and development, providing contrasts, well-joined transitions, and a moving balance. Its objective is to lend the person experiencing the space an orientation where he or she can locate themselves and the major features of the space, sense their movement throughout it, and deepen the grasp of the meaning of their environment. This should help to provide an understanding of the use, history, and nature or symbolism of the space.[40]

This scoring system incorporates the strong elements of the reviewed scoring systems in music, dance and the environment, to better capture and provide a system with which designers could conceive future spaces. It would be used by the architect and/or landscape architect to analyze the experiences which his or her path will capture and convey it to others involved in the process. It is therefore a tool of analysis, process, and design, and should be used in a flexible manner, adhering to its fundamental ideas while expanding the specific symbols, path-notes and such to include diverse situations not discussed in this essay.

Endnotes

[1] Johnson, Philip. *Interview*, in Peter, John. *The Oral History of Modern Architecture: Interview with the Greatest Architects of the Twentieth Century.* Track 5. 1994. Produced by Harry N. Abraham, Inc. New York USA OHMA-001.

[2] Corners, James. "Representation and the Landscape." *Word & Image* 8:3 (July-September, 1992): 243.

[3] Lynch, Kevin. *The Image of the City.* (Cambridge, MA: MIT Press, 1960): 107.

[4] Appleyard, Donald, Kevin Lynch and John R. Myer. *The View from the Road.* (Cambridge, MA: MIT Press, 1964): 17.

[5] Ibid.: 17.

[6] As Quoted in Pallasmaa, Juhani, *The Eyes of the Skin: Architecture and the Senses.* (Chichester: Wiley-Academy; Hoboken, NJ: John Wiley & Sons, 2005): 25.

[7] Ong, Walter J. *Orality and Literacy.* (London and New York: Routledge Press, 1991). As quoted in Pallasmaa: 24-25.

[8] Gropius, Walter. *Architektur.* (Frankfurt and Hamburg: Fischer, 1956): 15-25.

[9] Le Corbusier. *Precisions.* (Cambridge, MA; MIT Press, 1991).

[10] Gibson, James, J. *The Perception of the Visual World,* (Boston: Houghton Bifflin, 1950).

[11] Hall, Edward T. "Art, Space and Human Experience," in Kepes, Gyorgy.ed. *Arts of the Environment.* (New York: George Braziller, 1965): 52-59.

[12] Treib, Mark. "Must Landscape Mean? Approaches to Significance in Recent Landscape Architecture," *Landscape Journal* 14 no. 1 (1995): 47-62.

[13] Lynch, Kevin and Gary Hack. "Site Design," in *Site Planning*, 3rd edition. (Cambridge, Mass: MIT Press, 1984): 127-129.

[14] Krog, Steven. "Creative Risk Taking," *Landscape Architecture* 73, no. 3 (1983): 70-76.

[15] Ibid.: 243-275.

[16] Lynch, Kevin. *The Image of the City*. (Cambridge, MA: MIT Press, 1960): 113.

[17] Rastall, Richard. *The Notation of Western Music*. (New York, St. Martin's Press, 1982): 2-3.

[18] Cardew, Cornelius. "Notation-Interpretation, Etc." *Tempo* 58 (Summer 1961), 30.

[19] For more on open and graphic scores see Hanoch-Roe, Galia. "Musical Space and Architectural Time." IRASM 34 (2003) 2, 145-160.

[20] Other known examples of works which employ mobile-open forms are Karlheinz Stockhausen's *Klavierstück XI* (1956). This work is constructed of nineteen groups placed on one manuscript, to which the composer instructs that at the end of the first group, the performer should read the tempo, dynamic and attacks indications that follow, and look at random to any other group, which he then shall play in accordance with the latter indications; Pierre Boulez's *Third Piano Sonata* with arrangements of eight possible manners of ordering the five movements. The work includes visual layouts of poems by Mallarmé ("Un coup de dés"—The throwing of dice), Cummings and Joyce. The

Sonata's score resembles a road map, which is in its own way a kind of score (for 'performance' by an automobile driver. David Bedford's *Fun for all the Family* (1970), is constructed as a game chart. All players begin on the square marked "start," each player makes four short sounds, choosing pitches, either pp or mf during the duration of the square (each square lasts 20"). The performers split off into two groups, then four and finally eight distinct parts, eventually joining again at the end. William Duckworth's *Pitch City* (1969) is a work for any four wind instruments, and specifies pitch and note-to-note successions, but not register, rhythm, duration, instrumental timbre, or the precise synchronization of parts. Duckworth chooses to control mood, overall gesture and large-scale continuity but requires each of the four performers to follow a path from one of the corner F#'s to the F# at the center.

[21] Cage, John. "Form is Language," in *John Cage*. Edited by Richard Kostelanetz. (New York, Washington: Praeger Publishers, 1970): 135-140.

[22] See Halprin, Lawrence. *The RSVP Cycles: Creative Processes in the Human Environment*. (New York: Braziller, Inc., 1969).

[23] The Cell Blocks' principle is so organized that not only are all the parts independent and therefore can be reassembled, assembled and reassembled in infinite combinations, each combination generating a different quality, but the sequence can start from any point. In terms of development new cell blocks can be added, others omitted, so that over a period of several years the same score can be in operation but entirely new cell blocks can

be inserted to the extent that the original has very little resemblance to the new one.

[24] See Guest, Ann Hutchinson. *Nijinsky's Faune Restored: a Study of Vaclav Nijinsky's 1915 Dance Score : L'après-midi d'un faune and his Dance Notation System Revealed.* (Philadelphia: Gordon and Breach, 1991); Guest, Ann Hutchinson. *Choreo-graphics : Comparison of Dance Notation Systems from the Fifteenth Century to the Present.* (New York: Gordon and Breach, 1989).

[25] Hall, Edward T. *The Silent Language.* (Greenwich, Conn.: Fawcett Publications 1969); Birdwhistell, Ray L. *Kinesics and Context; Essays on Body Motion Communication.* (Philadelphia, University of Pennsylvania Press, 1970).

[26] Appleyard, et al, *The View from the Road*: 4.

[27] Ibid.: 4.

[28] Ibid.: 4.

[29] Thiel, Philip. *People, Paths, and Purposes : Notations for a Participatory Envirotecture.* (Seattle, WA: University of Washington Press, 1997).

[30] Eisenstein, Sergei. *Film Form: Essays in Film Theory.* (New York: Harcourt, Brace & World, Inc., 1949): 69.

[31] Mausner, Claudia. "Capturing the Hike Experience on Video: A New Methodology for Studying Human Transactions with Nature." Dissertation, (City University of New York, 2004): 231-232.

[32] Ibid.: 191.

[33] Halprin, The RSVP Cycles: 1.

[34] Ibid.: 191.

[35] Appleyard et al. *The View from the Road*: 19.

[36] Ibid.: 17.

[37] Ibid.: 19.

[38] Retrieved from http://www.centralpark2000.com/database/shakespeare_garden.html on 5/1/06.

[39] As expressed in Corners, James. "Representation and the Landscape." *Word & Image* 8:3 (July-September, 1992): 243.

[40] Many of the principles adhere to Appleyard, Lynch and Myer's principal objectives of highway design, see Appleyard et al, *The View from the Road*: 18.

List of Figures

Figure 1: Earl Brown *Avialable Forms* (1961) Brown, E. (1961). New York, NY: AMP/G. Schirmer.

Figure 2: Earl Brown *December 1952* Brown, E (1954). *Folio and four systems.* AMP/G. Schirmer; and Piet Mondrian *Composition 10, Pier & Ocean* (1915) http://www.artyfactory.com

Figure 3: John Cage *Aria* (1958), Edition Peters 6701, 1960 by Henmar Press

Figure 4: Rudolph Laban, *Labonotation Scores,* Kinkead, Mary Ann (1982). *Elementary Labonotation.* (CA: Mayfield Publishing Company).

Figure 5: Joan and Rudolph Benesch, *Benesch Score* Benesch, J and Bensch, R. (1982). *Reading Dance.* CA: Mayfield Publishing Company.

Figure 6: Joan and Rudoph Benesch, *Benesch Dance Notation* Benesch, J and Bensch, R. (1982). *Reading Dance.* CA: Mayfield Publishing Company

Figure 7: Valerie Sutton, *Sutton Dance Notation,* http://www.dancewriting.org

Figure 8: Valerie Sutton, *Sutton Dance Notation,* http://www.dancewriting.org

Figure 9: Ray Birdwhistle, *Body Notation.* Birdwhistle, Ray L. (1970). *Kinesics and context: Essays on body motion communication.* Philadelphia: University of Pennsylvania Press, 1970).

Figure 10: Appleyard, Lynch and Myer, *Highway Score.* Appelyard, D., Lynch, K. & Myer, J.R. (1964). *The View from the road.* Cambridge, MA: MIT Press.

Figure 11: Appleyard, Lynch and Mye,r *Orientation Diagram*. Appelyard, D., Lynch, K. & Myer, J.R. (1964). *The View from the road*. Cambridge, MA: MIT Press

Figure 12: Appleyard, Lynch and Mye,r *Confinement Diagrams*, Appelyard, D., Lynch, K. & Myer, J.R. (1964). *The View from the road*. Cambridge, MA: MIT Press

Figure 13: Philip Thiel, *Envirotecture Score – Space Diagram*, Thiel, P. (1997) *People, paths, and purposes : Notations for a participatory envirotecture.* Seattle, WA : University of Washington Press.

Figure 14: Philip Thiel, *Envirotecture Score – Path Event Diagrams*, Thiel, P. (1997) *People, paths, and purposes : Notations for a participatory envirotecture.* Seattle, WA : University of Washington Press.

Figure 15: Claudia Mausner, *HIKEN Sample Notation* (Image courtesy of Claudia Mausner)

Figure 16: Claudia Mausner *Hiken Sample Notation Key* (Image courtesy of Claudia Mausner)

Figure 17: Lawrence Halprin, *RSVP Cycle Diagram*. Halprin, L. (1969). *The RSVP cycles: Creative processes in the human environment.* New York: Braziller, Inc.

Figure 18: Lawrence Halprin, Score for the *Overhoff-Halprin Fountain* in Seattle, WA. Halprin, L. (1969). *The RSVP cycles: Creative processes in the human environment.* New York: Braziller, Inc.

Figure 19: Lawrence Halprin, *Motation Study – Nicolett Mall*, Minneapolis, MN. Halprin, L. (1969). *The RSVP cycles: Creative processes in the human environment.* New York: Braziller, Inc.

Figure 20: Galia Hanoch-Roe, Opening mesure of a path score.

Figure 21: Galia Hanoch-Roe, Path Stave.

Figure 22: Galia Hanoch-Roe, Path Note symbols and corresponding images (Images Courtesy of the Author).

Figure 23: Galia Hanoch-Roe, Season Symbols.

Figure 24: Galia Hanoch-Roe, Linearity Patterns.

Figure 25: Galia Hanoch-Roe, Edges Symbols.

Figure 26: Galia Hanoch-Roe, Enclosure and Confinement Symbols.

Figure 27: Galia Hanoch-Roe, Direction and Turn Symbols.

Figure 28: Galia Hanoch-Roe, Rhythmic Patterns.

Figure 29: Galia Hanoch-Roe, Speed of Pace.

Figure 30: Galia Hanoch-Roe, Slope Indication.

Figure 31: Galia Hanoch-Roe, Sensual Stimuli Symbols.

Figure 32: Galia Hanoch-Roe, Score of the Shakespeare Garden, Central Park, NY.

Figure 33: Galia Hanoch-Roe, Score of the Cherry Esplande, Brooklyn Botanical Gardens, NY.

Figure 34: Galia Hanoch-Roe, Linear vertical filmstrip of still photos (Images courtesy of the author).

Kim Chow-Morris

Rhythm of the Streets: Sounding the Structures of the City

> A damsel with a dulcimer
> In a vision once I saw:
> It was an Abyssinian maid,
> And on her dulcimer she played,
> Singing of Mount Abora.
> Could I revive within me
> Her symphony and song,
> To such a deep delight 't would win me,
> That with music loud and long,
> I would build that dome in air,
> That sunny dome! Those caves of ice!
> And all who heard should see them there,
> And all should cry, Beware! Beware!
>   Coleridge, *Kubla Khan*, 441

This excerpt from Samuel T. Coleridge's 1797 poem "Kubla Khan" fancifully imagines both sunny dome and icy cave summoned and constructed solely through music's sonic potential. One of the period's best known examples of the intersection of architectural structures and music, the words depict the possibility of the visual translation of sound. Russian composer Modest

Mussorgsky's 1874 work "Pictures at an Exhibition," too, reflects the popularity of such romantic era synaesthesia, with the sonic representation of a series of paintings by architect-designer Victor Hartmann (1833-1873) for the Academy of Artists in St. Petersburg in honor of Hartmann's unexpected death.[1] After successively musically recreating each of Hartmann's paintings, Mussorgsky's grand work concludes with a musical interpretation of Hartmann's completed design for "The Great Gate of Kiev:" an architectural tribute to Czar Alexander the Great II which may have been inspired by the 1791 construction of Berlin's Brandenburg Gate (Wright 10). While Coleridge's poem imagines the channeling of sonic power to erect an architectural edifice, Mussorgsky's work, on the contrary, interprets the architectural structures themselves sonically, approaching the relationship of the visual and the auditory from the opposite perspective.

Numerous other visual and musical artists have similarly explored the intersection of sight and sound. The one-hundred-eighty-three days of Karlheinz Stockhausen's performances in a specially-constructed dome for Expo '70 in Osaka, Japan, Morton Feldman's 1971 composition "Rothko Chapel," Brian Eno's musical relationships with visual artists of various media, and the many sound-architecture works of Iannis Xenakis, in honor of whom the *SoundaXis* conference was named, all offer worthy models for consideration and investigation.

Inspired by the *Architecture | Music | Acoustics* conference held at Ryerson University from June 7th to 10th, 2006 as part of Toronto's *SoundaXis* festival of music and architecture, architecture professor Ian MacBurnie and I determined to follow these trailblazers' leads, and explore our own sonic interpretation of visual structures focusing on the city of Toronto itself as a blueprint. Originally, MacBurnie suggested that he wished to hear the structures of Toronto *objectively* represented as sound in some manner for, as a relative newcomer to the city, he hoped to discern sonically the reasons for which he found that particular urban center so aesthetically displeasing in comparison with other cities which he had made home. 'Objectivity' is a contentious term in the field of music, where subjectivity and aesthetic choice frequently dominate debate; yet objectivity is easily embraced in the field of architectural science, where the very tangibility of buildings and structures have shaped theoretical discussions in concrete ways (Ripley 1). During several meetings in which MacBurnie and I engaged in a comparison of theoretical models within our respective fields, I related my discomfort with the concept of 'objectivity' and the idea that we can somehow consciously decide to break free from our own subjective aesthetic and intellectual choices.[2] We came to the reformed determination to embrace specifically chosen empirical, rather than objective, methods to shape the sonic rendering. After discussing at some length the translatability of the various parameters of urban structure and music, we decided that the fabric of the city streets themselves would become our primary focus.

Some perceive architecture as a means by which "to enclose space" (Friedman 8), dividing the world of the exterior from that of the interior. Walter Ong argues

> Sight isolates, sound incorporates. Whereas sight situates the observer outside what he views, at a distance, sound pours into the hearer. Vision dissects…When I hear, however, I gather sound simultaneously from every direction at once: I am at the center of my auditory world, which envelops me, establishing me at a kind of core of sensation and existence…By contrast with vision, the dissecting sense, sound is thus a unifying sense. (Ong 32)

Nonetheless, I urge here a broader definition of the field, one which will consider not only enclosing edifices, but also the architectural structures and patterns of the street *en pleine* air. I am not, however, without precedence in my aesthetic consideration of the urban streetscape. Los Angeles-based visual artists Dennis Keeley, Daniel J. Martinez, and Roland Young all captured the stark elegance of the curvilinear concrete streetscapes through their mid-1990s gelatin-silver prints of freeways, streets and bridge structures. Architectural giant Frank O. Gehry's chain-link, stucco and corrugated metal constructions—aspects of his so-called "urban junkyard" of disparate styles—were reportedly influenced by the aforementioned modernist works during his formative years in Los Angeles (Friedman 12-13). Toronto-born Gehry became, of course, one of the most fluid modern architects, embracing sound itself as a material element of construction in many of his works: Venice's whale-like Chiat/Day temporary office, Los Angeles' Walt Disney concert hall, and Seattle's Jimi

Hendrix-inspired Experience Music Project (Friedman 18; 110-123; 194-201).

Creating a soundscape that reflected the empirical architectural structures of a segment of the city of Toronto was a challenging task as a composer and musician. Early in the discussions with MacBurnie I pressed him to choose a linear pathway through a subsection of the city, since the fragile sonic medium of the musician necessarily exists in time, and is thus most readily translated to a linear format.[3] It required a total of five meetings with the architecture team, which evolved over time to include former Ryerson University School of Architecture students Matt Belaen,[4] Yidan Wang and Tom Smierzchalski, to come to a consensus on the blueprint of the city to be mapped. Over the subsequent months, we honed in on Queen Street's vibrant east-west trajectory to act as an experimental microcosm of the greater city.[5] Queen Street acts as one of the major arteries in Toronto, and acquires substantially different characters in each district along its path including, from east to west: the laid-back Beaches, known for its quaint shops and street festivals; residential Danforth-Coxwell; a once grotty but quickly gentrifying Queen Street East; the busy and upscale Downtown; the trendy Arts District; affluent Parkdale; and the sparsely populated reaches of Humber Park (see Figure 1). I determined that this dynamic roadway, with its embrace of both inner cohesion and disjuncture, could act as a single thread in the intricate tapestry woven by Toronto's city streets. We pulled it loose for closer examination.

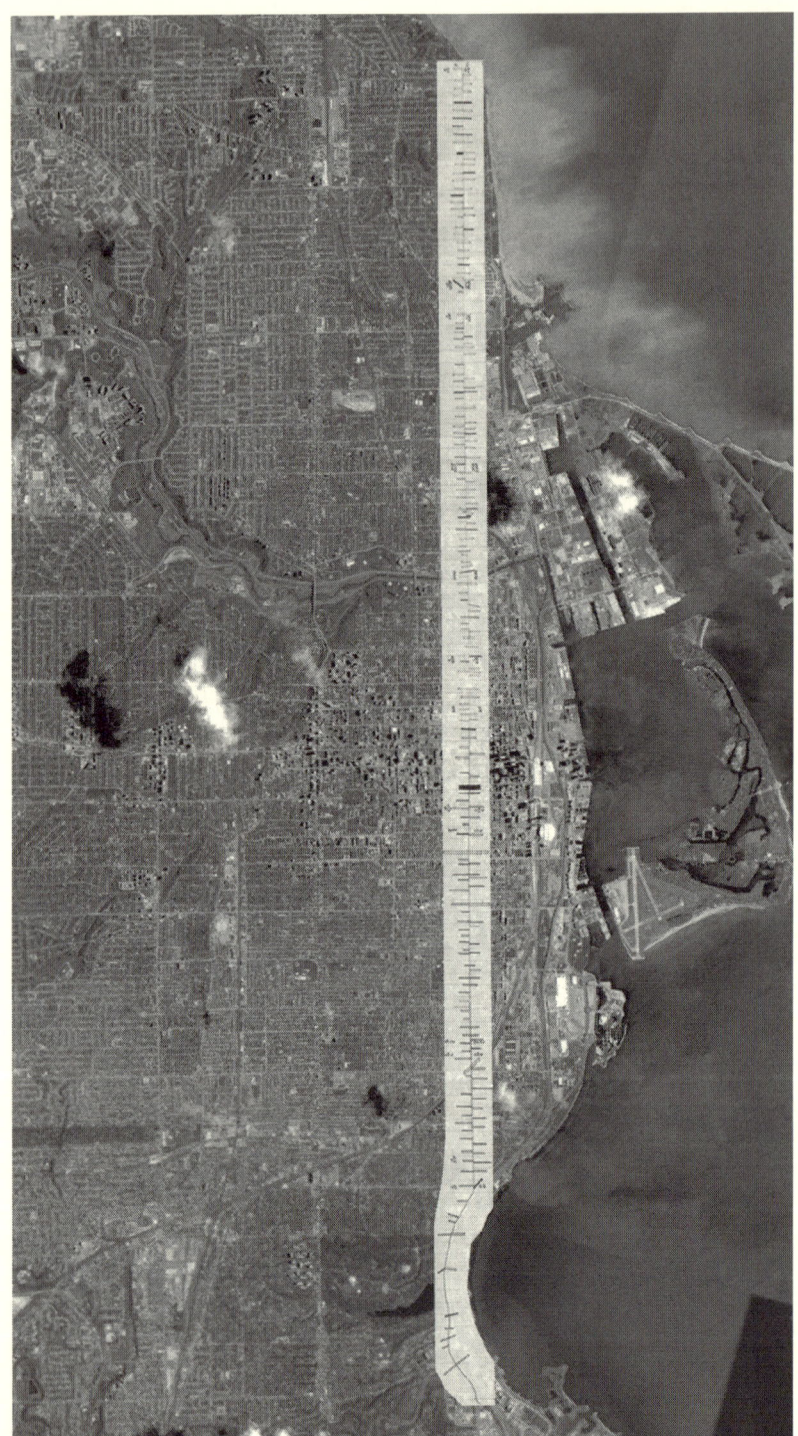
Figure 1: *Queen 501* score overlaid onto aereal view of Toronto.

Once Wang, Smierzchalski and Belaen had completed their multi-layered visual analysis of the street, I was handed a map of the topographical features they had jointly created using AutoCAD software.[6] As a musician accustomed to performing contemporary compositions, and inspired by the fanciful graphic notation of Ontario composer R. Murray Schafer (b. 1933)[7] that long graced the second floor Winter's College stairwell of my musical alma mater, York University, I instinctively read the map as a form of graphic notation in itself.[8] Interestingly, Belaen, MacBurnie and I each came to the independent opinion that the map was most aesthetically pleasing when read from east to west, in order that the piece "opened out" at the end, as the proximity of streets began to stretch through the Queensway corridor, thus creating a kind of rhythmic cadence for the conclusion of my composition (see Figure 2). In examining the architectural team's map, I found the rhythm of the crossroads of Queen Street to be of particular interest, and envisioned the interpretation of these north and south axis points as a major structural feature in my composition.

Although we had originally discussed contrasting instrumental orchestration for each major district of the street, in the dark hours of the night, as I gnashed my teeth and sank into the compositional process, I decided that the five-minute piece would possess greater cohesive integrity if performed with a smaller number of instruments and timbres.[9] I tightened up the orchestrational palette, but in so doing endeavored to reflect the multicultural landscape of urban Toronto through the inclusion of instruments from three cultural traditions: Euro-North American, Chinese and African. My choice of this particular triumvirate was intended to symbolize the rich cultural diversity of the city of Toronto which I was sounding, as evidenced by the 2001 Canadian census report. This recent ethnographic analysis revealed that forty-two percent of residents from the urban centre of Toronto use a non-English language as their first-learned tongue, and thirty-seven percent self-identify as "visible minorities," thereby underlining the inherent cultural diversity of the area (Statistics Canada np). The orchestrational palette also reflected my own musical training in western flute, Chinese wind instruments, and African drumming and dance.[10] Moreover, as both a performer and ethnomusicologist, I am particularly interested in contemporary compositions which successfully meld instruments and styles from diverse regions. My recent involvement as a bamboo flute performer in David Mott's 2006 world premiere of his piano concerto *Eclipse*, which included an accompanying orchestra of saxophone, cello, accordion, percussion, Gambian *kora* (plucked lyre),[11] Indian *tabla* (paired drums), Chinese *dizi* (bamboo flute), and Middle Eastern *oud* (fretted lute), was a particularly inspirational force (Mott 14-21).[12]

Motivated by Forward Kwenda's hypnotic piece "Mandarendare" (Yudkin 21), whose slowly shifting patterns I had analyzed so often for my introductory music classes at Ryerson University, I chose to use the African *mbira* thumb piano as a grounding ostinato in 6/8 time.[13] The foundational *mbira* ostinato sonically reflects both the repetition and subtle variation in the rectangular visual

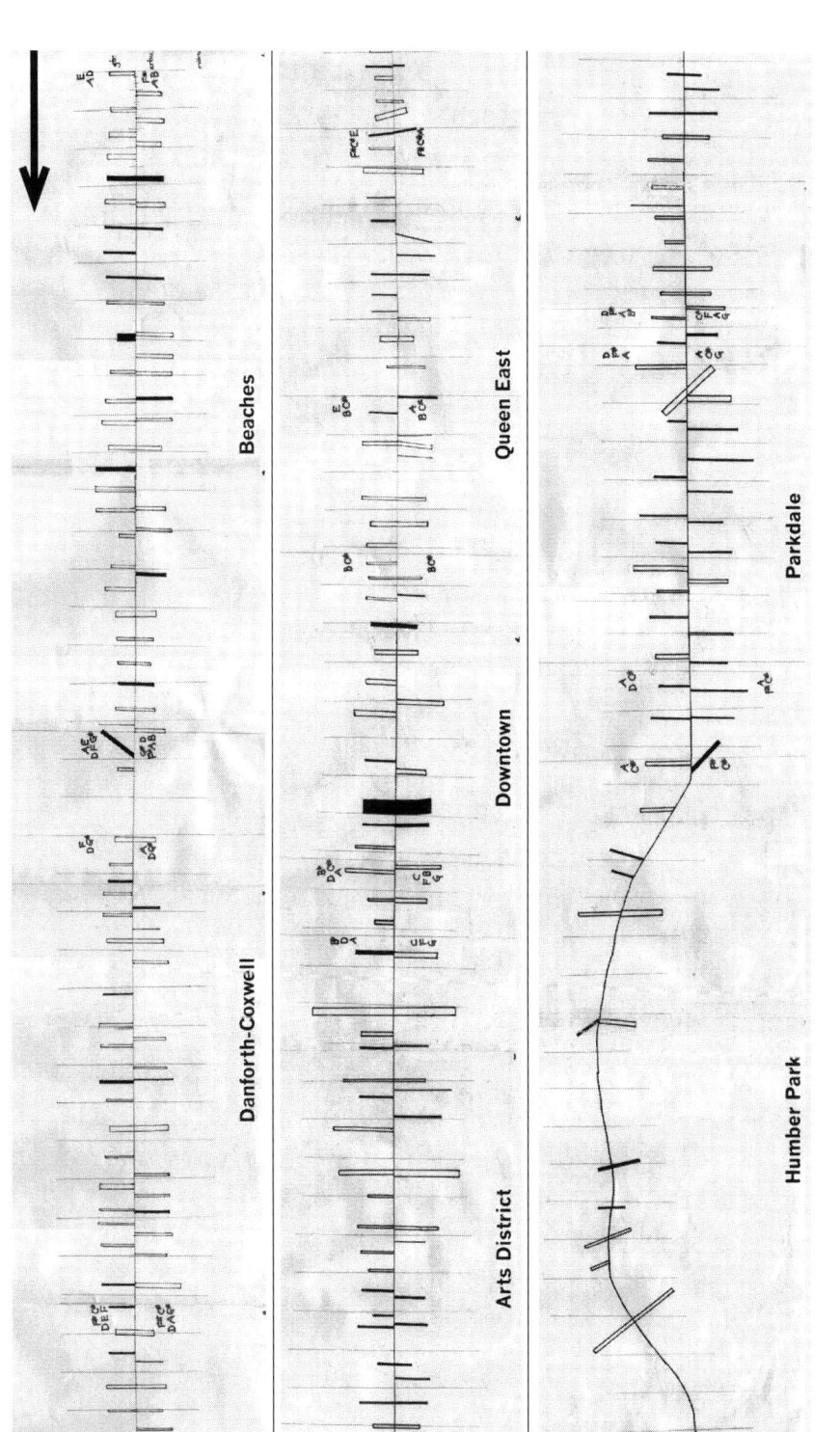

Figure 2: Complete score of *Queen 501* soundscape in three sections. The score is read from top right to bottom left.

patterning of Queen Street's city blocks, perhaps sonically invoking the modernists' Cubist visual art, despite the softness of the *mbira*'s timbre, and the lulling effect of the lilting 6/8 pattern. The *mbira* part, which I performed myself in the premiere of *Queen 501* (see Figure 3) is grouped into two-bar phrases that repeat up to four times at the discretion of the performer before transitioning to the next phrase (see Figures 4-6). Slight changes are gradually and unobtrusively brought into the ostinato pattern, which begins sparsely with a single beat per bar, then increases in rhythmic and textural density with the addition of more frequent melodic and harmonic notes, only to return once again to a more spacious pattern—albeit with slightly different pitches—at the western terminus of Queen Street.

With thanks to Carol Vernallis' in-depth explication of the subtle rhythmic counterpoint of the visual and auditory in popular music video (179-180), I eventually chose to apply the concept of empirical objectivity to the literal translation of the visual micro-rhythms expressed by the crossroads that Belaen, Wang, and Smierzchalski had mapped. Roads which ran north from Queen Street were assigned to the guitar, while those that ran south were allotted to the somewhat raspier Chinese bowed fiddle, *erhu*. I determined that the traditionally bowed *erhu* would play pizzicato, to balance the more pointillist nature of the western guitar.[14] Maintaining the relative spacing ratios of the crossroads, I carefully re-mapped them onto a ten page-long continuous horizontal axis which represented Queen Street, and reflected the continuity of the ongoing *mbira* ostinato. After superimposing bar lines on the resultant grid, I determined the tempo required in order to perform this soundscape in the allotted five minute time slot—approximately M.M. 60 per quarter note.

I directed performers of the "Queen 501" soundscape's June 10th, 2006 premiere at the conference—guitarist Jaroslaw Dabrowski and *erhu* player Patty Chan—to sound the crossroads within my superimposed bar lines from right to left (east to west), assuming a subdivision of four beats per bar, which provided an additional challenge to performers traditionally accustomed to reading scores from left to right.[15] The squarer duple subdivision was, I believe, easier to visualize than the lilting 6/8 of the *mbira* ostinato, yet added a significant polymetric intellectual challenge to the conception and performance of the piece. The performers' reading of the micro-rhythms was further challenged by the necessity of synchronizing the sounding of streets which ran both north and south from Queen Street. The unevenly spaced northern, southern, and bi-directional musical crossroads were enacted independently from—and played against—the quasi-regular blocking of the compound metrical pattern of the ostinato, emphasizing order within disorder, and disorder within order.

The density of the urban fabric and structural weight of each feature was also of importance to the sonic translation of the architects' work. The performers were instructed to express dynamically the relative presence and weight of each crossroad as evidenced by the proportionate width of the individual streets I had mapped from the blueprint of the city: tiny laneways were thus rendered piano, while arrival at major intersections such as Yonge Street were heralded

Figure 3: Guitarist Jaroslaw Dabrowski (center), erhu player Patty Chan (behind Dabrowski), and Kim Chow-Morris on mbira (front right) during the premiere of *Queen 501* at Ryerson University, June 10, 2006. Photo by MikeschMuecke.

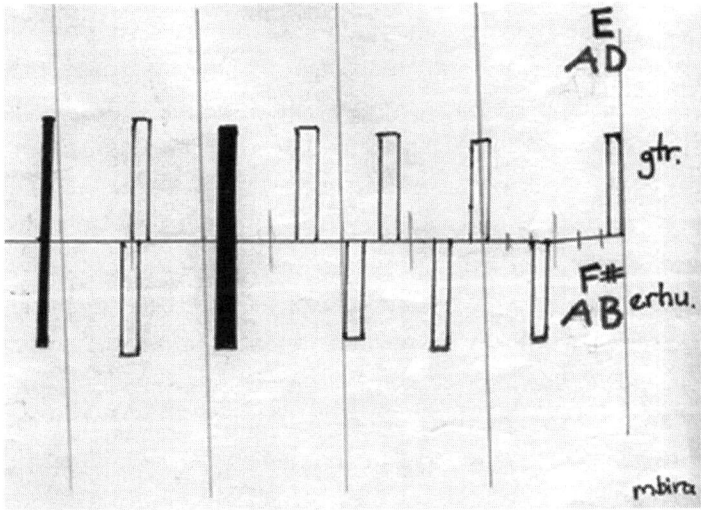

Figure 4: Beginning of *Queen 501* score showing instrumentation and initial chords.

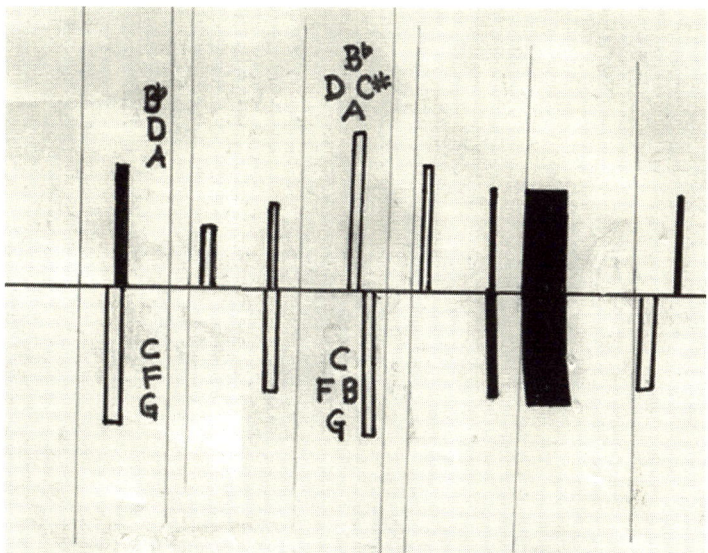

Figure 5: Middle of *Queen 501* score showing the intersection of Queen Street with Yonge Street downtown.

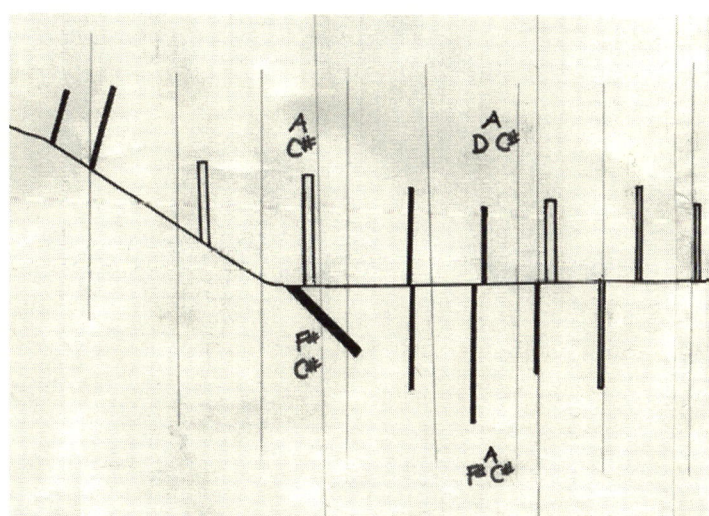

Figure 6: End of *Queen 501* score showing the bend of Queen Street toward the northwest between Parkdale and Humber Park.

by a fortissimo.[16] While the *mbira* ostinato continues at a relatively consistent mezzo piano to mezzo forte dynamic level, both the *erhu* and guitar come forward and recede in the musical texture in response to changes in street width, creating a continuously shifting overall dynamic spectrum.

The major districts of Queen Street are represented by discrete pitch sets from which the *erhu* and guitar performers each individually choose his or her notes at the moment of arrival at each crossroad: seven brief movements result. Areas of transition between the districts are marked by a brief combining of available pitch sets. In each movement, periods of relative architectural density are mirrored by tighter, smaller intervals and a greater frequency of dissonances between the three instrumental parts; in contrast, areas of relatively little density are governed by wider intervals between the instrumental parts and a higher prevalence of compositionally planned consonance. For instance, intervals of a major or minor second were frequently planted as choices in denser districts like that of Danforth-Coxwell, while perfect octaves, fifths, and fourths—the latter a consonant interval in this context— were imbedded as likely possibilities in districts of lesser density such as Humber Park. Interpretation of the graphic notation of the resultant compositional map required accomplished performers who were particularly sensitive to relativistic dynamic gradation and grid-based rhythmic interpretation with an internal polymetric sensibility.[17] The successful rendering of the performance map also required the performers to attain gradually a level of comfort with the shifting harmonies and blended timbres resulting from their spontaneous choices of pitch at each new crossroad.

The final textural layer of the composition juxtaposed the three live acoustic instrumental performances with a pre-recorded soundscape. The digital soundscape was created by sampling the ambient sounds of Queen Street on a handheld mp3 recorder from the westward-bound 501 Queen street car during its final run for the evening on May 14, 2006. In its original form, the listener can hear a myriad of streetscape sounds: the clang of the streetcar bell, the brittle murmurs of street chatter, revving car and motorcycle engines, the rhythmic swoosh of the street car doors, recorded music from open car windows and street-side shops, cell phone ring tones, the sound of change irregularly dropping into the metal fare box, and the fragmented discussions of streetcar patrons as they passed my microphone suspended at the edge of the open window near the front-most seat, behind a protective windscreen.[18] As I had hoped, the microphone's positioning was successful in capturing sounds from both the interior and the exterior of the streetcar in fairly equal measure. My inclusion of these sounds of enclosure and the exterior implicitly requests of the audience members a greater awareness of the aesthetic spectra of each of our unique sonic environments.

One of the most interesting aspects in the process of capturing the soundscape occurred at the point during the several hours of recording when a new streetcar driver, a driver trainer, and a retired Toronto transit driver all caught sight of my recording equipment. After several introductory questions about the nature of the recording, the four of us engaged in conversation about the soundscape composition project, which was itself captured on the recording. Coincidentally, the driver had completed an undergraduate degree in music at Humber College in Toronto, and had learned there about the creation of environmental soundscapes. The retired driver, too, had his own fair share of ideas for future streetcar routes that would yield potentially interesting soundscape recordings: in the course of his daily job, he had spent many years thoughtfully considering the distinctive sonic palettes of each of his various routes. Suitably, these conversational threads were incorporated into my "Queen 501" composition as part of the soundscape itself.

After obtaining the basic recording, the original live track was subsequently time-compressed to make the rhythms of the streetcar more apparent and to reduce the several hours of tracks to five minutes. The track was then manipulated to emphasize acoustically interesting peaks, and selectively amplified through the Soundforge 4.5 software program with late-night assistance from Toronto-based composer Patrick Rashleigh.[19] The layering of pre-composed empirically-derived acoustic rhythm lines with spontaneously chosen melodic notes from given pitch sets and digitally-manipulated ambient sounds results in a delicate interplay of pre-determined and the aleatoric patterns throughout the performance of the soundscape.

While an initial inspiration for my composition had been MacBurnie's desire to render the structures of Toronto sonically accessible in an empirical or objective manner, the process of compositional discovery that I undertook necessitated many subjective choices, including the choice of region to be mapped and the technical process of doing so, the selection and amplification of instrumental and soundscape timbres, and the choice of pitch sets, meter, orchestration, tempo, and aesthetic character, amongst others. In the final tally, "Queen 501" is clearly marked not only by forces of empiricism and of subjectivity, but also by acts of expectation and disruption: it is constructed on the edge of creative tension and play inherent in these recurrent dualisms. Our pairing of the fields of architecture and music can similarly be viewed as the enactment of a creative dualism, and throughout our months of exploration likewise framed acts of expectation and subsequent disruption that somehow suits the interpretation and experience of Queen Street itself. Yet as with Coleridge's "sunny domes" and "caves of ice," the ultimate juxtaposition of this too seldom-married duo resulted not in the fragmentation of a jarring binary opposition, but in the reunification of a paradoxically complementary pair.

Endnotes

¹ Synaesthesia—the crossing of the five senses of perception—was quite common in the Romantic period. Artists and literary scholars of the time frequently reported tasting colors, hearing textures, and feeling shadows. Some attribute the rise of synaesthesia to the prevalence of drugs during the era, while others view it as a force for creativity.

² I give a nod here to philosophers of subjectivity and intersubjectivity, Maurice Merleau-Ponty and his student Michel Foucault.

³ As Carol Vernallis explains, "[s]ound is process oriented. It ebbs and flows, and it begins and ends" (176).

⁴ Belaen worked for Robbie/Young & Wright Architects Inc in 2006, but has since gone on to pursue graduate studies at McGill University.

⁵ Our team also envisioned the possible textural layering of a set of street-based soundscapes in order to enact the city of Toronto on a more comprehensive scale, and considered my "Queen 501" composition a test case for our experiment.

⁶ Wang and Smierzchalski undertook extensive foundational mapping of the street, including analysis of economic shift from district to district, and the creation of a number of potential maps for my usage. Belaen completed the polished final AutoCAD map to be used for my composition based on their former work. Belaen also fluidly took over the coordination of the architectural team in April, May and June 2006, when MacBurnie's focus was necessarily shifted to other papers and pedagogical duties,

and acted as the liaison between the architects and myself, as musician-composer.

[7] Schafer is well known in recent years for his environmental theatre, and in particular the "Patria Cycle." He was a professor of music at Simon Fraser University before he resigned in order to focus on his writing, and returned to live near Haliburton, Ontario (Sadie 665; Koskoff 14; 345; 1059; 1105; 1219).

[8] Other composers who have utilized graphic notation include John Cage (1912-1992), George Crumb (1923-2006), Brian Eno (b. 1948), Morton Feldman (b. 1929), Gyorgy Ligeti (b. 1948), Krzystof Penderecki (b. 1933), and Karlheinz Stockhausen (b. 1928).

[9] The five minute temporal boundary was pre-determined based on the necessity of discussing the compositional process and theoretical implications of our work in the twenty-minute conference format at the Ryerson *Architecture | Music | Acoustics* conference.

[10] I began my training in western flute with Kay Hoehner and Anne Emond in St. Thomas and London, Ontario respectively, but continued my studies with Douglas Stewart (western flute), Chan Ka Nin, Ming Wong and Stephen Li (Chinese wind instruments), and Kathy Armstrong (Ghanaian drumming and dance) at the University of Toronto's Department of Music. I later went on to study Chinese wind instruments (*dizi, xiao, bawu* and *hulusi*) with Lu Chun Ling and the late Yu Xun Fa, in Shanghai, China.

[11] The *kora*, a harp-like instrument made from a calabash resonator and skin covering, is prevalent

in other West African countries, including Senegal, Guinea and Mali. Due to staffing difficulties, a keyboard was substituted for the intended *kora* in Mott's world premiere.

[12] A Canadian Broadcasting Company recording of the second movement of Mott's work, "Eclipse Part II: The Dark Shadowed Moon" and his Musicworks article discussing the significance of its composition were subsequently published. I was involved in the world premiere of the piece in 2006 as the *dizi* player for the chamber orchestra of world music instruments. The recording of this piece was taken into space by Canadian astronaut Steve MacLain in 2006.

[13] The *mbira* exists in many different formats, but is created with either metal or wood "tongues" of varying lengths attached to a calabash, box or board resonator. The keys, which vary greatly in number, are plucked by the thumbs or fingers. The instrument is also sometimes known as the 'thumb piano', and may be found in different forms throughout sub-Saharan Africa and Latin America (Randel 407).

[14] While most commonly sounded with a horse-hair bow, the *erhu* is capable of a wide range of extended techniques, including portamento, pizzicato, harmonics, two forms of vibrato (pressed and rolled wrist), and whinnying effects, thanks to the development of the folk instrument's technical capabilities by "Blind" A-Bing and his followers.

[15] Stockhausen's 1959 composition "Zyklus" similarly allowed for the reading of the musical notation from right to left, at the discretion of the performer.

[16] The Italian term "piano" refers to notes sounded quietly, while "fortissimo" refers to notes played very loudly.

[17] While the sonic effect of the work was perhaps somewhat hypnotic and lulling—described as "beautiful" by several audience members at its world premiere—the performers conversely found that the rhythmic and metrical aspects of the composition were quite challenging to perform, and thus required of them great concentration and mental acuity.

[18] I used a clip-on windscreen to reduce the "hiss" commonly produced when air—in this case blowing in from the open street car window—hits the microphone, which would have resulted in an elevated noise factor in the recording and subsequent lack of acoustic detail.

[19] I would like to thank most sincerely Patrick Rashleigh, a graduate from the York University graduate programme in musicology and ethnomusicology, for his generous contribution of time, creativity, and sound equipment.

References

Beranek, Leo L. *Concert Halls and Opera Houses: Music, Acoustics, and Architecture, Second Edition.* (New York: Springer-Verlag New York, Inc., 2004).

Beranek, Leo L. *Music, Acoustics & Architecture.* (New York: John Wiley & Sons, Inc., 1962).

Coleridge, Samuel T. "Kubla Khan." *Norton Anthology of English Literature. 7th Edition. Volume 2.* ed. (M.H. Abrams. New York: W.W. Norton and Co., 2000).

Friedman, Mildred, ed. *Gehry Talks: Architecture + Process.* (New York: Universe Publishing, 2002).

Harley, James. *Xenakis: His Life in Music.* (London: Taylor and Francis Books, 2004).

Hyatt, Peter. *Local Heroes: Architects of Australia's Sunshine Coast.* (Craftsman House, 2000).

Koskoff, Ellen, ed. *The United States and Canada: The Garland Encyclopaedia of World Music, Vol. 3.* (New York: Garland Publishing, Inc., 2001).

Mott, David. "Music is Energy: The Divine Sound in Live Music." *Musicworks* #95, Ed. David McCallum. (Toronto: Musicworks Society of Ontario, Inc., Summer 2006): 14-21.

Ong, Walter. *Orality and Literacy: The Technology of the Word.* (New York: Methuen, 1985).

Randel, Don Michael, ed. *The Harvard Concise Dictionary of Music and Musicians.* (Cambridge: Harvard University Press, 1999).

Ripley, Colin. *Architecture | Music | Acoustics: Ryerson University, Toronto Canada June 7-10 2006 Proceedings.* (Toronto: Ryerson Embodied Architecture Lab, 2006).

Sadie, Stanley. "Schafer, R(aymond) Murray." *The Norton/Grove Concise Encylopedia of Music.* (London: MacMillan Press, 1998).

Statistics Canada. "2001 Community Profiles." Released 27 June 2002, modified 30 November 2005. *Catalogue no. 93F0053XIE.* Online. Accessed 23 August 2006.

Vernallis, Carol. *Experiencing Music Video: Aesthetics and Cultural Context.* (New York: Columbia University Press, 2004).

Wright, Craig. *Listening To Music, Fourth Edition.* (California: Thompson Schirmer, 2004).

Xenakis, Iannis. *Formalized Music: Thought and Mathematics in Composition (Harmonologia Series No. 6).* (New York: Pendragon Press, 2001).

Yudkin, Jeremy. *Understanding Music, Fourth Edition.* (New Jersey: Pearson Prentice Hall, 2005).

Jim Lutz

Transpositions: Architecture as Instrument/Instrument as Architecture

The allied arts of music and architecture have historically intersected at points that are primarily theoretical or abstract in nature—shared ideas of compositional structure, aesthetics, acoustics, and the like. Setting aside the realm of the immaterial for a moment, this paper posits that there is another area of commonality to be found between the two disciplines in a more obvious and tangible form: the affinities that are possible between the tectonics of buildings and musical instruments. In developing the thesis that architecture can be informed by the tools of music, three areas of overlap between the two fields will be considered:

Forms and spaces: Is it viable for architectural space to be defined through the emulation of instrumental form?

Materials and finishes: Does the delicate artisanal nature of musical instruments preclude adapting elements of their construction to the more rigorous demands of architecture?

Structure and mechanics: Can the manner in which tensile and compressive forces are dealt with in musical instruments find valid architectural corollaries?

This argument is supported by examples drawn from the recent past that manifest the potential presented by musical instruments for those architects who have sought to create physical expressions of the relationship between sound and space.

Introduction

In a well-known exercise assigned in the architecture studios at the Cooper Union in the 1970s and 80s students were asked to select a musical instrument and explore it through a series of detailed drawings. All manner of instruments were subjected to this investigative process, traditional woodwind, reed, percussion and string

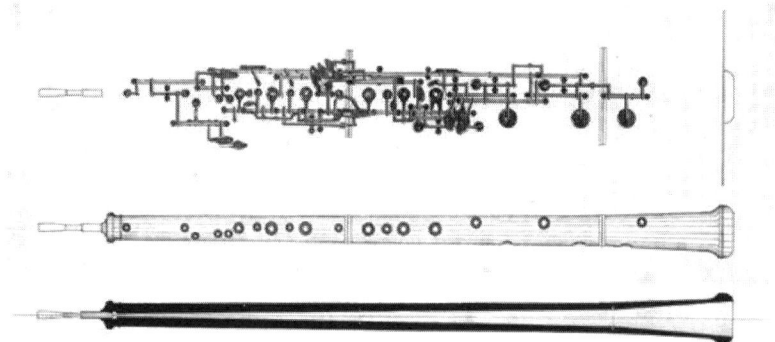

Figure 1: Drawing of an oboe. Stephen Isola. The Cooper Union. 1980/81.

instruments, as well as some unexpected subjects, an exploration of the lungs, trachea and larynx, for example, that carefully considered the instrumentality of the human voice (Figure 1). A young architecture student, Carlos Jiménez, now a respected architect and educator, recalls his experience in a class taught by John Hejduk in 1979.

> Each of us was to select a different musical instrument and draw it at full-scale [...]. I was fortunate enough to have selected an acoustical guitar, a hard instrument to draw in elevation, but certainly less anguishing to render than a clarinet, as I learned from watching one of my classmates.[1]

What was the pedagogical purpose of this exercise? While music and architecture have a long history of informing one another, this synergistic relationship has historically grown out of the theoretical underpinnings, compositional structures and acoustical phenomena shared by both. In this paper I draw from recent history to posit yet another way in which there has been experimental interplay between music and architecture: through the forms and spaces, materials and finishes, structural and mechanical concepts that are held in common by buildings and musical instruments. On this idea Daniel Libeskind has written:

> Buildings provide spaces for living but are also de facto instruments, giving shape to the sound of the world. Music and architecture are related not only by metaphor, but also through concrete space. Every building I have admired is, in effect, a musical instrument whose performance gives space a quality that often seems to be transcendent and immaterial.[2]

In support of this assertion, a brief look at some instruments designed by architects will serve as a useful prelude. From the nineteenth century, through the twentieth, and up to the present, a number of architects have designed musical instruments. English Arts-and-Crafts architect M. H. Baillie Scott (1865-1945), Scotsman Charles Rennie Macintosh (1868-1928), Germans Peter Behrens (1868-1940) and Bruno Paul (1874-1968), and the American architect Francis Henry Bacon, all designed art-case pianos. Each of these objects can be viewed as examples of the designer's architectural sensibilities extended and applied to the decorative arts. In the later part of the twentieth century we can see more eclectic examples as architect Alexander Gorlin looks to the de

Stijl movement for inspiration, and Richard Diebboll—a partner in Michael Graves' firm, who has designed dozens of art-case pianos—does so using the Post-Modern idiom associated with that office.

Relative to the issues of form, materiality and structure to be discussed here, however, it is three designs completed by architects in the last two decades that are of particular interest. Austrian architect Hans Hollein (b. 1934)—with his 1990 design for the Viennese company Bösendorfer—has re-imagined the materials and finishes. Red has joined the traditional black lacquer, and the case is inlaid with gold. The legs and pedal-lyre have been fashioned in solid brass. The wooden support typically used to prop open the lid has been replaced with an electric motor that now raises and lowers it.

Similarly, American architect Richard Meier designed a limited edition piano for Rudolf Ibach Sohn in 1995 (Figure 2). Like Hollein, metal legs and lyre have replaced the traditional wooden ones, and the top is likewise electronically operated. Meier has gone one step further, however, changing the traditional shape of the case by subsuming the signature "piano curve" within a rectilinear form. While the familiar compound curve can be viewed as a direct and rational response to the structural metal frame across which the strings are tensioned, function is here supplanted by form. As an aside, Meier's original idea to make all the keys, naturals as well as sharps and flats, the same color, was abandoned when it was pointed out to him by a musician that many pianists rely on the shadows cast by the keys while performing.[3]

Figure 2: Rud. Ibach Sohn grand piano. Richard Meier. 1995.

Daniel Libeskind, a classically trained musician and child prodigy, in his 2003 design for the German piano-maker Schimmel has, like Meier, chosen to alter the traditional form of the instrument by squaring its lines (Figure 3). While maintaining the traditional black lacquer finish, it is now embellished with titanium inlays. Ignoring materiality, Libeskind has chosen to make his strongest statement using scale. The instrument is over nineteen feet long, compared to the nine to ten feet of a typical concert grand. The instrument is so large, in fact, that it would not fit into the architect's own New York apartment.[4]

All of these designers have reconceived a traditional musical instrument by applying an architectural sensibility to issues of finish and materials, form

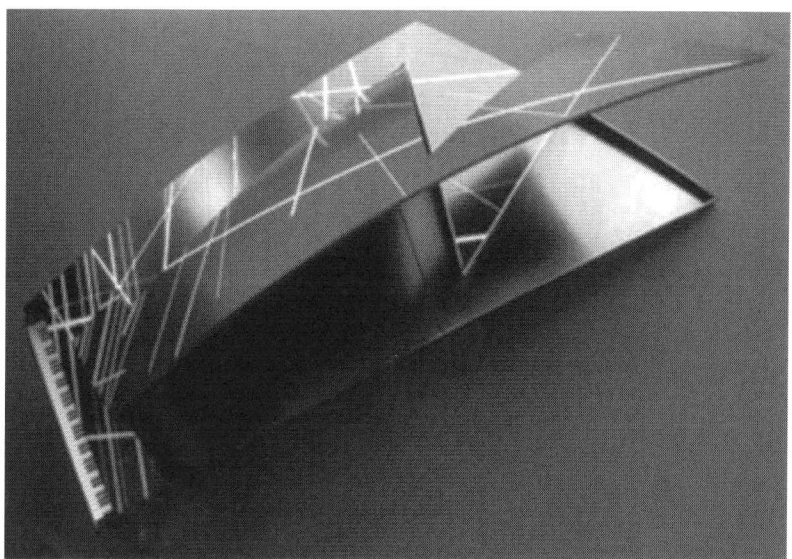
Figure 3: Schimmel grand piano. Daniel Libeskind. 2003.

and space, structure and mechanics. Using these same concerns let us now consider the reciprocal relationship—how musical instruments can inform works of architecture.

Materials and Finishes

Despite being recognized for the use of cutting edge computer technologies, hand-drawn sketches and study models are well-known parts of Frank Gehry's preliminary design process. The development of the Experience Music Project (EMP) in Seattle, commissioned in 1995, was no exception. Originally conceived as a structure to exhibit entrepreneur and philanthropist Paul Allen's personal collection of Jimi Hendrix memorabilia, the

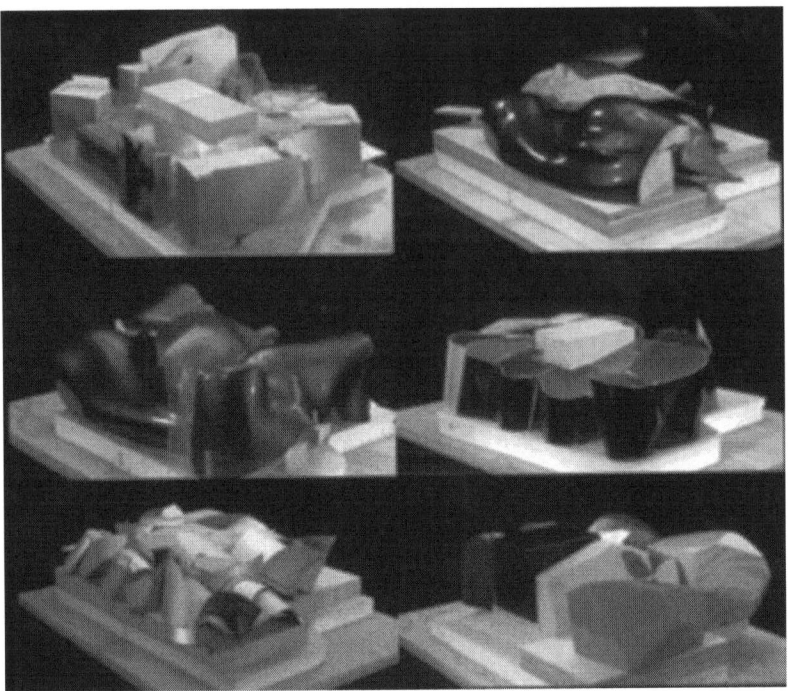

Figure 4: Experience Music Project. Study Models. Frank Gehry, Architect. 1995-2000.

structure eventually grew to address themes pertaining to a broader array of progressive music genres. In response to the building's stated purpose (a rock 'n roll museum) and his clients request for a "swoopy" building (to use Allen's term), it is perhaps not surprising that Gehry eventually came to employ bits of broken guitars in his initial design studies. At one stage, a flowing glass band reminiscent of a guitar's fret board was used, overlaid with a tangle of pipes and cables. Describing this building element, project architect Craig Webb said, "They're like guitar strings. A lot of people think it looks like the neck of a guitar with the frets on it. Frank took the guitar neck and said, 'Make a bunch of these'." Continuing his description of the fret-like form, he says, "[…] it started to undulate, like music. He [Gehry] was trying to get the building to look like music."⁵ (Figure 4)

Gehry himself recounts the process in this way,

Figure 5: Guitar fragment from Jimi Hendrix's performance at the Monterey International Pop Festival. 1967.

> We talked about broken guitars, and I did remember Jimi Hendrix breaking guitars on stage. There's a guitar shop right near our office in Santa Monica; the guy makes these electric guitars. We got a bunch of broken chunks of guitar, piled them all up and started to look at the colors. In the end I made one of the parts of the building the Purple Haze. It's really beautiful.⁶ (Figure 5)

As the structure became more abstracted during the design process, many elements present in the early schemes ultimately did not make it to the final building (the fret board survived, the attendant "guitar string" cables did not). Relative to this discussion and as Gehry points out, it is the *colors* that remain as the salient feature from the experimental use of the instruments. "I wanted to evoke the rock 'n roll experience without being too literal about it", he says, "The colors come from guitars". His staff in fact ascribes specific sources for the building's various colors: blue from the Fender

Mustang, gold from a Gibson Les Paul, and red from a Fender Stratocaster. Of the last one, Gehry says, "[...] the red will fade. We did that on purpose so the red will look like an old truck, a faded old red truck. I believe that it's going to be wonderful."[7] Whether known to Gehry or not, Fender had in fact used stock automotive paints as finishes on their early guitar models.

If Frank Gehry's work on the Experience Music Project provides us with an example of musical instruments providing the colors for an architectural work, his design for the Walt Disney Concert Hall in Los Angeles is an instance where the selection of architectural materials can be tied to instruments as well. Commissioned in 1988 and completed in 2003, the Disney Concert Hall features a "vineyard" style performance space set within an envelope of undulating metal-clad surfaces. The architect has purposefully contrasted the finish materials of the auditorium with those used in the ancillary spaces that serve it—133,000 square feet of wood paneling in the concert hall juxtaposed against a variety of finishes in the remainder of the public spaces. While acoustics certainly played a decisive role in the selection of the materials for the concert space, the choice consciously goes beyond pure science. Australian Liza Lim was commissioned by the Los Angeles Symphony to write a dedicatory piece for the hall's opening. Entitled *Ecstatic Architecture*, the composer eloquently describes the relationship between her work and the building.

The concert hall designed by Gehry is a precisely tuned 'instrument for listening' and one thought I had about connecting the orchestra to the hall came from observing things on a physical or material level. One of the architectural details in the hall that sparked my imagination was the use of Douglas fir for the wooden paneling of the ceiling. This is a wood often used to build stringed instruments, particularly cellos. I thought of the resonances of the cellos at the opening of my piece as a kind of moment of recognition between the wood of the instruments and of the hall, murmuring at one another. Extending this feeling about the material sensing each other's presence, the flutes and trumpets address the exterior metal. So the opening moments of the work are an orchestration of a metaphor about how 'inside' and 'outside' begin to communicate and talk together. The hall itself suggests this metaphysical relationship.[8]

Lim has described a process that has turned full circle, one where the material used in making musical instruments has inspired the choice of finishes for the architectural space, which in turn has become the point of departure for a musical composition.

Forms and Spaces

In designing the Disney hall, the architect and acousticians made a clear distinction early on between the concert hall proper and the noise-producing support spaces, going so far as to rename them the "Box" and the "Baggage" respectively. The clear distinction between a precious instrument and the utilitarian protective case that surrounds it is a poignant metaphor that has been taken up by several artists; Matisse has painted it, Arman has dealt with it as sculpture, and most recently, conceptual artist Christian Marclay has used the theme in installations (Figure 6).

Figure 6: Empty Cases (In Memoriam Tom Cora). Christian Marclay, artist. 1998.

Architect Steven Holl displays an empty violin case in his apartment as a kind of surrealist sculpture.[9] For architect Louis Kahn, the violin and its case provided a fitting concept for his design for the Theater of Performing Arts (1966-1973) in Fort Wayne, Indiana (Figure 7). As Kahn clearly noted

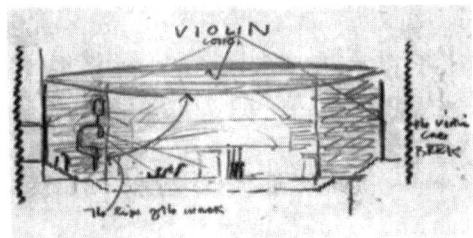

Figure 7: Schematic section sketch. Theater of Performing Arts. Fort Wayne, Indiana. Louis Kahn, Architect. 1966-1973.

on an early schematic section through the building, the "violin" was the stage and the 800 seat auditorium chamber, while the "violin case" was comprised of the public lobby and the galleries surrounding the former. Like Gehry's project, this differentiation was physically manifested through the use of different construction materials. In Kahn's building the chamber was built with a system of folded concrete walls, while the attendant lobbies were constructed of masonry.

Figure 8: Music Room. Halifax, Nova Scotia. Niall Savage Architecture. 2002.

The notion of a hard outer shell enveloping a finely crafted interior space has again been given form in a small performance space in Halifax, Nova Scotia (Figure 8). Architect Niall Savage in his design for the Music Room, has adopted Kahn's model.[10] Concrete blocks and steel joists combine to create a container into which an undulating liner of maple is inserted. As one architectural writer has described it, "The liner is like an instrument – continuous wooden ribbons curving and folding over floors, walls and ceiling making the effect like being inside a violin". Stradivarius specifically selected maple, a dense hardwood, for the backs of his violins, and soft spruce for the top plate knowing that the spruce would vibrate while the maple would reflect the sounds up and out of the instrument.

Despite its modest size, or perhaps because of it, this project successfully links musical forms and materials.

Structure and Mechanics

Casting an engineer's eye over the range of musical instruments that humankind has developed over the ages, Buckminster Fuller noted, "Slowly man evolved many musical instruments, all of which from a structural standpoint, were highly demonstrative of the full family of mechanical functions [...]".[11] Apparently concurring with Fuller's observation, architect and engineer Santiago Calatrava found formal and structural parallels with musical instruments in a series of three bridges he designed in the Netherlands between 1999 and 2004. Naming the trio after chordophones—the Harp, Cittern and Lute—the bridges do indeed depend upon a similar balance of tensile and compressive forces as their namesakes (Figure 9).

Figure 9: "The Lute." Bridge over the Hoofdvaart. Hoofddorp, Netherlands. Santiago Calatrava, Architect. 1999-2004.

Each bridge is a variation on the underlying structural idea, a cable-stayed steel pylon that is expressed as a spindle.

While the engineering concept actually derives from Calatrava's graduate thesis, the allusion to musical instruments resonated with one architectural critic who noted that the series of sister bridges "embody a special sense of movement, a musical, rhythmical quality [...]."[12] The Harp uses three groups of cables, one planar, the other two Gaussian in nature, the Lute carries two curving roadways suggesting the rounded sound box of its namesake, while the Cittern, a distant relation to the guitar, supports intersecting spans from one mast. While the cittern is uniquely western European in origin, dating to the Middle Ages, examples of the lute and harp can be found in several cultures with roots extending back many centuries. It is in fact lutes and harps from non-European regions that bear the closest similarity to Calatrava's designs: the kora from Africa, bow-shaped and angular harps from Borneo, Burma,

Figure 10: Egyptian wall painting depicting an angular harp. Circa 15th century BCE.

Figure 11: Luminous Veil. Dereck Revington, Architect. Toronto, Canada. 1998-2003.

Figure 12: Singing Ringing Tree (unrealized project). Tonkin Liu Ltd., Architects. Burnley, England. 2005.

the Urals and from ancient Egypt (Figure 10). Each of these, through their direct and clearly articulated form, prefigures the arrangement of support and strings found in the bridges. For some, the metaphorical lyricism is too literal. Frank Gehry has commented on Calatrava's work, "He's a brilliant musician, [...] a high-level intellect. But there is romanticism in his work that I would veer away from, which probably comes out of all that intellect, all that music. I try to purge myself of those romantic notions [...]."[13]

A similar parallel between a work of architectural engineering and a musical precursor can be found in the Luminous Veil project by architect Dereck Revington (Figure 11). Designed as a suicide barrier protecting the pedestrian walkway on the upper level of the Bloor Street bridge in Toronto, the range of taut, vertically strung steel cables that runs the length of the viaduct has been compared by some to an Aeolian harp, a zither with strings of equal length that are "played" when winds cause them to vibrate, an instrument whose origins can be traced back to biblical times. One writer has described the "fugue-like pattern for the vertical cables of the Veil's inner layer," going on to describe the bowstring masts that "tilt out like harps to pull the layers of cables."[14] After the architect noted Mozart's

Requiem as one of his inspirations for the project, some have speculated that the array may have been tuned to perform its own mournful composition when played upon by the winds.

The idea of "nature as musician" has been developed by others as well. Athanasius Kircher, the 17th century polymath with an active interest in acoustics, proposed a version of an Aeolian harp having architectural scale, including horn shaped elements meant to amplify and project the sounds. Some four centuries later, the British architectural firm of Tonkin Liu produced a design for a large-scale aerophone (Figure 12). Like Kircher's Aeolian harp, the design, entitled *Singing Ringing Tree*, would rely upon the wind blowing from the adjacent moor to compose random tunes as it passes over its 350 pipes. Here the syrinx, or panpipes, an instrument common to many cultures around the world, has provided the inspiration for the architectural monument.[15]

Summary and Conclusion

In these several examples we have seen that architects have looked at musical instruments as sources of inspiration in several ways. For some it was the materials and finishes that have intrigued them, as Frank Gehry's interest in color and substance attests when called upon to design structures with a music related purpose. For others, it was the forms taken by the tools of music and the mysterious and poetic possibilities of the spaces hidden inside of them. Louis Kahn succinctly characterized the functional interaction between the inner and outer shells of a modern performance space using a musical metaphor, and through this observation, inspired a generation of architects to similarly explore variations on the theme. In the case of Santiago Calatrava, it is the notion of structural and mechanical parallels that intrigues. The artful balance of compressive and tensile forces inherent in bridge design does indeed conjure the imagery of stringed musical instruments in many of his solutions.

As architecture continues to look beyond its traditional borders for opportunities for experimentation and intervention, the realm of music continues to provide a source rich with possibilities.

Endnotes

[1] Hays, K. M., *Sanctuaries: The Last Works of John Hejduk*, (The Whitney Museum of American Art, New York, U.S.A., 2003).

[2] Libeskind, D., *The Walls are Alive*, http://p196.ezboard.com/fcafeurbanitefrm7.showNexyMessage?topicID=142.topic, accessed July 13, 2002.

[3] Meier, R., Shapiro, D., Fischer, V., *Richard Meier: The Architect as Designer and Artist*, (Rizzoli, New York, U.S.A., 2003).

[4] Libeskind, D., *Breaking Ground: Adventures in Life and Architecture*, (Penguin, New York, U.S.A., 2004).

[5] Friedman, M. (ed.), *Gehry Talks: Architecture + Process*, (Rizzoli, New York, U.S.A., 1999).

[6] McGuigan, C., *Frank O. Gehry*, http://www.bbzine.com/archeplus/tabloid01/Qbloid104.html, accessed November 11, 1999.

[7] Friedman, M. (ed.), *Gehry Talks: Architecture + Process*, (Rizzoli, New York, U.S.A., 1999).

[8] Lim, L., *Ecstatic Architecture*, http://www.elision.org.au/repertoire/notes/27200.html, accessed February 2005.

[9] Coleman, D., "A Structural Pro and His Empty Space", *The New York Times*, February 5, 2006.

[10] King, A., Belisle, J., Eisler, L. (eds.), *Building Art*, (University of Calgary Press, Calgary, Canada, 2003).

[11] Fuller, B., *Nine Chains to the Moon*, (Doubleday & Co., New York, U.S.A., 1939, 1936, 1971).

[12] Tzonis, A. and Donadei, R., *Santiago Calatrava: The Bridges*, (Universe Publishing, New York, U.S.A., 2005).

[13] Filler, M., "Going Places", *Departures*, http://www.departures.com/ad/ad_0301_calatrava.html, accessed March/ April 2001.

[14] Weston, B., "Between Life and Death", *Azure*, May/ June 2003: 60-62.

[15] Dowdy, C., "Sound Investment: 'Singing Sculpture for a British Moor'", *Wallpaper*, 2005: 156.

List of Figures

Figure 1: The Irwin s. Chanin School of Architecture of The Cooper Union, *Education of an Architect* (Rizzoli, New York: 1988): 135.

Figure 2: High Museum of Art, *Richard Meier – The Architect as Designer and Artist* (Rizzoli, New York: 2003): 101.

Figure 3: Daniel Libeskind with Sarah Crichton, *Breaking Ground* (Riverhead Books, New York: 2004): Insert 2, page 11.

Figure 4: Experience Music Project, *Experience Music Project – The Building* (Experience Music Project: Seattle: 2000): 14.

Figure 5: Tom Wheeler, *The Stratocaster Chronicles* (Hal Leonard Corporation, Milwaukee: 2004): 129.

Figure 6: Jennifer González, *Kim Gordon, Matthew Higgs, Christian Marclay* (Phaidon Press, New York and London: 2005): 105.

Figure 7: Romaldo Giurgola, Jaimini Mehta, *Louis I. Kahn* (West View Press, Boulder, Colorado: 1975): 124.

Figure 8: Andrew King, Jocelyne Belisle, Lawrence Eisler (editors), *Building/Art* (University of Calgary Press, Calgary, Canada: 2003): 150.

Figure 9: Alexander Tzonis, Rebeca Caso Donadei, *Santiago Calatrava – The Bridges* (Universe Publishing, New York: 2005): 174.

Figure 10: Max Wade-Matthews, Wendy Thompson, *The Encyclopedia of Music* (Hermes House, London: 2003): 16.

Figure 11: B. Weston, *Azure* magazine, "Between Life and Death" (May/June 2003): 60.

Figure 12: C. Dowdy, *Wallpaper* magazine, "Sound Investment: 'Singing Sculpture for a British Moor'" (2005): 156.

Yu Zhang

Altar and Studio: Musical Design in 18th-century Chinese Architecture

In this study I am concerned with musical design in 18th-century Chinese architecture. The goal is to explore how certain archi-music practices express their inherent socio-cultural meanings by examining two surviving examples of imperial buildings in Beijing: the Altar of Heaven (rebuilt in 1749) and the Zither Rhythm Studio (built in1757)—both constructed at the direction of Emperor Qianlong (乾隆). Through on-site surveys and literature review of historical documents it was found that, (1) the terrace plan of the Altar was deliberately designed under the "huangzhong" tonal measurement (黃鍾律尺), and (2) the Studio and its surrounding landscape were encircled by water-sound produced "music" (水樂). To explain the real design concept in each case, the influence from ancient Chinese ideas on the "sage-king" (聖王) notion are discussed here. At the conclusion of this study, the above two archi-music masterpieces can be considered as the materialized representation of Emperor Qianlong's sage-king ambition.

Introduction

In the mid-18th century, the imperial city of Beijing, as the center of the stable and prosperous Qing Dynasty (1644–1911), was perhaps at its zenith. While Beijing's basic layout, much as it is today, had been completed in the fifteenth and sixteenth century, the city was largely renovated during Emperor Qianlong's reign (1736–1799). According to Dai Yi (戴逸), the distinguished Qing historian, no other Qing ruler had as great an impact on imperial Beijing. For three decades after 1738 Qianlong carried out an ambitious building program. He improved the city's water-control system, repaired the city's roads and walls, and renovated palaces and villas. During the 1740s and early 1750s many temples were erected and the major state altars were rebuilt; many buildings in the Forbidden City and the Beihai (北海) Park were built by his direction.[1]

Among those structures of the Qianlong Era, two surviving ones display the apparent collaboration between architecture and music: one is the Altar of Heaven (rebuilt in 1749) in the southern suburb of Beijing; the other is the Zither Rhythm Studio (built in 1757) in the Beihai Park in the center of Beijing (Figure 1). As the Qing archives reveal, it was Emperor Qianlong who exerted substantial influence on both building projects, brought musical elements into the architecture, and even employed music philosophy in guiding the architectural design. In the following paragraphs I will examine how the Altar of Heaven and the Zither Rhythm Studio were

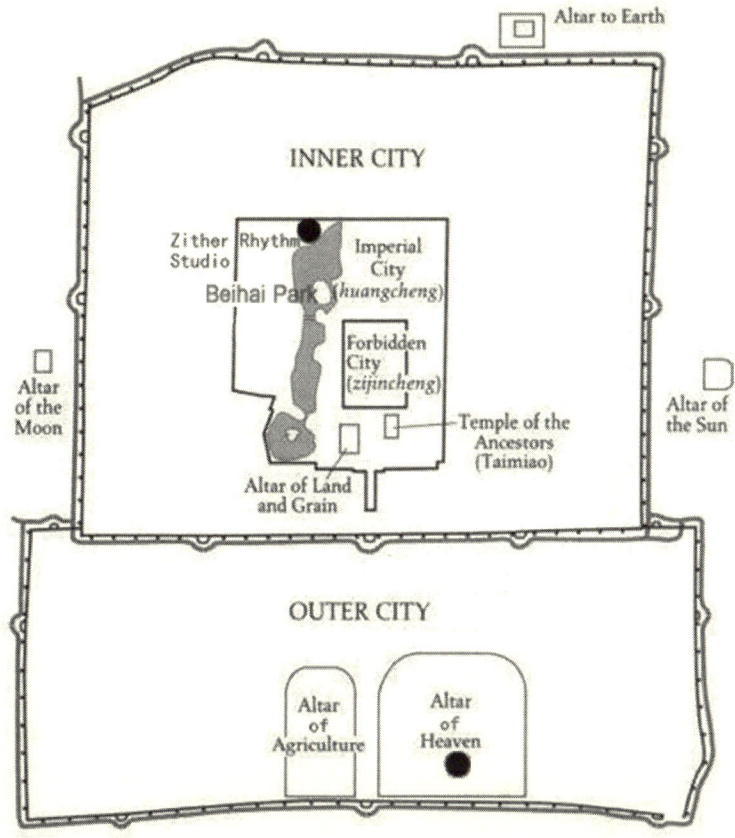

Figure 1: Plan of imperial Beijing in the 18th century. The dot in the lower position marks the site of the Altar of Heaven; the upper one, the site of the Zither Rhythm Studio.

designed by incorporating musical ideas, and why such archi-music practices were implemented. However, to form the background of the study, one important aspect of ancient Chinese thoughts ought to be discussed here: the 'sage-king' notion.

193

'Sage-King' Notion and Emperor Qianlong

In traditional China, the ideal status for the emperor to achieve was being a 'sage-king'. Confucian ideology defined a 'sage-king' not only as having attained the ultimate level of political domination ("king outside" 外王, in the Confucian term), but also to follow strict disciplines of moral cultivation ("sage inside" 內聖).[2] The combination of political leadership and moral authority offered ideological legitimacy to the dynasty.

Here is an almost perfect example of 'sage-king' behaviors; it concerns Emperor Qianlong. Even from his early prince age, Qianlong was imbued with a sense of being a 'sage-king' (Figure 2). When crowned, he continued to work hard to achieve the sage-king status. He successfully established himself as a fellow Confucian scholar, and was greatly admired for his martial and literary accomplishments. During Qianlong's reign, his empire expanded to over ten million square kilometers; meanwhile, the arts and culture flourished in China. Qianlong supported the arts, created libraries, and constructed many gardens. His calligraphy can still be found in almost every well-known place in China. He was also one of the most productive poets of his time, credited with more than 42,000 poems.

'Sage-King' and Architecture

In a sense, the 'sage-king' notion could be transplanted onto imperial architecture—respectively, the 'king' aspect to the Altar of Heaven, and the 'sage' aspect to the Zither

Figure 2: Court portraits of Emperor Qianlong, revealing his duality of the sage-king ambition. (left) formal attire in Emperor Qianlong's enthronement ("king outside"); (right) literati dress as a well educated scholar ("sage inside").

Rhythm Studio. It was the Altar that the emperor came to every year "to speak to heaven" and pray for a bountiful harvest. Heaven was supposed to give the ruling dynasty a "mandate" to rule the people; hence the Altar could be viewed as a typical site for displaying political domination ("king outside"). In contrast, the Zither Rhythm Studio—as a garden architecture with a tranquil atmosphere—may offer a perfect place for emperors to cultivate their "sage leadership inside".

To behave like a sage-king, Emperor Qianlong annually presented himself at the Grand Sacrifice (大祀) ceremony in the Altar of Heaven for a total of sixty years, from 1736 until 1795, no matter whether it was windy, rainy, or snowy on that day of ceremony.[3] Qianlong also kept visiting the Zither Rhythm Studio after it was built in 1757, and quite enjoyed his reclusive life there.

'Sage-King' and Music

Music was one of the main themes that ancient Chinese texts elaborated upon. What is music? According to *Shi Ji* (史記, *Records of the History*, 1st cent. B.C.E.), Music is happiness. When somebody is moved by the outside environment, he hears sound; when people feel happy hearing sound, and even dance with it, then music is born. Music thus has a strong influence on the person's temper and mind, and even on the customs of society. For example, truthful, elegant songs show the honesty of society; cheerful songs encourage the mood of the army; but evil and dirty songs would lead people to sins and crime. Again, in *Yue Ji* (樂記, *Records of the Music*, 3rd cent. B.C.E.)—the first book on musical theory in China—music is defined as an echo of the harmony between heaven and earth. So that from the harmony with heaven people can enjoy happiness.

Since music can influence the temper and mind, this could be applied to education. Also, music is an effective medium when people sing to glorify the heaven, and to achieve harmony with heaven and earth. Consequently, for a 'sage-king' in ancient China, he performed music not only for entertaining himself. Instead he ought to use the music as a tool for educating his people to obey his authority, and he should earnestly choose the proper music for sacrificing heaven and earth; music was thus imbued with political functions.

To achieve the 'sage-king' status, Emperor Qianlong paid great attention to music, and not just for amusements but chiefly for regulating order in the world. Under Qianlong's reign the imperial Bureau of Music was established in 1741; the ritual music for various sacrifice ceremonies was under revision from 1738 to 1742; and a new imperial book on musical theory was compiled in 1746.[4] In general—by the end of 1740s—a complete system of court music had been established. What followed in the next decade was an interesting phenomenon in the sense that two archi-music masterpieces came into being: namely the Altar of Heaven and the Zither Rhythm Studio.

Case Study I: Altar of Heaven

The Altar of Heaven, popularly known as the Circular Mound Altar ("*yuan-qiu*", 圜丘 in Chinese), was built in 1530 and enlarged in 1749 (the 14th year of Emperor Qianlong's reign). It consists of three circular terraces of white marble—decreasing in diameter—surrounded by balustrades made of the same material. From 1530 until 1911 the altar served as a place for holding the ceremony to worship Heaven at every winter solstice, hence symbolizing the relationship between earth and heaven at the heart of Chinese cosmogony, and also the emperor's special role within that relationship[5] (Figure 3).

As is known to many common Chinese people, the Altar of Heaven is noteworthy for its extraordinary reliance on the number '9'. In ancient Chinese number symbolism the number '9' represents infinity and extremity. It was

Figure 3: Bird's-eye view of the Altar of Heaven. Three circular terraces of white marble are decreasing in diameter.

a magic number. The highest heavens were referred to as the "ninth heaven." The land ancient Chinese people inhabited was poetically named the "nine states" ("*jiu zhou*", 九州) which means that the country encompasses so much territory that it is beyond measure. In the Forbidden City, there are nine rows with nine gilded knobs on the double doors of the major gates which represent the supreme power of the emperor. The circular Altar of Heaven, however, is an architecture example in which the number '9' is used more typically. The upper one of the three circular terraces was used to measure its diameter as 9 "*zhang*" (丈, a kind of Chinese traditional unit of measurement equaling 3.2 meters), the middle one 15 "*zhang*", and the bottom one 21 "*zhang*"; the total number of the three terraces is 45, the result of 9 x 5[6]. Furthermore, the steps of each flight, the slabs and pillars of each balustrade are 9 or multiples of 9 in number, symbolizing that god lived above the "nine heavens."

However, there is one aspect of the terrace dimensions that has always been overlooked—the "*zhang*" unit measuring the diameter was actually in a reduced length. According to the measured survey in 1998 by the School of Architecture, Tianjin University, the diameter of the three circular terraces from top to bottom are respectively

23.6 meters, 39.3, and 54.9. Since the same lengths were recorded as 9 *zhang*, 15, and 21, one "*zhang*" unit could thus be converted into approximately 2.6 meters—surprisingly, this is quite different from 3.2 meters, the normal length of the "*zhang*" unit in traditional Chinese life.

Why was the "*zhang*" unit reduced when applied to the Altar? Imperial archives suggest that it was a deliberate design.[7] On March 29, 1750, such a design plan was authorized by Emperor Qianlong. As it was stated in this very plan, a set of "ancient" measurements (古尺) were to be used that exactly equaled 0.81 times of the normal measurement, that is, 0.81 x 3.2 = 2.6 meters—just as the measured survey in 1998 demonstrated. Now, it is clear that the plan of the altar terrace was intended to apply the "ancient" measurement. But what is its function?

The key to understand the reduced "ancient" measurement is to be found in the ancient Chinese *luxue* (律學) theory, the study of the tonal system. There are twelve standard pitch pipes (十二律管) within an octave, representing the whole system of pitches in Chinese music. Among them, the "*huangzhong*" (黃鍾, literally "yellow bell") pipe was the fundamental one on which the length of the other pipes in any given scale was based. Recorded in *Han Shu Lu Li Zhi* (漢書・律曆志, *Records of Tonal System and Calendar*,[8] *History of the Han Dynasty*, 1st century AD), the "*huangzhong*" pipe, as the origin of the system of pitches, also acted as the origin of measurement:

> What are the units of length? They are Fen, Cun, Chi, Zhang, and Yin.[9] Their use is to

measure the lengths of objects. Their origin is the length of the huangzhong pipe.

度者,分、寸、尺、丈、引也,所以度長短也。本起黃鐘之長。……

That means the standard units of length come from the "*huangzhong*" pipe and the system of pitches. Such a method has its own scientific basis. As we know, the pitch level produced by a pipe actually depends upon its length. The changes in length of a pipe certainly result in pitch level changes, and vice versa. The auditory changes are always much more recognizable than the visual changes. Taking a violin for example, the sharp or flat tone can easily be sensed by the ears but it is difficult to judge with the eyes whether the length of a string has been shortened or not. As for a pipe, its length would be adjusted when people find its tone changing. By this method, the length of the pipe selected can be constantly ensured. Such a method could also be qualified for shaping the standard for weights and measures (度量衡)[10] (Figure 4).

The ancient Chinese considered the twelve pitches to be absolute tones in nature, and the fundamental "*huangzhong*" pipe was especially granted authority by the rulers. Therefore, the length of the "*huangzhong*" pipe was always under the emperor's control. The emperor could adjust it slightly, according to what he thought most closely matched his interpretation of ancient records, in order to better control the ideological legitimacy of the dynasty.

For the Qing Dynasty (1644-1911), the length of the "*huangzhong*" pipe was finally fixed by 1713. Regulated by the imperial book *lulu Zhengyi* (律呂正義, *Exact Implication on Musical Theory*, 1713), the tonal measurement based on the "*huangzhong*" pipe equaled 0.81 times of the normal measurement—identical to the "ancient" measurement. In fact, "ancient" means the ancient measuring method based on the "*huangzhong*" pipe.

Below are some analyses on the Altar design:

1. Compared with the normal measurement, the "*huangzhong*" tonal measurement (黃鍾律尺) was much more authoritative, since

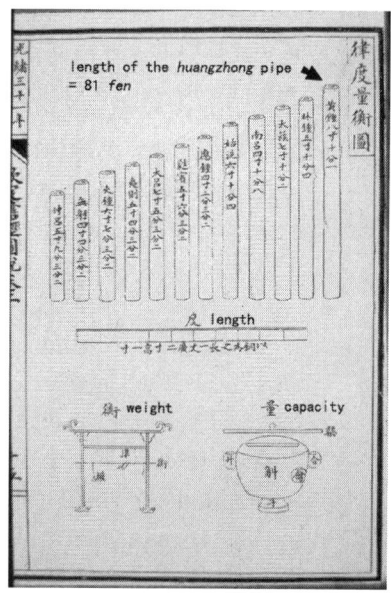

Figure 4: The relationship between measurement and the system of 12 fundamental pitches. The "huangzhong" pipe (the first pipe from the right direction, and also the longest one among the twelve pipes) was taken as the standard of lengths (度), capacities (量), and weights (衡).

for two thousand years the tone was considered to be absolutely fundamental in nature. The Altar of Heaven involved the musical element, hence reflecting perfect harmony between heaven and earth, and symbolizing the high legitimacy of the dynasty.

2. As mentioned above, from 1738 to 1742, the ritual music for various sacrifice ceremonies was under revision. Twelve types of special melodies were established for use in different sacrifice ceremonies and places. With Qianlong's

authorization the music of the "*huangzhong*" melody (黃鍾調) was designated as the special type for the Grand Sacrifice in the Altar of Heaven. Therefore, the "*huangzhong*" tonal measurement in the Altar terrace helped the architecture echo the performing "*huangzhong*" melody loudly.

3. The length of the "*huangzhong*" tonal measurement, regulated as 0.81 times of the normal measurement, had a close relationship with the number '9', because 0.81 = 0.9 x 0.9. While the number '9' had been repeatedly used in the Altar, the regulated length of "*huangzhong*" measurement intensified such reliance.

In conclusion, it has been found that there are intertwined correlations between the following four elements: (i) the Grand Sacrifice in the Altar of Heaven, (ii) the "*huangzhong*" tonal measurement for architecture, (iii) the "*huangzhong*" melody for ritual music, and (iv) the magic number '9'.

Case Study II: Zither Rhythm Studio

While the grand imperial garden Beihai located in the inner city of Beijing has been in existence since the 10th century, most of the buildings now standing were constructed during Emperor Qianlong's reign. Among those constructions, the Zither Rhythm Studio (韻琴齋, "*yunqin zhai*" in Chinese) was built in 1757 (the 22nd year of Qianlong's reign). The scenic objects of this place were clear and simple, and the

Fig 5. The Zither Rhythm Studio (left), and the surrounding environment. A roughly square pool is located in the center of the courtyard. The water sound is produced from some corners of the pool.

environment was calm and peaceful, so Emperor Qianlong and his crown son used the studio for reading. There was a roughly square pool located in front of the Studio. Since a stream dropped to form a tiny waterfall, giving off musical sounds, the name of "Zither Rhythm" was given to the building (Figure 5).

Yet one may pose two questions to such a design: First, why did Qianlong name the studio after the "zither" rather than the other musical instruments? And secondly, what is the reason for arranging the water-sound-produced "music" instead of real zither music?

In order to answer the first question, it is necessary to return to the history of Chinese musical instruments. For the ancient Chinese, musical instruments were not only simple tools of sound-making; they were also a kind of regulator that harmonized worldly matters, and a kind of key to resolve disorder in natural phenomena. The Chinese zither (古琴, "*guqin*" in Chinese) is extremely typical of those musical instruments, for it represents both the sage ruler's political ideal, and the well educated scholar's self-cultivation.

According to a Chinese legend, the Yellow Emperor (黃帝, *Huangdi*) once made a 5-string zither to play the song of *Qing Jiao* (清角). Later, when the *Shun* Emperor (舜帝) played another zither song named *Nan Feng* (南風), he held the musical performance as a kind of ceremony, rather than entertainment. Concerning the 5-string zither, it was said that the body of the zither was of 0.81-*zhang*-long—this length, as we remember, was the origin of measurement. Besides, the major string, or in other words, the thickest string, was placed in the middle of all the strings, which then is the emperor of strings. The minor string was placed on its right side, performing like the minister, and the other strings were all placed according to their order of thickness and length, so that the superior political domination of the emperor would be reflected in the layout of the zither strings.

Also, in traditional China, a well educated scholar was expected to be skilled in four arts: zither, chess, calligraphy, and painting. Zither ranked first, indicating its high position in a scholar's life. Usually, zither was employed as an important medium for scholars and poets expressing their emotions.

Now we are able to understand why Emperor Qianlong, in his attempt to be the 'sage-king', chose "zither" as the sole musical instrument he proposed to play. Only this kind of instrument could be the perfect 'sage-king' symbol.

To answer the second question concerning the arranging of water-sound-produced "music" instead of real zither music, it may be useful to search into Emperor

Qianlong's poems, finding clues that are relevant to the Studio. Although he wrote a total of fifteen poems focusing on the Zither Rhythm Studio, we will here only examine two that have been loosely translated into English.

Here is one of Qianlong's poems, dated 1765.[11]

> Though part of the water surface was already iced, the spring hasn't frozen yet; the soft water sound brings the sense of the warm season.
> Bamboos near the studio grow densely, echoing when the wind blows through.
> Water sounds agree with each other, composing a euphonic song.
> I can't help laughing at Yuanming, who put on a pose of playing zither without strings.

> 鏡浦雖冱凝,流泉故不凍。泠泠常作聲,已覺春溫貢。齋傍竹特茂,清籟和吟鳳。回應有相投,底藉八音眾。寄意笑柴桑,無弦猶撫弄。

And here are some verses from another of Qianlong's poems, dated 1772.[12]

> The studio faces the spring and the rocks, borrowing their scenes and sounds.
> The inscription "zither rhythm" always makes visitors surprised,

for there is no real musical instrument in existence.
Such an idea is similar to Tao Yuanming's, though mine is somehow advanced.

斯齋臨石泉,原屬相假借。來源凝沍堅,乳竇淙奚藉。韻琴題簷額,虛語徒成訝。雖然更有進,頗似陶潛舍。

What Emperor Qianlong alluded to in his poems were the great poet Tao Yuanming (陶淵明, 365–427) and his odd behaviors. In Tao's late years, when joining friends' parties, he always took out a zither without strings, put on a pose of playing it, and sighed with his feelings: "Once I recognize the charm in the zither music, there is no need to produce tones over strings any more! (但識琴中趣,何勞弦上聲)" According to Qianlong, the design conception of the Studio was quite like Tao's idea, yet superior to Tao's. Tao removed the strings, while holding the body of his zither. However, in Qianlong's "zither" studio, there was neither a zither nor a player. Instead, the springs in the pool performed as the strings; and the rocks along the pool, as the body of the "zither." Visitors were reminded to listen to the "music" when seeing the inscription "Zither Rhythm Studio" hanging outside the studio building.

To some extent, the water-sound-produced "music" could be appreciated as the highest form of musical work.[13] The "music" is continuous even on the coldest days of winter, since the water under the surface of the pool stays unfrozen. The "music" only fades out when people go away from the studio. Further, people do not have to sit down to listen to it. They just turn their attention toward it, and then realize it is always already going on. For Emperor Qianlong in the Studio, such music quieted his mind, and effectively cultivated his sage leadership inside.

Conclusion

In the past, very little has been written or said about the archi-music designs of the Altar of Heaven and the Zither Rhythm Studio. While in fact the musical design in the above architecture has always been in existence but not always apparent. Furthermore, the musical elements add extra socio-cultural meanings to the architecture. The Altar of Heaven attained ideological legitimacy from the "*huangzhong*" tonal measurement, and the Zither Rhythm Studio involved social responsibility because of the zither virtue. For Emperor Qianlong, such archi-music exercises represented his sage-king ambition: political leadership, moral authority, and ideological legitimacy combined.

However, it is inaccurate to credit all the design concepts to Qianlong, though it was he who directed the programs and finally authorized the designs. The "*huangzhong*" tonal measurement as the "ancient" dimension could date from the "ancient" 1st century AD, while the "music" without zither strings could be traced back to the poet Tao Yuanming of the 5th century. Therefore, further research on archi-music works beyond the 18th-century imperial cases should be conducted.

Endnotes

¹ Dai Yi 戴逸, *Qianlongdi jiqi shidai* (乾隆帝及其時代, *Emperor Qianlong and His Era*, Beijing: Zhongguo renmin daxue press 中國人民大學出版社, 1996): 461-464.

² For more details on this matter, see Jianfei Zhu, *Chinese Spatial Strategies: Imperial Beijing 1420-1911* (London; New York: Routlegde Curzon, 2004): 43-44. Zhu expounds the duality of the traditional Chinese political system similar to the "sage-king" notion: of *li* (禮) and *shi* (勢), *wangdao* (王道) and *badao* (霸道), Confucianism (儒家) and Legalism (法家). According to Zhu, the layout of Beijing is that of symbolic representation and functional practice; of a formal plan and an actual space.

³ The ceremony was always held at the Winter Solstice in December. Due to the cold weather, it wouldn't be easy to keep presenting at every of the ceremonies for sixty years.

⁴ The imperial book was named *lvlv Zhengyi II* (律呂正義後編, *Exact Implication on Musical Theory II*, 1746) after *lvlv Zhengyi* (律呂正義, 1713), an earlier book directed by Emperor Kangxi (康熙), the Grandfather of Emperor Qianlong.

⁵ The role of "Son of Heaven" (天子), the interlocutor between humankind and the celestial realm, was played by the Chinese emperors over many centuries.

⁶ The result of 9 x 5, as a matter of fact, was in complete conformity with "the Supreme number of 9 and 5" (九五之尊) in the "*Book of Changes*" (易經, *I Ching*). The arrangement of putting number 9 and 5 together was used

exclusively in China by the ancient emperors, and that's why it was used here.

⁷ See *huangchao wenxian tongkao* (皇朝文獻通考 *Dynasty Document Collected*), vol. 93; *Qinding daqing huidian zeli* (欽定大清會典則例 *Imperial-ordered Qing Collected Regulation*), vol.76, vol. 126; *Qing shilu* (清實錄 *Qing Records*, XIII, Beijing: Zhonghua shuju yingyin 中華書局影印, 1986), vol. 359: 950-952

⁸ Ancient Chinese scholars often associated the study of tonal system with astronomical phenomena, calendar, weights and measures, Yin-yang (陰陽, feminine and masculine), the five elements (五行), and even social and political consideration, giving a comprehensive explanation and making the subject a huge theoretical system.

⁹ 10 *Fen* (分) equals 1 *Cun* (寸). 10 Cun equals 1 *Chi* (尺). 10 *Chi* equals 1 *Zhang* (丈), and 10 *Zhang* equals 1 *Yin* (引).

¹⁰ Guan Zengjian and Fu Guimei, "On Liu Xin's 劉歆 Metrological Theory", in *Historical Perspectives on East Asian Science, Technology and Medicine,* ed. Manuel Omar Estela Benavides: 477-488 (Singapore University Press, 2001)

¹¹ Emperor Qianlong, *Yuzhi Shiji* (乾隆禦制詩集, *Qianlong Imperial-Compiled Poem Collection*), collection iii, vol. 43.

¹² Ibid., collection iv, vol.1.

¹³ The western interpenetration between music and environment sound was first put into practice by Erik Satie (1866-1925) in his *"furniture music"*, and then largely developed in John Cage (1912-1992)'s well-known work, *4'33"*.

References

Attali, Jacques (1977) *Bruit: Essai sur l'économie politique de la musique.* (Presses Universitaires de France).

Beihai and Jingshan Park Administration 北海景山公園管理處 (compiled, 1994) *Beihai* 北海. (Beijing: China Esperanto Press).

Chao Pian, Rulan (1997) "Music and Confucian Sacrificial Ceremony", *Enchanting Powers: Music in the World's Religions*, ed. by Lawrence E. Sullivan. (Cambridge: Harvard University): 237-262.

Dai, Yi 戴逸 (1996) *Qianlongdi jiqi shidai* (乾隆帝及其時代, *Emperor Qianlong and His Era*). (Beijing: Zhongguo Renmin Daxue Press 中國人民大學出版社).

Fu, Xinian (2002) *Chinese Architecture*, ed. by Nancy S. Steinhardt. (Yale University Press).

Giskin, Howard. and Walsh, Bettye S. (ed. 2001) *An Introduction to Chinese Culture Through the Family.* (State University of New York).

Guan, Zengjian. and Fu, Guimei (2001) "On Liu Xin 劉歆's Metrological Theory", *Historical Perspectives on East Asian Science, Technology and Medicine*, ed. by Manuel Omar Estela Benavides. (Singapore University Press): 477-488.

ICOMOS (1998) *World Heritage List, Temple of Heaven (China), No. 881.*

Keswick, Maggie (1986) *The Chinese Garden: History, Art and Architecture.* (New York: St. Martin's Press).

Liu, Gui-teng 劉桂滕, "Humble Exploration of the Court Ritual Music of Qianlong Period, Qing Dynasty" (清代乾隆朝宮廷禮樂探微), *Musicology in China* 中國音樂學, No. 3 (2001): 43-67.

Needham, Sir Joseph (1965) *Science and Civilisation in China*, Vol. 4, Physics and Physical Technology, Part 1, Physics. (Cambridge University Press).

Rachel, Daniel R. (2000) *The Science and Applications of Acoustics*. (New York: Springer-Verlag).

Rawski, Evelyn Sakakida (1998) *The Last Emperors: A Social History of Qing Imperial Institutions*. (University of California Press).

Steinhardt, Nancy Shatzman (1999) *Chinese Imperial City Planning*. (University of Hawaii Press).

Watt, James. "The Qin and the Chinese Literati", *Orientations Magazine*, No.11 (1981): 38-49.

Zhu, Jianfei (2004) *Chinese Spatial Strategies: Imperial Beijing 1420-1911*. (London; New York: Routledge Curzon).

John Sands

Transgressing Boundaries: Considering a Societal Function of Music and Architecture Through Markus Pernthaler's Helmut-List-Halle

> *When a writer of the past centuries expressed an opinion about his craft, was he immediately asked to apply it to the other arts? But today it's the thing to 'talk painting' in the jargon of the musician or the literary man to 'talk literature' in the jargon of the painter, as if at the bottom there were only one art which expressed itself indifferently as one or the other of these languages, like the Spinozistic substance which is adequately reflected by each of its attributes.*
>
> Jean-Paul Sartre, *What is Literature?*, 1947

> *Our culture no longer bothers to use words like appropriation or borrowing... Today's audience isn't listening at all—it's participating. Indeed, audience is as antique a term as record, the one archaically passive, the other archaically physical.*
>
> William Gibson, *Wired Magazine*, July 2005

It's strange, this comparison of music and architecture. It's strange because everyone with whom I end up in a conversation about it approaches the topic with some degree of incredulousness. It is simply difficult to ideate a concrete basis for such a comparison, and that is, I suspect, partly because most of us are unable to reconcile immediately the vast differences between the two; the affective devices of architecture differ greatly from those of music, though historically each discipline has shown an astonishing capacity for appropriating convincingly and meaningfully the theoretical tropes of the other. (I am reminded of Vitruvius' lengthy excursus in Book V, Chapter IV of the *Ten Books* wherein he gives a rather thorough lesson on Greek musical scales, explaining how different modes were used by the ancients for different moods or occasions. What is not explicitly stated in this passage, though, is that Vitruvius, our predecessor, was appropriating music to validate his own architectural credentials—architects should, after all, be trained in music, he says—and his earlier explanation of the most decorous utilization of the Greek orders. The evolution of concert music some seventeen hundred years later required, in turn, an architectural validation: the concert hall.) The difficulty in negotiating a persuasive contemporary comparison of music and architecture, as Sartre reminds us above, lies in the fact that there is little basis, at least formally, for such a juxtaposition. In short, for our comparison to be fruitful we must examine *what* music and architecture do rather than *how* they do it, leaving the practitioners of each the freedom to plot their own course. But if architecture and music are able to transcend the nature specific to each—and I believe they can and sometimes, in ideal circumstances, do—then we might begin to locate between the two a shared goal. That is my proposition to you: that the common ground of music and architecture, beyond all topical elements—form, proportion, harmony, and so on—and beyond the more-than-occasional overlap in parlance, might be better and more convincingly assessed through a consideration of shared societal and cultural function.

This comparison we are undertaking finds a convincing home, perhaps not surprisingly, in a corner of southern Austria. The city of Graz is the provincial capital of Styria and haven for noted architects since the aftermath of the Second World War. Situated along the river Mur, Graz is known as *'Österreichs heimliche Liebe'* or 'Austria's secret love' but the city's important cultural, social, and architectural initiatives have gone unnoticed by few. With a population of just over 285,000 (many of whom are university students), the Styrian capital has in recent years garnered several accolades for progressive environmental, social, and cultural undertakings that include an award from Greenpeace in 1993 for climate protection that lead to the designation of *Ökostadt* or eco-city, and later in 1996 the European Union's 'Sustainable City' award. In 1996 Graz was named Europe's Human Rights Capital by the United Nations. Graz was also granted the singular distinction of being named Europe's *Kulturhauptstadt* for the year 2003.

Three major architectural projects were built for the *Kulturhauptstadt* events, including the famous *Kunsthaus*

Figure 1: Exterior view of the Helmut-List Halle. Photo by Gerald Liebminger, from http://www.helmut-list-halle.com/presse/HLH048.jpg, accessed December 5, 2006.

designed by Peter Cook and Colin Fournier, and the so-called *Murinsel* by Vito Acconci. The third project is the *Helmut-List-Halle*. Planned in but four months and built in ten, it was designed by Graz architect Markus Pernthaler, whose projects in the Styrian capital—such as the master plan of the main square in 2002—have increasingly earned him a reputation as a sensitive builder. The building was commissioned by Graz resident Helmut List, who is chairman of AVL, a developer of sustainable automotive technologies. Particularly relevant to the work of AVL is the use of acoustics as a means of calculating engine efficiency. The hall was to be a reflection of AVL's technological expertise and aesthetic conscientiousness, having in its conception the issues for which Graz has become known. It was to be a place for the fellowship of art and science, not dissimilar to the work of AVL in automotive design. As List himself notes:

> With this project we wanted to bridge the gap between science and art in a future-oriented and sustainable way. This bridging synergetically unites acoustic know-how and

artistic competence and thus makes scientific progress exploitable for new challenges to be met with regard to cultural productions and socio-political issues.[1]

The visual evidence makes plain the fact that this is a building of the twenty-first century, but in the formal grammar there is something of a wistful (though unsentimental) remembrance of years past. Indeed, the steel substructure of an old *Fabrikshalle* situated on the site slated for demolition provided the framework for a series of three volumes to house a foyer, the concert space itself, and a backstage area. The substructure of the factory imposes through its formal economy an *inherent aesthetic logic,* as Jürgen Habermas might say,[2] of an industrial and functional architecture, i.e. the economic and efficient use of space and of economical and efficient materials; in this case, steel, glass, and concrete. The steel frame allows for buoyant glass volumes contrasted and anchored by the necessarily weighty central hall.

Each component of musical production is compartmentalized formally but unified by spatial organization. The offices, conference rooms, dressing rooms, and catering facilities line the foyer and backstage areas via extensions of the central concrete volume, connecting the behind-the-scenes activities of musical production with the public aspects of concert-attendance. The south façade of the hall is lined with solar panels that generate electricity—26,000 kilowatt hours per year—that is directed into the power grid, integrating the musical culture of Graz into

Figure 2: View of concert hall interior. Photo by Gerald Liebminger, from http://www.helmut-list-halle.com/presse/HLH020.jpg, accessed December 5, 2006.

the ecological initiatives for which AVL—and the city as a whole—has garnered praise in the past.

Taken alone, the concert hall block itself is a technical and compositional masterpiece. AVL developed the acoustic system with the input of some of Austria's most renowned musicians, including, among others, conductor Nikolaus Harnoncourt. Housed in concrete and lined with solid hardwood, the hall boasts incredible crispness of sound along with a freedom of spatial configuration, which I shall later argue is crucial to the relationship of music and architecture in this building. The hall has neither a built-in stage nor seating and can thus be arranged in a variety of layouts, rising to the challenges posed by contemporary composers whose music increasingly spurns the spatial protocols imposed by more traditional concert venues. Peter Oswald, director of one of the resident festivals at *Helmut-List-Halle, steirischer herbst,* notes: "With *Helmut-List-Halle* new standards are being set for contemporary art production; the power of experimentation of great temperaments can *finally transgress the boundaries of spatial inadequacies*" (emphasis mine).[3]

Before going any further it is important to our comparison here to note that Gottfried Semper keenly linked architecture and music (albeit for aesthetic purposes) at their core, suggesting that music and architecture share the same *ur*-impulse. He writes:

> Artistic enjoyment of nature's beauty…is by no means the most naïve or original manifestation of the artistic impulse. A feeling for this rather is undeveloped in uncomplicated primitive man, who…enjoys recognizing a wreath, a string of pearls, a curl, in choral dances and the rhythmic tones that attend these, in the beat of an oar, et cetera, nature's creative law as it gleams through in the regularity of space and time sequences. These are the beginnings out of which have grown music and architecture, the two highest purely cosmic (non-imitative) arts, whose legislative support no other art can forego.[4]

We should draw from Semper's text that architecture and music are fundamentally spatial and temporal,

Figure 3: Interior view of concert hall. Photo by Gerald Liebminger, from http://www.helmut-list-halle.com/presse/HLH002.jpg, accessed December 5, 2006.

equally reliant, as it were, on both. As each of these dimensions gained clarification by scientific means—or problematization, perhaps more importantly, by political ones—both architecture and music faced disciplinary challenges to even their most basic tenets that yielded reconceptualizations of each throughout the last century.

Frank Lloyd Wright, for example, saw the proliferation of the automobile in the 1920s as the death of the city, heralding the rebirth of Jeffersonian democracy in America. The freedom to move across the landscape on vast transcontinental highways, Wright predicted in his plan for *Broadacre City*, would lead inevitably to expansive sprawling cities, reorganizing both urban and suburban

Figure 4: Exterior view of Helmut-List Hall. Photo by Gerald Liebminger, from http://www.helmut-list-halle.com/presse/HLH043.jpg, accessed December 5, 2006.

fabric along with the human relationships in space and time that such reorganization implies. "It will haphazard build itself," Wright wrote in *Living City*,[5] and it did—at least topically. The great roads he imagined were a means of communication in their own time, and a prelude to the advances our generation saw realized toward the end of the last century. In his polemical response to Le Corbusier's condemnation of American urbanism, Wright wrote of a coming revolution in how information would be transferred, invoking in the same stroke of the pen environmental concerns, the banner architecture waves today under the term 'sustainability:'

> As the citizen sits in his car, he may press any variety of buttons or turn an indicator and obtain any section he desires of the modern newspaper—the forests saved and millions of tons of waste paper eliminated. He picks up sound and sight whatever he is interested in, learns by listening where the day's specialties are to be found; where events of interest are occurring or are going to occur, near or far

away. All over the surface of the globe, in fact, if he pleases, he may listen in.⁶

In the early 1920s, during the same time that Wright developed his *Broadacre* plan for a decentralized urban model, the German musicologist Heinrich Besseler, developed a theory of *Gebrauchsmusik*—literally music for use—based on his understanding of dance suites from the seventeenth century. Besseler noted a difference in dance music in that certain suites in the genre were composed to be danced to while other suites of the same genre were simply listened to. He suggested a "technical and qualitative contrast between '*Vortragsfolge*' and '*Gebrauchsmusik*'."⁷ In other words, Besseler pointed out an inherent difference in the processes that necessitate or facilitate the composition of these types of music: either edification of an audience or audience inclusion. Besseler took this idea one step further in 1926, blurring the distinction between performer and listener:

> One would presuppose fundamentally different approaches to music where the…essentially concert-determined characteristics were missing. Perfection of reproduction would count as inessential, the listeners would not constitute a limitless crowd taking in what is performed in passive devotion, but would approach the music as a genuine community of like-minded individuals with an active attitude and in active expectation. Such art would

therefore always correspond to a concrete need, it would not have to find its public but grow out of it. Such an art is *Gebrauchsmusik*.⁸

Here I would like to draw attention to Besseler's use of the subjunctive tense in the preceding passage. He, like Wright, proposed something that, at that time, did not exist, at least not in the idealized form either one of them describe. The function of so-called *Gebrauchsmusik*, as Besseler saw it, *would* be social in nature in that music *would* be understood as a community activity. By extension, the musical work is not something that *would* be objectified. Rather, the shared experience of creation would be the object, wherein all participants actively engage one another. Music *would* be the unifying agent and organizing phenomenon.

In this analytical moment, Besseler theorizes a music different philosophically and theoretically than the art music of the day. And a music that is arguably not music, at least in the Kantian sense of music as aesthetic object, marks a radical shift away from the philosophy of art that developed, as the noted musicologist Carl Dahlhaus reminds us, after the mid-eighteenth century in Europe. One factor of note that led to the push for functional music lies in a 'Romantic' phenomenon made possible by the concert. This phenomenon, the complete objectification of music, seemed to many to serve no social purpose. Erich Doflein sought a fundamental shift away from the objectification. Writing for the journal *Melos* Doflein notes in 1927:

> We place the works before us, instead of using and utilizing them. This aesthetic placing-in-front-of-oneself of works may generally seem to be taken for granted, as something deriving quite naturally from the Romantic tradition, from the tendency to make absolute not only the individual work but also the individual himself; this necessarily stems from the structure of the works that we are used to listening to in the concert hall.[9]

Such observations were in line with criticisms of others within the movement favoring *Gebrauchsmusik*. Besseler saw the concert hall and the culture that emanated from it as detrimental to the experience of music. His assessment of the concert was, quite simply, a control mechanism that governed every aspect of music from its composition to its ultimate performance. "Today's situation," he writes, "presents the possibility of illuminating other types of approach to music that are usually held to be invalid and are thus ignored but that, despite their rudimentary condition at present, permit the interpretation of analogous attitudes in earlier epochs."[10] For Besseler *eigenständige* music insisted at one level on a detachment from the music, and at a more philosophical level, the subconscious acceptance of a certain arbitrariness of the musical experience as well as the social experience.[11]

In roughly the same time period, we see an architect on one continent forecasting the death of the city as the result of incredible technological progress, highlighting the inadequacies of previous models of social cohesion based on spatial organization. On another continent we find a possible solution by a musicologist theorizing a new music that would, ostensibly, be a mechanism by which social cohesion is maintained through musical—temporal—participation. The prediction of instantaneous attainment of information and communication led by Frank Lloyd Wright to a necessary awareness of global (and environmental) issues as well as a new model of a decentralized urbanism. The theory of *Gebrauchsmusik* as laid out by Heinrich Besseler suggests that a society growing increasingly apart politically, and as a result, spatially, necessitates a reconsideration of the social function of music that could unify and encourage equal participation. Both theories underscore the importance of the individual, but with a careful consideration of her participation in the collective. Wright's model for individualized transportation in the automobile as well as land ownership for all citizens evolved from the model of Jeffersonian democracy while Besseler's theory fosters democratic participation of all people in the social experience of music. Wright's model relies on science and technology to compensate for the spatial issues that arise as a result of decentralization. Besseler's relies on the inexplicable universality of art to bring people together in shared involvement and, he suggests, political reconciliation.

And so we are left with a mass of complex issues, all of which come to the fore in a consideration of *Helmut-List-Halle*. The aesthetic issues of functionalism as they pertain to both music and to architecture find some strange synthesis in the reconceptualization of spatial and social relationships such as Wright and Besseler prevised. As a proper concert hall, we might reasonably expect a building that houses that which aesthetics has taught us to be functionless, but this building's purpose—as a vehicle by which the shared experience of music is made possible—is realized in a radically different manner than many other concert halls. The industrial connotations of the architecture suggest to us what would have been, in years gone by, a place of production and utility. Pernthaler was aware of the extraordinary fusion of ideas he was making when he writes: "The consolidation of art and science, technology and modern cultural output finds its *formal counterpart* in the synthesis of old industrial architecture and contemporary formal language" (emphasis mine).[12]

I suggest that this clash of ideals evident in Pernthaler's *Helmut-List-Halle* proposes a reconsideration of the ethics of architectural and musical aesthetics. For the greater part of the two and a half centuries preceding us the public spaces of western art music, while differentiated vastly formally and acoustically, shared, for better or worse, one basic feature: the fixed and rigid and ultimately hierarchical orientation of the audience toward the performer. But the new freedom to "finally transgress the boundaries of spatial inadequacies" allowed in *Helmut-List-Halle* marks two subtle but significant shifts. Music as an architectural problem is no longer one of simply producing an acoustic envelope; architecture, as a result, becomes a musical problem: music, not architecture, takes on the fundamental role of spatial organizer, allowing for what Reyner Banham calls "a range of spatial experience and cultural responses…"[13] The industrial architectural aesthetic of utility demands of the musician and concertgoer an acknowledgment (if I may paraphrase Karsten Harries) of what it seems Heinrich Besseler believed is music's ethical function.[14] The *Helmut-List-Halle* welcomes this paradox by allowing an industrial architecture to transcend its own functional utility and create a space and time for the possibility of music whose long-disavowed utility might once again, at long last, be embraced.

Endnotes

[1] Helmut List, "AVL–Science and Art." Available: www.avl.com.

[2] Jürgen Habermas, "Modern and Postmodern Architecture," in *The New Conservatism: Cultural Criticism and the Historians' Debate*, trans. Shierry Weber Nicholsen (Cambridge, Mass.: The MIT Press, 1989): 12.

[3] Peter Oswald, "Die Halle." Available: www.avl.com.

[4] Gottfried Semper, *Style in the Technical and Tectonic Arts; or Practical Aesthetics*. Trans. Harry Francis Mallgrave. (Los Angeles: Getty Research Institute, 2004): 82.

[5] Frank Lloyd Wright, *The Living City* (New York: Horizon, 1958): 144.

[6] Frank Lloyd Wright, "Broadacre City: An Architect's Vision," *New York Times* (20 Mar 1932): 8.

[7] Heinrich Besseler, "Beiträge zur Stilgeschichte der deutschen Suite im 17. Jahrhundert" (Universität Freiburg, 1923), p. 28. Trans. in Stephen Hinton, *The Idea of Gebrauchsmusik: Musical Aesthetics in the Weimar Republic with Reference to the Works of Paul Hindemith*. (New York: Garland, 1989): 7.

[8] Heinrich Besseler, "Grundfragen des musikalischen Hörens," in *Jahrbuch der Musikbibliothek Peters für 1925* (Leipzig: 1926), p. 38. Trans. in Stephen Hinton, *The Idea of Gebrauchsmusik*:10.

[9] Erich Doflein, "Wandel der Bedeutungen," *Melos* vi (1927), p. 170. Trans. in Stephen Hinton, *The Idea of Gebrauchsmusik*: 18.

[10] Heinrich Besseler, *Studien zur Musik des Mittelalters*, *Archiv für Musikwissenschaft* (University of Freiburg, 1926), p. 144. Trans. in Stephen Hinton, *The Idea of Gebrauchsmusik*: 9-10.

[11] See Ibid.

[12] Marcus Pernthaler, "Wissenswertes zur Helmut-List-Halle." Available: www.Helmut-List-Halle.com.

[13] Reyner Banham, *The Architecture of the Well-Tempered Environment*. (Chicago: University of Chicago Press, 1984): 18.

[14] Karsten Harries, *The Ethical Function of Architecture* (Cambridge, Mass.: The MIT Press, 2000).

Acknowledgments: I would be remiss to omit special thanks to Daniel J. Bowles and to Nathanael Oster for assistance with translations over the course of this project.

List of Figures

All figures are photographs by Gerald Liebinger, from the official Helmut-List-Halle website http://www.helmut-list-halle.com/content/05_presse/pressefotos.php, accessed on December 5, 2006.

Garth Ancher

Translating the Intangible Qualities of Miles Davis' Jazz Rock Fusion into Architecture

The School of Contemporary Music at the University of Tasmania (UTAS) in Launceston, Australia, has been seeking relocation from the outskirts of Launceston, to the inner city arts campus, effectively uniting all the arts-based faculties of UTAS onto one campus. Currently the contemporary music faculty operates at a level of anonymity on a separate university campus surrounded by the faculties of education, nursing and science. The proposed relocation and development of the new contemporary music school provided the opportunity to explore the possibilities of music influencing architecture.

The Inveresk Railyards is the proposed site for the music school and is rich in the history of Launceston's evolution. After researching the history of jazz—in particular Miles Davis' jazz-rock fusion—and the various industries that have inhabited the site over the past 150 years, parallels became clear. Themes of reinvention, adaptation and resourcefulness are shared between the continuous development of jazz as an art form and the development of the former railyards site into an arts precinct. These themes have a parallel in the music school itself which bases its teaching philosophy on reinterpretation and experimentation. There is also further potential to translate the undetermined aspects of jazz, including improvisation and performance, into architectural propositions. Davis' fusion embodies all these characteristics and is the predominant metaphor for the Launceston School of Contemporary Music.

Launceston is a small city in the north of Tasmania, with an estimated population of 68,000. The city is located at the juncture of the North Esk, South Esk, and Tamar rivers. The proposed site was previously swampland used for agricultural purposes and in 1871 the Launceston Railway Station and Workshop was established as part of the Launceston and Western Railway. The workshops were gradually expanded until World War II, when the premises were used to manufacture munitions. Operations continued to run on the site until 1994. In 2002 the Queen Victorian Museum and Art Gallery and UTAS's School of Visual and Performing Arts relocated into the former railyard workshops. The School of Architecture is set to move into the old Exhibition Building on this site in 2006.

The project partly responds to Markus Bandur's assessment[1] of how art has been perceived since the acceptance of Hegel and Schopenhauer's philosophies of aesthetics. According to Bandur, Hegel and Schopenhauer's philosophies produced a hierarchical system of ranking the arts, based on the art forms' ability to evoke sensual pleasure in an individual. Architecture and music had previously been considered as the leaders of the arts but architecture lost importance in the new system while music retained its position at the top of the arts. According to Bandur this caused architects to opt for functionalism over aesthetics. Bandur argued that the result of the new criteria of pleasure and aesthetics segregated the arts into individual areas of specialization. During this period any notion of functionality was disregarded in favor of pure aestheticism. Bandur cites institutions as examples of this: art schools for pottery and painting, conservatoriums for musicians, and architecture schools for architects. Bandur believes that valuable cross-pollination between the arts had been lost.[2] These examples equate to a more focused but pared down education. The addition of the music school to the arts precinct would see all the arts represented at the same campus, rejuvenating the chance for integration between disciplines. According to Bandur's argument in *The Aesthetics of Total Serialism*, all art forms have much to gain from cross-pollination. Furthermore, jazz especially can have a beneficial effect on architectural design because of music and architecture's potential to engage and influence each other on a formal and functional level.

Understanding how the intangible qualities of fusion could translate into a building means examining how music has influenced architecture in the past. For centuries, amphitheaters and concert halls have been designed to function acoustically, and musical harmony and proportion have been effectively translated into building façades. However more recent examples of less determined aspects of music driving architectural design are more relevant in terms of this project. Steven Holl designed the Stretto House (Dallas, Texas, 1989-92) "as a parallel to Bartók's *Music for Strings, Percussion and Celeste*."[3] Holl acknowledges the importance of rhythm, form and proportion in architecture and music but focuses on the translation of unknown qualities, such as composition, arrangement and manipulation, and how these qualities have a stimulating effect on the listener. Holl examines the contrast between Bartók's expression and technique and attempts to recreate it in the formal and spatial treatment of the Stretto House.

Another work, Toyo Ito's *Tower of Winds* project (Yokohama, Kanagawa, 1986) was inspired by the ephemeral nature of music. The *Tower of Winds* was designed to be a temporary structure that changes in response to outside forces such as traffic noise. This architectural improvisation and spontaneity is an example of how a building can change in accordance with the mood of its environment or users. The utilization of intangible qualities by Holl and Ito in these two projects was especially useful in understanding how to translate the intangible qualities of fusion into an architectural proposition.

Miles Davis' jazz rock fusion exemplifies an even more potent link between music and architecture. Davis' fusion is defined by its simple structure and spontaneous nature, and any attempt to draw inspiration from it requires an understanding of jazz, the context in which fusion was created, and some analysis of fusion itself. "Jazz is a serious art music, capable of sustaining intellectual and emotional interest on par with any other art form."[4]

The roots of jazz can be traced back to ancient West Africa where songs were used within tribal communities to exert influence between tribes. In the nineteenth century European ignorance lead to the view that West-African music was a primitive form of music. This belief of West-African music as being inferior can be traced back to a fundamental difference in the hierarchy of elements, specifically melody and rhythm, used by each respective culture.[5] Western European music emphasized melodies (instrumental solos) with rhythm (percussion) as accompaniment; however West-African music emphasized rhythm (drums) with the melody (voices) as the accompaniment. Not surprisingly, today West-African music is revered as one of the most "complex, subtle and sophisticated forms of music in the world."[6]

In the late 19th century slaves were transported from West Africa to America. At this point musicologists believed that the earliest forms of jazz evolved in southern North America. During this period the West-African slaves were discouraged from practicing their native religious customs, language, and language arts.[7] However, some slave owners encouraged music and dance because it improved morale among slaves and increased their productivity. Slaves would sing the European songs enjoyed by their owners instead of their traditional songs but apply their vocal style to the structures and harmonies found in European music.

Fundamental elements of jazz were born when the dynamic rhythmic language and expressive pitch-bending of African vocal music became fused with structures and harmonies borrowed from the European music favored by white slave owners."[8] Borneman states that the fusion between the vastly different music of the two cultures resulted in a diverse range of music, however the surviving product from that period was the beginnings of what is now referred to as jazz.[9] This melding of contrasting cultures formed the basis of jazz, but is also embodied in Miles Davis' fusion.

Another significant difference between Western-European and Western-African music is that the type of scale used in European music differs from the one used in traditional West African music.[10] European music generally operates on a diatonic scale, an eight-note scale that consists of five tones and two semi-tones. West African music generally uses a 'non-hemitonic pentatone' scale, a six-note scale consisting of five tones. According to Borneman: "West Africans who are not familiar with European music will tend to become uncertain when asked to sing in a tempered scale."[11] Borneman cites the example of a West-African singer who has never heard western music attempting to sing a diatonic scale, to highlight the manner in which jazz scales evolved. He explains that as the singer approaches the third and seventh notes of the diatonic scale he invariably utilizes pitch-bending techniques such as increased vibrato and varying timbre. These techniques are inherent in West-African language and are used to form the 'foreign' notes. The altered notes on the third, seventh (and later the fifth) notes of the diatonic scale led to the creation of the 'shout' scale and 'blues' scale, which are cornerstones in the development of jazz.[12] The creation of the blues and shout scales highlight qualities of adaptation and resourcefulness. These qualities are central in the development of fusion and can also be linked to improvisation and live performance.

Jazz has continually evolved since its conception. From the early 1890s to the early 1920s jazz was associated with alcohol, drugs, and prostitutes; a public perception that was countered by the 'clean' swing bands (in the 'big band era') of the 1930s and 1940s. However during the 1940s the swing style of jazz gave way to the more adventurous bop and hard bop styles that in turn were tempered by cool and east-coast jazz in the 1950s. Then modal jazz developed in the early 1960s to provide greater freedom for improvisation and melded with rock-inspired rhythms in the late 1960s to form fusion.

Fusion is not considered to be true jazz by purists of the art form but rather a hybrid style of jazz and rock born from a desire for commercial success. Fusion embodies the resourceful nature inherent in jazz as it combines rock with modal jazz; an earlier jazz style based on Medieval and Renaissance scales. This makes jazz—and fusion in particular—an ideal design generator for a school that bases its teaching philosophy on experimentation and rejuvenation.

The three main aspects of fusion that have been used as design drivers for the project are:

- the improvised nature of the melodies that promote feelings of spontaneity and randomness
- the way fusion is structured or the form of the music
- the concept of live performance

As noted earlier, Miles Davis was a leading figure in the bop, hard bop, cool, modal, and fusion styles of jazz. "Davis' creativity and his influence as both a player and conceptualist was sustained for more than four decades, an example which introduced the idea of permanent conceptual development into jazz life."[13] Davis' contribution to the evolution of hard bop, cool, modal, and fusion jazz captures the inherent intangible qualities of the jazz genre. For example, throughout his career Davis was constantly reinventing, adapting, and borrowing from music outside jazz to develop playing styles.

Modal jazz differed from previous forms of jazz since it was based on scale progressions as opposed to chord progressions. Modal scales were commonly used in Medieval and Renaissance times and had been resurrected by avant-garde classical composers at the turn of the twentieth century.[14] Cooke explains that using these scales meant musicians could perform solos with an unprecedented level of melodic improvisation. Furthermore, he argues that this led also to the 'static' or unemotional nature of modal jazz. This highly improvised form of jazz directly evolved into what is known as fusion. Davis described this improvisation as follows:

> You can give a cat some chords and say play it like that. Or give him some notes and say play those notes like this, but it will be different every time you play it… and then they fuck it up… and that's when you come up with something new.[15]

The improvised nature of modal scales translates to a building that changes based on ideas or events that are not preconceived. This is realized by facilitating impromptu performances, as mentioned before, such as façade and surface patterning, triangulated roof forms, and the utilization of interactive technologies. The music school also features internal courtyard spaces that are designed for informal use by students and staff. These spaces have bench-seating that can be arranged into configurations for small or large groups. The seating can also be joined together to form a stage for impromptu performances (Figure 1).

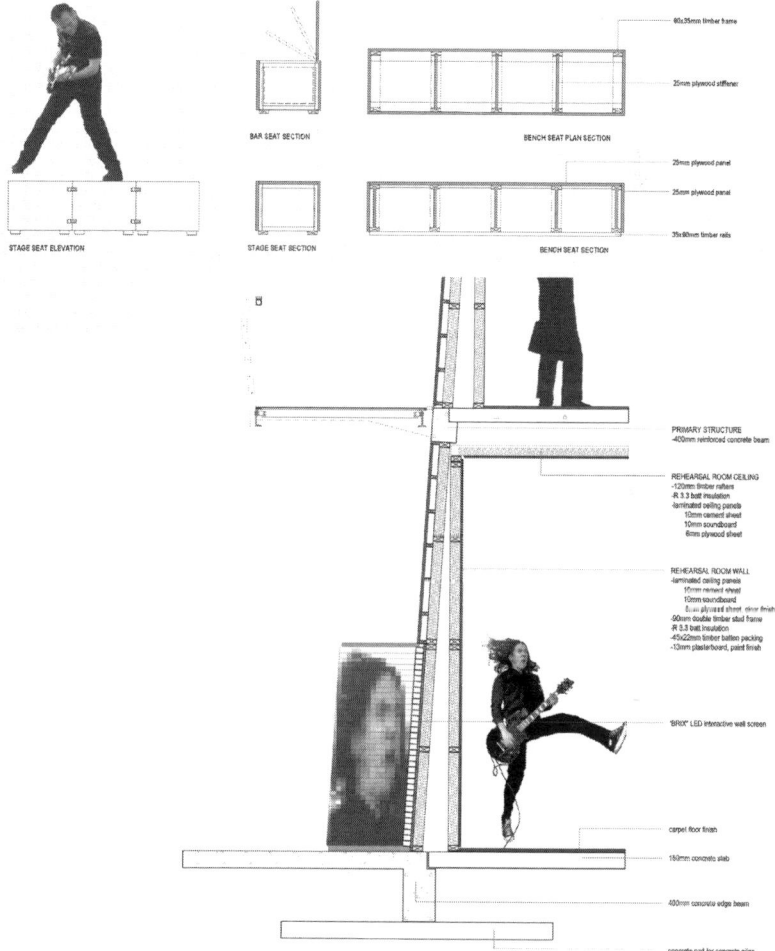

Figure 1: Plan and detail of custom-designed timber bench seats that can be arranged into configurations to suit groups or individuals.

The secondary foyer space for the concert hall also functions as an internal courtyard for times when the concert hall is not in use. This space features bench-seating that can be converted into a bar area for pre- and post-performance drinks, and during intermission. A large section of glazing along Invermay Road and selected internal surfaces of the building will be interactive in a translation of the ephemeral quality of improvisation. The users of the school and concert hall will inadvertently influence the internal skin of the building by triggering computer-controlled light-emitting diode (LED) screens that capture images of users. The exterior screen is a double-glazed LED screen that can be clear or display an image (Figure 2). This screen will be used to promote up-coming events at the music school and concert hall. The interior will feature interactive walls similar to the *brix* and *light brix* virtual brick wall systems

Figure 2: The LED screen as seen from Invermay Road.

designed by HeHe.[16] The *brix* wall consists of a wall of plastic bricks. A camera in the wall captures an image that is transferred onto the wall by each brick acting as a pixel to form the image. The *light brix* wall consists of a wall of plastic bricks containing lights that turn on and off as they are touched.

The interior technologies, expressive forms, façade patterns, and interactive elements mean that the building will constantly change with spontaneous movements and images of the users and the atmosphere that they create.

The complex sound of fusion belies its relatively simple structure, a structure that displays the resourceful nature of fusion, as highlighted in Davis' 1970 release *Bitches Brew*, a double album that proclaimed jazz-rock fusion as the jazz of the future.[17] Jazz-rock fusion was not unlike modal jazz; the major difference being the adaptation of rock inspired bass riffs. Cooke explains that the adopted bass lines were used in an attempt to match the popularity of rock music at the time. Fusion continued the tradition in jazz of appropriating selected elements from other musical genres, and reinventing them to create a distinctive sound. Fusion consists of a rock-inspired riff-based rhythm section, which is overlaid with improvised melodies inspired by modal jazz. This composition of order and spontaneity has been translated into the building structure, influencing form in space.

Initially I explored the use of tensegrity structures throughout the music school by expressing the contrasting layered nature of fusion (Figure 3). Tensegrity structures work using a simple system of tension and compression

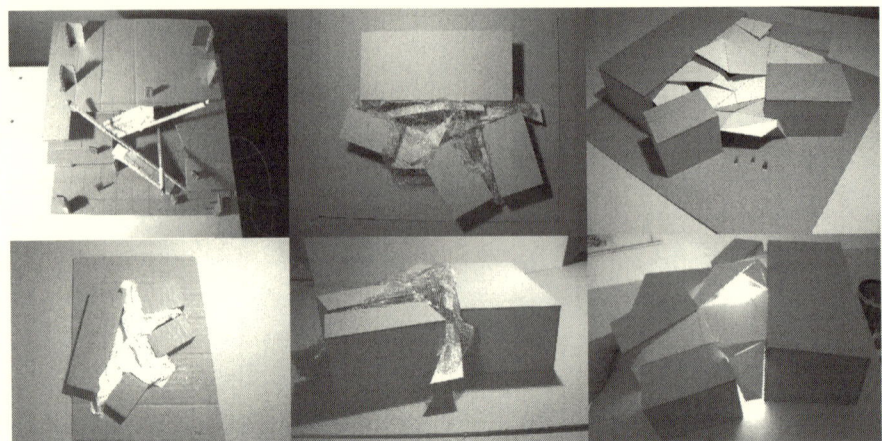

Figure 3: Early card and computer models exploring the proposed tensegrity structures.

that seemed to be a perfect translation of the composition of fusion. However, I discovered that tensegrity structures were too impractical to use as structural elements, particularly in the environment of a music school where acoustic performance and the quality of sound insulation are paramount. However, the way tensegrity structures use tension cables and compression rods in a co-dependent way led to the idea of using contrasting structures within the School that were completely dependent upon each other in order for the School to operate.

The primary concrete structure is expressed as regular and solid in a translation of the rhythmic structure of fusion. This is overlaid with the secondary steel structure that is expressed as lightweight, irregular, and transparent, in a translation of the improvised melodies that rise above the riff-based rhythms of fusion (Figure 4). The triangulated roof form is designed to express the spontaneous and random nature of fusion. The solid concrete frames of the four pavilions support the faceted

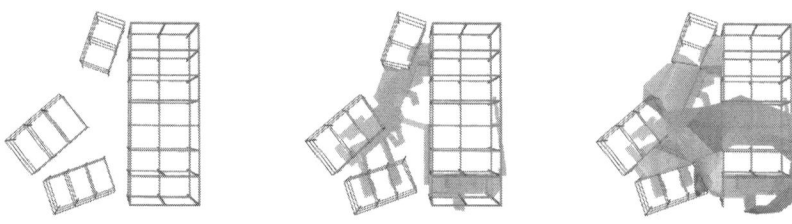

Figure 4: Diagram of the primary, circulation and roof structures

roof that grows into a geometric three-dimensional spontaneous pattern.

The form has been created from joining basic geometric shapes (triangles) in an irregular way. This technique has been used in the façade treatment and the interior faces of the building by using rectangles in what are almost literal fusions. The two structures have been designed to be symbiotic; they do not compete but rely on each other in order for the building to function (Figure 5). For example, the primary structure houses the specific functions of the music school (such as practice rooms and lecture rooms) while the secondary structures house the circulation and informal meeting spaces.

Fusion was originally created from improvised recordings; consequently live performance is an essential aspect of fusion. The concept of performance has been translated into the building by employing the users as performers, tapping into the idea that people like to view or be viewed. Conversation and interaction between the users can be expressed as an informal performance. The atrium space of the music school features a series of stairs, ramps, and platforms that have been designed to facilitate viewing or being viewed. These changes of level offer points to linger as a voyeur, or parade while using the building on a daily basis or when visiting the concert hall for a special event.

Figure 5: The view of the back entry to the Music School, showing the connection of the regular and irregular structural systems.

The bar and secondary foyer of the school are designed to light up at night and offer an impromptu performance to a passer-by in the street.

The undetermined aspects of Miles Davis' fusion have been used as inspiration for the design of the Launceston School of Contemporary Music. Intangible qualities such as adaptation, reinvention, spontaneity, improvisation, and performance have been interpreted into the building through its structure, form, material, and various functions. It is intended that the school will translate these undetermined qualities of fusion into an architectural speculation, transforming the ephemeral into a series of spatial and tactile experiences.

It is important to note that because of the nature of jazz-rock fusion, the music school could take on any type of

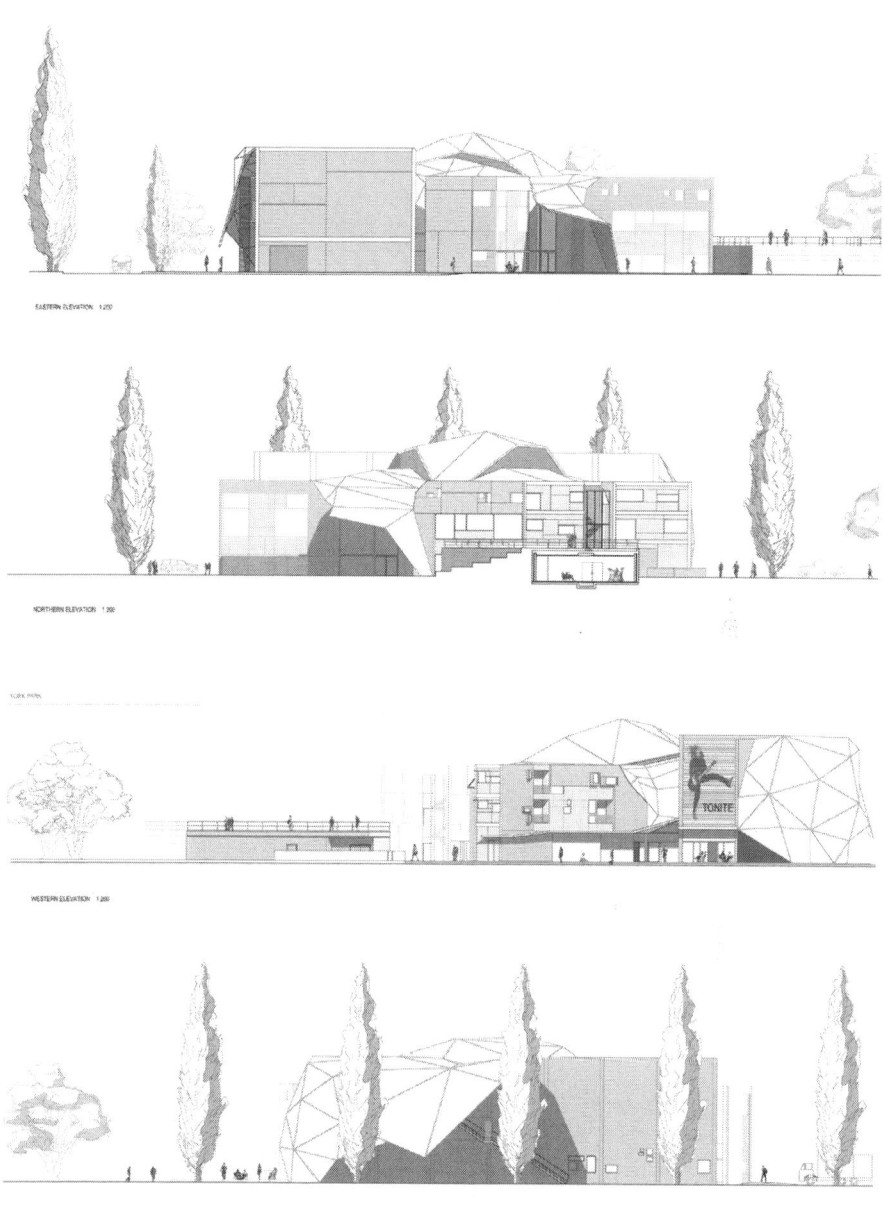

Figure 6: Elevations of the Music School.

form and appearance. The essential part of this project is the process of creating the form, appearance, and atmosphere, so that the experience of jazz-rock fusion is translated into the experience of the architecture. The music school needs to be completely responsive to its users and must be left open to outside influences, i.e. anything that can change the mood of the school through visual, auditory, and tactile means.

The translation and continuous interaction with users and outside influences would benefit the music school and its students as they would be encouraged to push the boundaries of contemporary music to new and exciting realms.

Endnotes

[1] Bandur, M., *Aesthetics of Total Serialism*, (Birkhåuser, Basel, Boston, Berlin: 2001): 5.

[2] Ibid.: 6.

[3] Martin, E., *Pamphlet Architecture: Architecture as a Translation of Music*, (Princeton Architectural Press, New York, 1994): 56.

[4] Cooke, M., *The Chronicle of Jazz*, (Thames and Hudson, London: 1997): 8.

[5] Borneman, E., 'New Perspectives on the History of Jazz', in Boreman's, *The Roots of Jazz* (Da Capo Press, New York: 1959): 4-5.

[6] Ibid.: 4.

[7] Smith, C.E., *New Orleans and Traditions in Jazz*, 'Jazz: New Perspectives on the History of Jazz', (Da Capo Press, New York: 1959): 23.

[8] Cooke, M., *The Chronicle of Jazz*: 8.

[9] Borneman explains that jazz was not necessarily the best musical style to come from this blend of West African and Western European music, what was not recorded is now lost forever.

[10] Borneman, E., 'New Perspectives on the History of Jazz', in Boreman's, *The Roots of Jazz*: 7.

[11] Ibid.: 7.

[12] Ibid.: 7.

[13] Carr, I., in Mervyn Cooke, *The Chronicle of Jazz*: 216.

[14] Ibid.: 147.

[15] Davis, M., *Hot Docs: Miles Electric-A Different Kind of Blue*, SBS documentary 10 pm, 07-05-2005.

[16] Evans, H., and Hansen, H., *Light Brix* and *Brix*, http://www.hehe.org, August 2005. HeHe describe themselves as a non-profit making organisation for production. Featuring work on traffic design, pollution monitoring, public advertisement, meteorology, architecture and public lighting.

[17] Cooke, M., *The Chronicle of Jazz*: 170.

List of Figures

All figures courtesy of Garth Ancher.

References

Bandur, M., *Aesthetics of Total Serialism*, (Birkhåuser, Basel, Boston, Berlin: 2001).

Borneman, E., 'New Perspectives on the History of Jazz', in Boreman's, *The Roots of Jazz* (Da Capo Press, New York: 1959).

Cooke, M., *The Chronicle of Jazz*, (Thames and Hudson, London: 1997).

Martin, E., *Pamphlet Architecture: Architecture as a Translation of Music*, (Princeton Architectural Press, New York, 1994).

Smith, C.E., *New Orleans and Traditions in Jazz*, 'Jazz: New Perspectives on the History of Jazz', (Da Capo Press, New York: 1959).

Mikesch Muecke and Miriam Zach

Resonance: Music and Architecture[1]

Things we do and experience have resonance. It can die away quickly or last a long time; it can have a clear center frequency or a wide bandwidth; be loud, soft or ambiguous. The present is filled with past experience ringing in various ways and now is colored by this symphony of resonance.[2]

[...] Tell me (since you are so sensible to the effects of architecture), have you not noticed, in walking about this city, that among the buildings with which it is peopled, certain are *mute*; others *speak*; and others, finally—and they are the most rare—*sing*?[3]

Let us begin with a recent example of experiencing the resonance in both architecture and music. Following other connoisseurs of the building arts we, too, had consumed drawings and photographs of Peter Zumthor's Thermal Baths in Vals, Switzerland, through ubiquitous architecture journals but to experience the building in person is another matter. Zumthor's constellation of bath chambers organized around a central indoor and peripheral outdoor pool, with walls constructed of local granite stacked high, creates a sophisticated yet also primitive environment for the visual and auditory senses. On our first visit we explored the bath spaces with their different water temperatures as intensely as possible. The grotto bath remains our favorite. Up to our waists in water we would move slowly through the short tunnel that connects the large indoor bath with this much more intimate bath space. The grotto bath had a square footprint and was very tall. Lit only by small lights recessed into the floor the space felt enclosed and private. Upon entering we noticed two other bathers already suspended in the clear water, holding on to the tubular brass handrail running along the four walls. After adjusting visually to the dimly lit space we became aware of a slight hum in the air, and noticed the content and yet mischievous expressions on the other bathers' faces. What was going on here? Apparently the rough-granite-clad surfaces of the bath made the sound of mere breathing audible. Further vocal tuning would allow each inhabitant to quickly find the sympathetic resonance between body and space by humming slowly through a range of different frequencies. After adding our own frequencies to the impromptu performance we really didn't want to leave this powerful space that coddled our bodies in a vibrating medium of air while caressing the rest with warm clear water.

We recall this experience so vividly because it combined utter vulnerability—barely clothed and without any tools or gadgets for defense—with a heightened sensory experience of sight and sound. From this perspective the Vals Thermal

Baths transported us back to a much more primitive time when humans first became aware of the power of their voice and other sounds. Stephen J. Waller argues that the Paleolithic-age cave art in France—in deep caves like *Lascaux* as well as open air sites like the *Vallon des Roches*—was the result of particular acoustic and cultural conditions. Waller suggests that Paleolithic stone-tool makers, creating percussive sounds as part of their work, would cause the apparent echo of what would have sounded like galloping animals emanating from places in the cave or valley where there were no animals visible. In these places the Paleolithic artists would feel the need to paint what can be heard but is invisible. Sound becomes a generator for the visual arts.

Several thousand years later the Greek architect Polykleitos would design the semicircular amphitheater at Epidauros, Greece (ca. 300 BCE) which is still in use today, and continues to accommodate dramatic performances without the aid of amplifying technologies. The shape of the theater in its natural surroundings, carved out of a hill side, becomes a precise amplifier of sound when the performers stand in the *skene*. Here, as in the Paleolithic age the creators of visual and aural art understood how to work with nature to advance their arts. By the time the Roman writer, architect, and engineer Marcus Vitruvius Pollo (ca. 80 to 25 BCE) writes his book *De Architectura,* the aural concerns of designers have become infused with interior spaces as much as with natural settings.[4] Vitruvius expounds in Book 5 of *De Architectura* on musical theory, using Greek nomenclature to explain the types of modulation, notes, and tetrachords. He also insists on architects knowing about basic acoustic principles, mentioning the use of resonance by actors who, when accompanying themselves to a lyre in a wooden theater, and "when they want to sing in a higher key, turn toward the stage doors and thus avail themselves of the harmonic support that these can provide for their voices."[5]

By the Renaissance architecture and music began to have a more formal relation than existed during the apex of Greek and Roman integration of both arts. On March 25, 1436 Guillaume Dufay's motet *Nuper Rosarum Flores* premiered at the consecration of Florence Cathedral. Dufay (1397-1474) had written this polyphonic motet including two tenor parts with the same cantus firmus and isorhtyhmic symmetries, apparently with the double-skinned dome of the cathedral in mind (designed by Filippo Brunelleschi between 1420-1461), confirmed by recent scholarship (see Charles W. Warren's essay in *The Musical Quarterly*, vol. 59, No. 1). When, fourteen years later, the polymath Leon Battista Alberti wrote his Vitruvius-inspired *De Re Aedificatoria*, numbers rather than acoustics had definitively become the new focus of the relationship between music and architecture. Rudolf Wittkower paraphrases Alberti when he writes that "music is geometry translated into sound, and that in music the very same harmonies are audible which inform the geometry of the building."[6] There exists now a clear structural separation of music *from* architecture. While the listener can hear the same harmonies that are in use in architecture in the music, there is little connection between music and its architectural space. Music has been geometrized and lost its connection to the material, i.e. spatial experience of sound. Not surprisingly the Renaissance architects focused their efforts on metric proportions of spaces rather than their acoustic properties. Especially the golden section ratio (1:1.618) and the Fibonacci number series (a+b=c, i.e. 1, 2, 3, 5, 8, 13, etc.) were used as a generative device for many buildings. The country estates designed by Renaissance architect Andrea Palladio (1508-1580), for example the exquisite Villas Rotonda and Barbaro at Maser, in Northern Italy, all make use of formal ordering devices like symmetry, squares, and harmonic proportions while simultaneously connecting the architectural spaces to the surrounding country side. However, while Palladio's treatise *I Quattro Libri dell' Architettura* was filled with knowledge about how to make buildings, it did not explicitly dwell on how these constructions might sound.

That is not to say that beautiful acoustic spaces didn't exist in the Renaissance, but they were few and far between. Music itself had of course advanced tremendously since the Medieval times. In the space of three hundred years the simple yet beautiful monophonic sound structures by such composers as Hildegard von Bingen (1098-1179), in her *O Viridissima Virga, Ave* from the *Canticles of Ecstasy*, had given way to relatively complex polyphonic compositions in the Renaissance, like those of Maddalena Casulana (1540-1583) who set her own, and the poetry of others, to intricately woven four-voice contrapuntal textures in her famous *Il Primo Libro di Madrigali a quattro voci* in 1568. Many of these compositions would be performed in sacred spaces with long reverberation times, although even private dwellings had much better acoustic characteristics due to higher ceiling heights and resonating materials than can be found in today's residences.

On the architecture side it was not until 1727 that the Swiss mathematician Leonhard Euler (1707-1783) published the first post-Vitruvian theoretical treatise on sound with his *Dissertatio Physica de Sono*. The German Jesuit Athanasius Kircher (1601-1680) had written an earlier sound treatise, the *Phonurgia Nova* (1673), in which he offered amazing examples of architectural devices to overhear servants in a house, or to make statues appear to speak (Figures 1 and 2). While the work had breadth, it did not have the depth of Euler's theoretical comprehension. Elsewhere German physicist Ernst Chladni (1756-1827) laid down the experimental principles of acoustics with his research on vibrating plates. He invented a technique to make vibration processes visible by drawing a violin bow over a metal plate sprinkled with powder, published in 1787 in his book *Entdeckungen uber die Theorie des Klanges*. This inspired the Swiss scientist Hans Jenny (1904-1972) in the twentieth century to explore the physical patterns produced by sound waves in various mediums such as fluids, powders, and liquid paste in his book *Cymatics: The Study of Wave Phenomena* (1967).

The first signs of an applied, post-Epidauros engagement between music and architecture would have to wait until 1723 when Johann Sebastian Bach (1685-1750) became cantor at the *Thomasschule*, and started to play organ and direct the choir at the adjacent *Thomaskirche* in Leipzig, Germany. This relatively small Lutheran church with

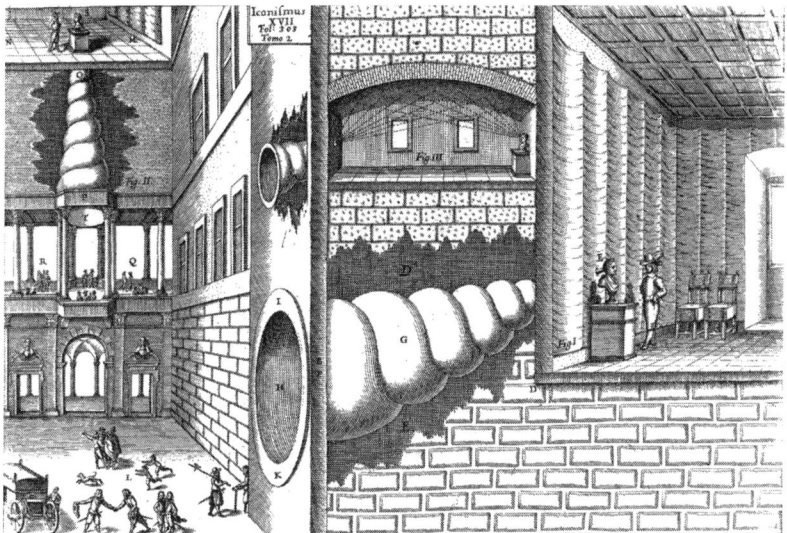

Figure 1: Image from Kircher, Athanasius. *Musurgia Universalis*. (Rome, 1650) showing among other things a technique to make a statue appear to speak.

Figure 2: Image from Kircher, Athanasius. *Phonurgia Nova*. (Rome, 1673) showing a projected installation of listening horns to overhear servants and guests in a house.

a shorter reverberation time than any of the medieval cathedrals in existence then in Europe made it possible for Bach to compose complex polyphonic melodies using contrapuntal techniques. The relatively dry space allowed the listener to distinguish chord progressions clearly, allowing for an unprecedented complexity of music in a public space. While this transformation took place in the sacred realm of church music, a similar change occurred in the profane spaces of dramatic performances. In the mid-seventeenth century opera as a genre came to the fore in Italy, although it took another one hundred years to build a proper edifice for its performance. Giuseppe Piermarini's design for the opera house *La Scala*, built appropriately on the site of the demolished church Santa Maria alla Scala in Milano between 1776 and 1778, became the starting point for many other public performance spaces that began to transform the way music, architecture, and the dramatic arts interacted for the next 250 years.

For the aural connoisseur the first version of the shoe-box shaped *Gewandhaus* theater in Leipzig, Germany, was the *non-plus-ultra* of acoustic performance in the 1700s. The building looked nothing like Epidauros, and yet the capacity of its interior surfaces to resonate with instrumental music would make it the precursor for several high-performance interiors that would follow in its footsteps. However, the acoustics of many of these large performance spaces continued to be based on an incompletely understood science. It took until 1962 before the acoustics expert Leo L. Beranek (b. 1914) published his ground-breaking book *Music, Acoustics & Architecture*.[7] In it Beranek analyses a series of performance halls throughout history, and provides also a language to describe the acoustical characteristics of these buildings, realizing that, to understand music, acoustics, and architecture, we need a common language to describe all three. And yet architects continued to conjure Epidauros without reaching this earlier epitome of dramatic performance. The architect Gottfried Semper (1803-1874) came close with his design for a theater in Munich, Germany, a project that incorporated the semi-circle of Epidauros into a Renaissance-style performance space. Initiated by Semper's acquaintance, the composer Richard Wagner (1813-1883), and funded by the King of Bavaria, the project, however, was never realized. Instead Wagner created his own, smaller version in Bayreuth (without giving Semper credit for the initial idea). While he advanced both musical and spatial experiments in the Bayreuth Theater, which came to represent for quite some time the ultimate intersection of all the arts, paradoxically Wagner insisted in his design on separating the instrumental music production, i.e. the orchestra, visually from the audience and the vocal performers in favor of creating a sensual *Gesamtkunstwerk* in which instrumental music could be heard as if coming from nowhere. A section through the building shows the orchestra pit with its curved roof pointing toward the stage. The almost completely enclosed space supports the actors aurally on-stage but is acoustically detrimental for the projection of instrumental music to the audience.

It is quite possible that the size of Wagner's orchestration grew larger not only because of his compositional demands for increased dynamics but also due to the idiosyncratic layout and design of the Bayreuth theater. However, while Wagner's building has to be seen as a step backwards for acoustics, his musical explorations which moved to the edge of atonality, became the foundation for the work of composer and music theorist Arnold Schoenberg (1874-1951). In turn Schoenberg's twelve-tone music was liberated by the athematic serial compositions of Karlheinz Stockhausen (b. 1928) who, in the next twenty years, experimented increasingly with spatial constructs for his compositions, culminating in his performance of the piece *Spiral* in the German pavilion at the EXPO '70 in Osaka, Japan, where the audience was suspended in the equatorial plane of a sphere. Incidentally it was during this World Exposition that Iannis Xenakis (1922-2001) would perform his electro-acoustic piece *Hibiki Hana Ma* in the Japanese Steel Federation pavilion.[8] Both Stockhausen's and Xenakis' compositions exhibited a unique sensibility to the relationship between sound and space. Several of Xenakis' works, *Psappha* for example, require the audience to sit in a circle surrounded by a number of speakers. Architectural space becomes an instrument.

Peter Zumthor has expanded the sensory understanding of architecture to include its role as musical instrument. He writes: "Listen! Interiors are like large instruments, collecting sound, amplifying it, transmitting it elsewhere."[9] As if to take a page from Zumthor—and expanding the space of sound installations to include the exterior—the group Music Architecture Sound Sculpture (M.A.S.S.)[10] has been creating earth-harp installations for a number of years. They also transformed one of the icons of modernism in Chicago, Mies van der Rohe's Crown Hall, originally built on the IIT campus between 1950 and 1956, into a stringed instrument with which the group explored the resonance between the building's materials (glass and steel) and the space they enclose.[11] The experimental compositions/performances in Crown Hall approach the full-scale musical tempering of a building, in the sense of the German word for both atmosphere and tuning, or *Stimmung*. Here the composition and the production of music converge in the playing of an architectural space. The experimental approach to this convergence has an impact on how composers approach their craft. Zumthor recalls that John Cage mentioned in one of his lectures that he is "not a composer who hears music in his mind and then attempts to write it down. He has another way of operating. He works out concepts and structures and then has them performed to find out how they sound."[12] Relating this approach to architecture, Zumthor suggests that asking questions about such initially non-visual concerns as site, purpose, and building materials may then lead to architectural designs that, just like Cage's compositions, have the potential to reach an audience—whether for music or architecture—at a much deeper level than would be created by "the mere arrangement of stylistically preconceived forms."[13]

Furthermore, Zumthor's admittedly narrow reading of architecture as being primarily about a material expression creates a resonating link to music. He writes that architecture is always concrete matter. Architecture is not abstract, but concrete. A plan, a project drawn on paper is not architecture but merely a more or less inadequate representation of architecture, comparable to sheet music. Music needs to be performed. Architecture needs to be executed. Then its body can come into being. And this body is always sensuous.[14]

The sensuousness of the combined music-and-architecture body demands an active, perceptive receiver of both space and sound. An example from the arts might illustrate this symbiotic relationship. In 1977, during the international art event Documenta 6 in Kassel, the artist Joseph Beuys (1921-1986) installed in the main exhibit space Fridericianum a pump that transported honey through a long transparent plastic hose from a basement stair well into a third-floor meeting space—coined the Free International University—used by the artist for impromptu discussions with Documenta visitors and local citizens about the social dimension of art. During the long discussions participants could see and hear the honey flow through the plastic hose, sometimes coming to a standstill, only to soon after, and with a loud slurp, rush forward through the pipe, not unlike the discussions between Beuys and his audience.[15] Here the sound works as both an interrupter of the routine we associate with art exhibits, and as a symbolic reference to the difficulty of improvised verbal communication, those awkward fits and starts that occur as we try to tackle difficult subject matters.

An absent-minded perception of both sound and space is impossible under these circumstances.

A more direct enfolding of music and architecture can be located in the work of the Austrian sound artist Bernhard Leitner (b. 1938) who initially studied architecture in Vienna, then moved to New York in 1968, and now works again in Vienna. He is one of the first designers to focus in his work on the artistic spatialization of sound. Leitner's method of representing visually the path of sounds through a space by drawing solid and dashed lines with arrows on photographs that usually depict an individual standing or moving through his sound-altered environment, represents a useful yet inadequate means to communicate his art. As a step to make his spatial and musical compositions more accessible to listeners who cannot replicate his surround-sound installations, Leitner published in 2003 the CD *Kopfräume-Headscapes* which requires the listener to wear headphones for the effect of the recorded sounds moving around in his/her head. Even though his sound/space experiments might inspire both architects and musicians to borrow ideas from his designs which range from free-standing spaces to furniture and wearable devices, Leitner admits that he is not really interested in using music in his work because the brain "is immediately distracted if musical parameters are present. It [is] important to me that these sounds not be musical."[16] Of course, the perception of music is culturally conditioned, and thus open to change. Bernd Schulz points out that with respect to music, sound and noise are physically one and the same thing, for every sound and noise can be comprehended as the sum or integral of its sinus tones. At most it can be said that the number of frequencies comprised by acoustic events regarded as 'sound' is limited, whereas 'noise' encompasses practically all frequencies within the human hearing range.[17]

Given this broad definition, Leitner's sound art would qualify as music, even if he, for reasons of communicating his art, may think otherwise. It is perhaps useful to remember that both our reception of sound in general and music specifically are culturally conditioned. For example, when actor Joe Pesci is sent to jail, once again, for disrespecting the small-town judge in the 1992 comedy *My Cousin Vinny*, he sleeps soundly while around him the clamor of prisoners, the sound of sirens, and the shouting of jail guards would make everyone else sit up straight in his or her bunk bed. For Vinny, who can't deal with the hi-fi environment of a rural setting,[18] since he is used to the low-fi soundscape of noisy New York, the background sound chaos is the equivalent of a lullaby. And yet, there is no time to sleep.

Conclusion

> I listen to the sound of the space, to the way materials and surfaces respond to touching and tapping, and to the silence that is a prerequisite of hearing.[19]

More recently the creative resonance between music and architecture has begun to bear fruit in unusual locations. For example, the Music Technology Group at the Pompeu Fabra University in Barcelona, has created an interactive piece of furniture, the *reactable*, that allows users to transform—with the help of an audio synthesizer, some open-source software, and a few select electronic components—their audio-spatial environment instantly into a musical and architectural event. The collaborative nature of the device, its intuitive "zero manual, zero instructions"[20] approach to learning, affords a playful interaction between sound and space.

Another group, Pe Lang and Zimoun, both currently working in Switzerland, have created over the past few years a series of hybrid music-architectures using simple mechanical devices like electro-magnets, metal plates, eccentric couplings, paper, and sensors. Again the effect is a curious mix of sophistication and playfulness that makes the intersection of sound and space accessible to newcomers of the genre. Their crisply designed website includes witty videos and a dossier that explains their theoretical and practical approach to this interdisciplinary embrace.[21]

Finally, in November 2000 [The User], a placeholder for the Canadian-based artistic collaboration between the architect Thomas McIntosh and the composer Emmanuel Madan, led to the installation of an ongoing sound/space experiment in which anyone with either a telephone, an internet connection, or *in situ* can pipe sounds into the abandoned Silo #5, located in the old port of Montréal, and then listen to how the sound is transformed within the acoustic wonderland of the tall, cylindrical space.[22] What is perhaps most perplexing about accessing the silophone over the internet is the concentrated wait time as the chosen or uploaded sound is prepared by special software to be played through the silo's speakers. The anticipation of music in space, the waiting in silence, the absence of not knowing when and what kind of sound may be heard—the site is accessible 24/7 by anyone—is perhaps as important as the aural event itself.

We anticipate that this suspense—this expectation of the future—will continue to transform both music and architecture, sound and space, through cross-disciplinary experiments that may lead to a fertile, creative, and delightful resonance.

Endnotes

¹ This essay on resonance is consciously partial, in the sense of being both incomplete, i.e. fragmentary in nature, and of showing some bias toward parts of the history of music and architecture we know from our respective research, practice, and scholarship. For the omissions we take full responsibility, and we look forward to amending the contents in a future edition.

² Website http://www.brainyquote.com/quotes/quotes/p/paullansky184887.html, accessed Februay 13, 2007.

³ Valéry, Paul. "Eupalinos or the Architect," in *Dialogues*, edited by Jackson Mathews, 63-150. (New York: Pantheon Books, 1956): 82.

⁴ Vitruvius' main treatise was lost until the early fifteenth century when Poggio Braciolini found a fairly complete copy of the manuscript in the library of the monastery in St. Gallen, Switzerland. See more information about Vitruvius and his influence on Renaissance architects like Andrea Palladio in Tavernor, Robert and Richard Schofield. "Introduction," in *The Four Books on Architecture (I Quattro Libri Dell'architettura)*, vii-xix. (Cambridge, MA: MIT Press, 1997): vii.

⁵ Vitruvius, Pollio. *Ten Books on Architecture*. Translated by Ingrid D. Rowland. (Cambridge: Cambridge University Press, 1999): 68.

[6] Wittkower, Rudolf. *Architectural Principles in the Age of Humanism*. 4th ed. (London: Academy, 1973): 9.

[7] Beranek, Leo Leroy. *Music, Acoustics & Architecture*. (New York: Wiley, 1962).

[8] See Sven Sterken's essay on page 21 in this volume.

[9] Zumthor, Peter. *Atmospheres: Architectural Environments, Surrounding Objects*. (Basel; Boston: Birkhäuser, 2006): 29.

[10] See http://www.massensemble.com

[11] The CD *Acoustics and Light* with ten performance pieces recorded in Crown Hall is available at the M.A.S.S. website http://www.massensemble.com

[12] Zumthor, Peter, Maureen Oberli-Turner, and Catherine Schelbert. *Thinking Architecture*. 2nd, expanded ed. (Basel; Boston: Birkhäuser, 2006): 31.

[13] Ibid.: 31.

[14] Ibid.: 66.

[15] I still remember the sweet scent of honey permeating the Fridericianum, even if I did not meet Beuys in person.

[16] Schulz, Bernd and Bernhard Leitner. "The Whole Corporeality of Hearing: An Interview with Bernhard Leitner," in *Resonanzen: Aspekte Der Klangkunst = Resonances: Aspects of Sound Art*, 81-88. (Heidelberg: Kehrer, 2002): 82.

[17] Schulz, Bernd. "Introduction," in *Resonanzen: Aspekte Der Klangkunst = Resonances: Aspects of Sound Art*, 14-18. (Heidelberg: Kehrer, 2002): 14.

[18] We are using here the definition of R. Murray Schafer who distinguished between a hi-fi soundscape, where every sound can be distinctly heard, and a low-fi soundscape where different sounds blur into each other. For more

information see Schafer, R. Murray. *The Soundscape : Our Sonic Environment and the Tuning of the World*. (Rochester, Vt.: Destiny Books; distributed in the United States by American International Distribution Corp., 1993).

[19] Zumthor, Oberli-Turner, and Schelbert. *Thinking Architecture*: 86.

[20] See http://mtg.upf.edu/reactable/, accessed February 17, 2007.

[21] See http://www.untitled-sound-objects.ch/, accessed February 17, 2007.

[22] See http://www.silophone.net, accessed February 17, 2007.

References

Beranek, Leo Leroy. *Music, Acoustics & Architecture*. (New York: Wiley, 1962).

Schafer, R. Murray. *The Soundscape: Our Sonic Environment and the Tuning of the World*. (Rochester, Vt.: Destiny Books; distributed to the book trade in the United States by American International Distribution Corp., 1993).

Schulz, Bernd. "Introduction," in *Resonanzen: Aspekte Der Klangkunst = Resonances: Aspects of Sound Art*, 14-18. (Heidelberg: Kehrer, 2002).

Schulz, Bernd and Bernhard Leitner. "The Whole Corporeality of Hearing: An Interview with Bernhard Leitner," in *Resonanzen: Aspekte Der Klangkunst = Resonances: Aspects of Sound Art*, 81-88. (Heidelberg: Kehrer, 2002).

Tavernor, Robert and Richard Schofield. "Introduction," in *The Four Books on Architecture (I Quattro Libri Dell'architettura)*, vii-xix. (Cambridge, MA: MIT Press, 1997).

Valéry, Paul. "Eupalinos or the Architect," in *Dialogues*, edited by Jackson Mathews, 63-150. (New York: Pantheon Books, 1956).

Vitruvius, Pollio. *Ten Books on Architecture*. Translated by Ingrid D. Rowland. (Cambridge: Cambridge University Press, 1999).

Wittkower, Rudolf. *Architectural Principles in the Age of Humanism*. 4th ed. (London: Academy, 1973).

Zumthor, Peter. *Atmospheres: Architectural Environments, Surrounding Objects*. (Basel; Boston: Birkhäuser, 2006).

Zumthor, Peter, Maureen Oberli-Turner, and Catherine Schelbert. *Thinking Architecture*. 2nd, expanded ed. (Basel; Boston: Birkhäuser, 2006).

Author Biographies

Garth Ancher

Garth Ancher is a third-generation architect and grandson of one of the founders of Modernism in Australia. In 2005 he completed his architecture degree at the University of Tasmania, graduating with first-class honors. As a professional musician Mr. Ancher used his final-year honors project to explore the potential of infusing architecture and music. In 2006 his Launceston School of Contemporary Music was awarded the SWT Blythe Student Award. Currently Mr. Ancher is working for a large design-based firm in Dublin, Ireland.

Kim Chow-Morris

Kim Chow-Morris received a Bachelor of Music with honors from the University of Toronto (1994) and a doctorate in ethnomusicology from York University (2004), with a specialization in Shanghai region's improvisatory instrumental genre known as *Jiangnan sizhu* (south of the Yangtze River silk and bamboo music). She has taught courses on Music and Media, Musicianship, Chamber Music, Musicology, Symphony Orchestra, Harmony, Counterpoint, World and European Music History, and Music Cultures of the City, amongst others.

In her most recent research she analyzes Taoist influence on eastern Chinese instrumental repertoires, and the instrumental traditions of Xinjiang, China. She currently teaches in the Department of Philosophy and Music at Ryerson University, in Toronto.

Chow-Morris is an accomplished soloist on four Chinese wind instruments—*dizi, xiao, bawu,* and *hulusi*—which she studied under the two foremost Chinese flute masters, Lu Chun Ling and the late Yu Xun Fa. She has taught private lessons in Chinese *dizi, xiao* and western flute for York University, and founded Chinese orchestra classes for both York University and the University of Toronto. She has performed traditional and contemporary music for western and Chinese wind instruments in Canada, China and the United States, and her performances have been broadcast on Fairchild Television, OMNI TV, CBC radio, and across China on the nation's largest television station, CCTV. She has also accepted invitations to perform for dignitaries such as former Canadian Prime Minister Jean Chretien, China's Premier Wen Jiabao, the mayor of Zhouzhuang, China, and others. Her ensemble's self-titled CD *Yellow River Ensemble* is forthcoming in 2007 from the Yellow River Recordings label.

Galia Hanoch-Roe

Galia Hanoch-Roe holds a doctorate of musical arts and a bachelor degree of landscape architecture. Her teaching, practice and research interests include an interdisciplinary approach to design, concentrating on community participatory planning, environmental education and natural building techniques. Galia was trained as a classical pianist and has performed in recitals and chamber music throughout the US, Canada, and Israel. She completed her studies at the Rubin academy in Israel (B.M), Rutgers University (B.L.A.), Yale School of Music (M.M.) and CUNY graduate school in New York City (D.M.A). She was an instructor at the music department at Haifa University where she received distinguished teaching awards, and has lectured and taught seminars on music and architecture to students of both disciplines at a range of academic settings including the Israeli Technion and Tel-Aviv University departments of architecture. Galia has participated in various conferences and published in a range of topics in music and the arts, including articles on "Frozen Music and Fluid Architecture," published in the *Proceedings of the ISAMA conference* 1999, ISBN 84-930669-0-7; "Beethoven's Ninth: An "Ode to Choice" as Presented in Stanley Kubrick's *Clockwork Orange*," published in the *International Journal of the Aesthetics and Sociology of Music,* Dec. 2002, "A musical-Textual Portrait of Death: Franz Liszt's *Les Morts*," published in *Motar 6*, 1998; and "A Catalogue of Liszt's Original Death-related Works," published in the *Journal of the American Liszt Society*, 41, 1997.

Jim Lutz

Jim Lutz is an architect and assistant professor in the Architecture Program at the University of Memphis (USA). He holds a Master of Architecture degree from Syracuse University and a Bachelor of Arts in Architecture from the University of California, Berkeley.

Since 2000, the nexus of sound and space has been the focus of his academic research. He has presented papers on the topic to the Association of Collegiate Schools of Architecture (ACSA), Society of Architectural Historians (SAH), College Art Association (CAA), The American Institute of Architects (AIA), Southeast College Art Conference (SECAC), College Music Society (CMS), and the Society for Education, Music and Psychology Research (SEMPRE), among others. He is the co-author of "Thinking Outside the (Music) Box: Collaborations between Composers and Architects," published in *Collaborative Creativity* (Free Association Books [UK]:2004). He is also co-instructor of "Seeing Music/Hearing Architecture", an interdisciplinary course offered at Rhodes College (USA).

Kourosh Mahvash

Currently pursuing his academic and research interests by studying toward a Master of Interdisciplinary Design for the Built Environment (IDBE) at the University of Cambridge, Kourosh Mahvash has a diverse background in architecture and design. His main areas of research include "poetics of technology," phenomenology, inter- and cross-disciplinary design, and sustainability.

Kourosh received his First Professional Master of Architecture from the Faculty of Fine Arts, Tehran University (1995), and for four years worked as a registered design architect in his home country of Iran. The main body of work in this period includes museum and public projects; among them his award-winning thesis on Tehran

Municipality's Zoological Gardens (1995), and the winning competition entry and subsequent design of a municipal museum of natural history (1998).

Following his immigration to Canada, Kourosh obtained his Post-Professional Master of Architecture degree from the Faculty of Architecture and Urban Planning, Dalhousie University (2002) where the focus of his studies was an interdisciplinary study of light and lighting. After graduation, he immediately started teaching design studios and co-teaching building technology courses at Dalhousie. While the main theme of his design studios has been interdisciplinary design and phenomenology, lighting and sustainability comprised the core of his teaching responsibilities in building technology courses.

Having recently moved to Vancouver, he is currently working as Sustainability Researcher for Hughes Condon Marler Architects. Kourosh has independently worked on a number of multidisciplinary performance pieces and graphic design projects. He has also exhibited his lighting installations in Halifax and Banff.

Mikesch Muecke

Mikesch Muecke is Associate Professor of Architecture in the College of Design at Iowa State University, and he holds degrees from the University of Florida (B. Design, 1989, M. Arch, 1991) and Princeton University (Ph.D. in Architectural History and Theory, 1999). Born in Germany to a journalist and a homemaker he has enjoyed working as a newspaper photographer, carpenter, and shade-tree mechanic (mostly on Citroëns and Renaults) in Europe. In 1979 he left Germany for a year to travel, work as a painter in Alberta, Canada, pick flowers and apples in an orchard in Watsonville, California, play clarinet in the Caribbean Sea off Isla de Mujeres in Mexico, and renovate low-income apartments on the south-side of Chicago. In 1980 he returned to Germany to fulfill his tour of civil-service duty to the State by working as a maintenance man in an orphanage for fifteen months. During this time he lived in an agrarian commune with nine other idealists, then moved into a retired circus trailer for another two years with his then partner (now wife), the musicologist, organist, and music professor Dr. Miriam Zach.

Currently Mikesch complements his academic pursuits of exploring the intersection of music and architecture by creating accessible designs for the elderly in Florida with Miriam—in her affiliation as Assistant Professor at the University of Florida—through their design-build company misumiwaDesign. For updated information please direct your favorite browser to www.polytekton.com

John Sands

John Frank Sands is a doctoral fellow in architectural history and theory at the University of Pennsylvania School of Design. His background is in music, and he holds a degree in Composition Theory, magna cum laude, from the Blair School of Music at Vanderbilt University. His music has been performed throughout the United States and in Graz, Austria. Along with winning the 2003 Glimmerglass Opera Fanfare Competition, John Sands has been honored with the Sue Brewer Award for excellence in Music Theory and Composition, as well as membership in the national music honor society Pi Kappa Lambda. His research interests include theories of functionalism, postwar Austrian architecture, and architecture and the body. His guilty pleasure is Palm Springs Modernism.

Sven Sterken

Sven Sterken is an engineer-architect. Before graduating at Ghent University, Belgium, in 1998, he studied in Pretoria and Paris. In 2004, he obtained a Ph.D. in architectural history at Ghent University with a dissertation on the spatial and media work of the composer, engineer and architect Iannis Xenakis. As part of his doctoral research, Sven Sterken has been a visiting scholar at the Chandigarh College of Architecture (Chandigarh, India), and the Getty Research Institute (Los Angeles, USA). In 2003 he took part in the Visiting Teachers Programme at the Architectural Association in London, England.

After a research residency at the Jan van Eyck Academy in Maastricht, Netherlands, in 2004, Sven Sterken is now a lecturer and researcher at the Sint-Lucas Higher Institute for Architecture in Brussels, Belgium. He publishes regularly about architecture and the visual arts. In 2006, Sven Sterken was awarded a Scott Opler Emerging Scholar Fellowship for Membership by the Society of Architectural Historians.

Miriam Zach

Miriam Zach, Ph.D., organist, harpsichordist, and musicologist, was named International Woman of the Year (1992 and 1997) by the International Biographical Centre in Cambridge, England for her distinguished service to music. Her CD *Hidden Treasures: 300 Years of Organ Music by Women Composers* (1998) was recorded in Princeton University Chapel.

She currently holds the position of Assistant Professor in the Honors Program at the University of Florida—where she was named Professor of the Year (2000-2001)—and teaches music history, and music & health courses. She specializes in Baroque music as well as the works of Olivier Messiaen.

After completing degrees at Northwestern University and the University of Chicago she lived in Germany for five years, teaching piano at the *Universität Bielefeld*, singing in the *Kantorei St. Nicolai* in Lemgo, completing the national organist exam, and touring Europe with her husband Dr. Mikesch Muecke. Among her mentors she counts German organist/composer/music professor Jobst-Hermann Koch, and musicologist/professor Dr. David Kushner.

As founder and director of the International Women Composers Library she continues to organize annual International Festivals of Women Composers which have been crossroads for networking among women composers and their advocates for the past decade. She maintains her own music studio in Gainesville, Florida, giving lessons in piano, harpsichord, and pipe organ. In 2003 Miriam Zach became co-principal with Mikesch Muecke in the design/build architectural practice misumiwaDesign. In 2005 she published *For the Birds: A Women Composers' Music History Speller* with Culicidae Press.

Yu Zhang

Yu Zhang is currently a Ph.D. student in the School of Architecture at Tianjin University, Tianjin, China. He earned a Bachelor of Architecture (2003) and a Master of Architecture (2006) from the same school. Zhang's academic interests include Chinese architectural culture and imperial architecture of the Qing Dynasty (1644-1911). His paper *"Architectural Aesthetics in Researching Traditional Chinese Musical Thoughts"* presented at the 3rd International Conference on East Asian Architectural Culture in Nanjing, 2004, provided a new perspective from which to study Chinese architecture by analyzing the historical literature on music. His Master's thesis (February 2006), in which he focused on "the interplay of traditional Chinese architecture and music," was selected as one of the top five excellent Master's theses of the year in his school. Advancing research on the same topic will be made in Zhang's future Ph.D. studies.

In the future, Yu Zhang plans to pursue a career in architecture introducing more cross-cultural dialogues between China and the West. During the past two years, Zhang has translated several western academic books into

Chinese versions. Lately, the Chinese translations of Fil Hearn's *Ideas that Shaped Buildings* (MIT Press, 2003) and Danièle Pauly's *Le Corbusier: The Chapel at Ronchamp* (Birkhäuser V/A, 1997) are awaiting publication.

In the field of classical music, Yu Zhang has trained in cello for the past twenty years. He used to be the principal cello player in the Tianjin University Student Orchestra.

Index

Symbols
[The User] 265
1958 World Fair in Brussels 31

A
Absolute silence 59
Absorption 62
Abstract knowledge about a place 56
Abstract morphological sound patterns 38
Abyssinian maid 145
Academy of Artists in St. Petersburg 146
Acconci, Vito 216
Accordion 152
Accumulation of fragments, detours and incidents 80
Accumulation of meaningful events 80
Acoustically homogenous space 38
Acoustical guitar 171
Acoustic envelope 226
Acoustic space 36
Acoustic wonderland 266
Adaptation, reinvention, spontaneity, improvisation, and performance 244
Aeolian harp 184, 185
Aesthetic-associative manner of translation into music 94
Aesthetic character 161
Aesthetic spectra 159
Africa 183
African drumming and dance 152
African *mbira* thumb piano 152
Alberti, Leon Battista 254
Aleatoric patterns 160
Allegro Vivace 118
Allen, Paul 175, 176
Alphabetic construction of component parts 93
Altar of Heaven 15, 191, 192, 194, 197, 198, 201, 207
 and Grand Sacrifice ceremony 195, 202
 and number 9 197, 202
Alternative modes of listening 43
Al Fine 8, 9
Ambiance 118

283

Ambient sound 159
Ambient sound recording 68
Ambiguity 58
Analytical and active mode of listening 39
Ancher, Garth 15
Ancient West Africa 234
Andante Religioso 118
Anguished cry 59
Apparent echo 253
Appleyard, Donald 101, 104, 112, 122-123
Appleyard et al. highway score 116
Architectural space and total sensory experience 54
Architecture's melting into regained fluidity 85
Architecture-as-instrument 15
Architecture I Music I Acoustic Conference 12, 54, 146
Architecture and urbanism as science 34
Architecture as frozen music 70
Architecture as instrument 169
Architecture Mikesch 8
Architecture without drawing 113
Arman 180
Array of graphic symbols 114

Art-case piano 172, 173
Artistic spatialization of sound 263
Asceticism and abstraction 44
Associative sound recording 67
Attack and touch 88
Audio synthesizer 265
Auditory sense and extension of space 60
Aural connoisseur 258
Aural documentation 67
Aural experience 69
Australian aboriginals 69
AutoCAD 151
Avant-garde 31

B

Bach, Johann Sebastian 256
Bacon, Francis Henry 172
Balance of compressive and tensile forces 186
Balustrades 197
Bandur, Markus 232-233
Band music 61
Banham, Reyner 227
Bartók, Béla 233-234
Bayreuth 259
Bedford, David 138
Behrens, Peter 172
Beihai Park 192, 202
Being inside a violin 181
Belaen, Matt 149, 151, 154
Belvedere Castle 130-132

Benesh, Joan and Rudolph 14, 96, 98, 112
Benesh and Sutton dance staves 115
Benesh system 98
Beranek, Leo L. 258
Besseler, Heinrich 15, 222, 224-225, 227
Beuys, Joseph 262
Bingen, Hildegard von 255
Birds 80
Birdwhistell, Ray 99-100
Blacksmiths 66
Blended timbres 159
Bloor Street bridge, Toronto 184
Blueprint of the city 155
Blues scale 236
Body odor 100
Bonnemaison, Sarah 72
Boredom 123
Borneman, E. 235
Borneo 183
Bösendorfer 173
Boulez, Pierre 89, 137
Boundaries of music and architecture 11
Box and Baggage 180
Brandenburg Gate 146
Brass 173
Brittle murmurs of street chatter 159
Brix and light brix virtual brick wall system 240
Broadacre City 15, 220
Broken guitars 176

Brown, Earl 14, 90-92, 95
Brunelleschi, Filippo 254
Bucket with a 'potatoid' plan 42
Buildings as instruments 172
Burma 183

C

Cable-stayed steel pylon 182
Cage, John 14, 91-94, 122, 138, 261
Calatrava, Santiago 15, 182-184, 186
Calder mobile 91
Calligraphy 194, 204
Cannon 66
Casual logic, linearity, continuity and predictability 89
Casulana, Maddalena 255
Catalogue of sounds 65
Catching trains 94
Cathedral 57
Caves of ice 145, 161
Cedar Key, Florida 12
Cello 152, 179
Cellular phones 80
Cell blocks 95
Cell phone ring tone 159
Center of auditory space 60
Central Park, New York City, NY 120
Chan, Patty 155

Chandigarh 25
Charles Moore
  and House Near New York 57
Cherry Esplanade in the Brooklyn Botanical Gardens, NY 127
Chess 204
Chinese architecture 191
Chinese bowed fiddle, *erhu* 154
Chinese cosmogony 197
Chinese *dizi* 152
Chinese *luxue* theory 199
Chinese music 199
Chinese musical instruments
  as key to resolve disorder in natural phenomena 203
  as regulators to harmonize worldly matters 203
Chinese number symbolism 197
Chinese standard for weights and measures 200
Chinese system of pitches 200
Chinese traditional unit of measurement and *zhang* 198
Chinese units of length 199
Chinese wind instruments 152
Chinese zither 203
Chladni, Ernst 256
Choice of movement 90
Choral dances 219
Chordophone 182
Chow-Morris, Kim 14, 145
Church bells 66
Cinema 105
Circular Mound Altar 197
Circus trailer 8
Cittern 182, 183
Clang of a streetcar bell 159
Clarinet 171
Coherent scoring system for linear paths in space 96
Coleridge, Samuel T. 145, 146, 161
Collage and juxtaposition 29
Colored light and electronic music 38
Comparison of music and architecture 214
Composite notation 107
Compositional map 158
Compositional sophistication 37
Compositional technique 37
Compound curve 173
Computer-controlled light-emitting diode (LED) screens 240
Concert hall design and instrument building 40
Concrete poetry 95
Concrete shell 42
Confining walls 102

Confucian ideology 194
Constructing with sound 64
Construction trailer conversions 8
Context 55
Contextual soundscape 53
Contextual sound piece 68
Continuous body movement 99
Continuous transition between two discrete states 32
Cook, Peter 216
Coolness 61
Cooper Union 170, 171
Cora, Tom 180
Corners, James 80, 84, 134
Creative priorities and hierarchies 89
Creative symbiosis 11
Crispness of sound 218
Criteria of a musical drawing 92
Cross-pollination between the arts 233
Crossroads 6
Cubist visual art 154
Cultural and musical sounds 65
Cultural phenomena 64
Culture 55
Culture of the visual 57
Curl 219
Czar Alexander the Great II 146

D

Dabrowski, Jaroslaw 155
Dahlhaus, Carl 223
Damsel with a dulcimer 145
Dance 95
Dancer-choreographer 95
Dance notation system 100
Darkness 64
Davenport, Iowa 12
Davis, Miles 16, 231, 232, 234, 236, 237, 244
  and *Bitches Brew* 241
Da Capo 8
Deafness 60
Degree of curviness 132
Designing visual sequences 104
Design process 64
Detection of body heat 100
De Stijl movement 172
Dialectics of instrument and architecture 14
Diatonic scale 236
Diebboll, Richard 173
Diffusion of music 41
Diffusion of sound 35
Digitally-manipulated ambient sound 160
Digital soundscape 159
Direction of the action 96
Direct sound recording 67
Dissociation between visual and aural perception 33
Distinction between symbol and drawing 92

287

Distribution of sound sources 40
Divergent thought mode 16
Diversity and richness of soundscape 64
Documenta 6 in Kassel 262
Doflein, Erich 223
Dominance of visual culture 63, 66
Domination of the emperor 204
Douglas fir 179
Duckworth, William 138
Dufay, Guillaume 254
Duration and dynamics 88
Duve, Thierry de 55
Dynamics 88
Dynamic and spatial visual art 38

E

Earth-harp installation 260
East-coast jazz 237
Eccentric couplings 265
Eclipse 152
École-des-Beaux-Arts 96
Ecstatic Architecture 178
Edges 102
Edge of creative tension 161
Edge of visual space 60
Edge symbols 121
Egypt 184
Eisenstein, Sergei 105
Ekha 5

Ekhe 5
Electro-acoustic music 37
Electro-magnets 265
Elements of soundscape 63, 68
Emperor Qianlong 15, 191-192, 194-197, 199, 201-204, 206-207
and poetry 205
Empirically-derived acoustic rhythm lines 160
Empirical objectivity 154
Enactment of a creative dualism 161
Enclosure 99
Eno, Brian 146
Environmental or sculptural actions 95
Environmental scoring technique 110
Environmental soundscape 160
En pleine air 148
Ephemeral architectures and virtual spaces 39
Epidauros 253, 256, 258, 259
Erhu 158
Ethnographic analysis 152
Euclidian space and acoustic space 38
Euler, Leonhard 256
Evolution of musical scores 77
Expansion of the realm of perception 55

Expectation and disruption 161
Experience Music Project 175, 178
EXPO '70 in Osaka, Japan 39, 146, 260
Expression 88
Expressive pitch-bending 235
Extravaganza or efficiency 37

F

Fabric of city streets 147
Fabrikshalle 217
Faded old red truck 178
Feeling space 58
Feel of a place 56
Feldman, Morton 146
Fender Mustang 177
Fender Stratocaster 178
Fernorchester 37
Fibonacci series 23, 24, 28, 255
Fifth (interval) 158
Fire engines 66
Florence Cathedral 254
Flute, western 152
Folded concrete walls 181
Folk 94
Footsteps 67
Forbidden City in Beijing, China 120, 192, 198

Forehead-mounted microvideo camera 106
Forms and spaces 170
Form and proportion in architecture and music 233
Form and structure 21
Fortissimo 158
Found objects 68
Fournier, Colin 216
Fourth (interval) 158
Free International University 262
Fret board 176, 177
Fridericianum 262
Fugue-like pattern 184
Fuller, Buckminster 182

G

Gabo, Naum 30
Gadgets 252
Galloping animals 253
Gambian *kora* 152
Garth Ancher 16
Gastmeier, Bill 72
Gebrauchsmusik 15, 222, 224, 225
Gehry, Frank O. 15, 148, 175-179, 181, 184-185
 and Chiat/Day office 148
 and Experience Music Project 149
 and Walt Disney concert hall 148

General morphology 34
Gentle cool breezes 57
Geography of a place 80
Geometric sound recording 67, 68
Geometry 70
Gewandhaus theater in Leipzig, Germany 258
Gibson, Benoît 13
Gibson, William 213
Gibson Les Paul 178
Gilded knobs 198
Glassblowers 66
Glissandi 31, 32
Goethe, Johann Wolfgang von 85
Golden Section 23-24, 29, 70, 255
Gorlin, Alexander 172
Granite 252
Graphic notation 31, 92-94, 158
Graphic score 93
Graph paper 28
Graves, Michael 173
Gravesano 41
Graz, Austria 215
Greek musical scales 214
Greek orders 214
Greenpeace 215
Grid-based rhythmic interpretation 158
Gropius, Walter 83
Grotto bath 252
Grounding ***ostinato*** 152
Guitar 158

Guitar strings 176
Gurgling fountains 57

H

Habermas, Jürgen 217
Hall, Edward 14, 83, 99
Halprin, Ann 95
Halprin, Lawrence 14, 108, 109, 110, 119
 and Motation Studies 110
Hanoch-Roe, Galia 13, 14
Hard bop, cool, modal, and fusion jazz 238
Harmonic manipulation of sensory experiences 57
Harmonic proportions 21
Harmony 87, 134, 215
Harmony between heaven and earth 196, 201
Harmony of natural and artificial rhythms 56
Harnoncourt, Nikolaus 218
Harp 182, 183
Harries, Karsten 227
Hartmann, Victor 146
Hauberstock-Ramati 91
Hegel, Georg Wilhelm Friedrich 232
HeHe 241
Hejduk, John 171
Hendrix, Jimi 149, 175, 177
Henry, Peter 72
Heschong, Lisa 61
Hierarchic forking paths 120

Highways 101
Highway experience and path experience 104
High priest 79
HIKEN™ Trail Notation 106, 107
History 55
Holistic experience of the path 134
Holistic scoring/notation system for designers 14
Holl, Steven 56, 70, 180, 233-234
  and Stretto House 70
Hollein, Hans 15, 173
Holy of holies 79
Homogenous diffusion of sound 41
Homophony 134
Honey flow 262
Horse-drawn carriage 66
Huangzhong 15, 199, 207
  and tonal measurement 191, 201, 202
Huangzhong melody 202
Huangzhong pipe 200, 201
  and origin of measurement 199
Human hearing range 264
Human intelligence in a particular state of crystallization 39
Human scale 55
Human voice 171

Humber College, Toronto 160
Humming 252
Hybrid music-architectures 265
Hyperbolic paraboloid 30, 32

I

Ideaogram 93
Identity 55
Ignace, Paul 91
Imagination 54
Immaterial and dynamic spaces 43
Immersion 40
Immersive experience 44
Imperial book on musical theory 197
Imperial Bureau of Music 197
Impromptu performance 252
Improvisation and performance 232
Improvised nature of modal scales 238
Inaudible sound 70
Independent melodic voices 134
Indeterminacy of forms 92
Indian *tabla* 152
Industrial and functional architecture 217
Infinite range of variation 94
Instrumental tapestry 14

291

Instrument as architecture 169
Instrument for listening 179
Intellectual and phenomenological realms 21
Intellectual and phenomenological resonance 13
Internal polymetric sensibility 158
International Orienteering Federation 106
International Style 30
Interpersonal communication 99
Interpretive sound piece 69
Intersection of music and architecture 12
Intersection of sound and space 13
Inveresk Railyards 231
Iowa State University 11
Isola, Stephen 171
Isolation 62
Isotropic acoustic space 44
Ito, Toyo 234

J

Jail guards 264
Japanese Steel Federation 39
Jarring binary opposition 161
Jazz 94
Jazz-rock fusion 231, 234, 241, 246
Jazz fusion 16
Jeffersonian democracy 220, 225
Jenny, Hans 256
Jiménez, Carlos 171
Johnson, Philip 79

K

Kahn, Louis 180, 181, 186
Keeley, Dennis 148
Keynote sounds 63, 68
Kinesthetic sensation 101
King of Bavaria 259
Kircher, Athanasius 185, 256
Koestler, Arthur 6
Kopfräume-Headscapes 263
Kora 183
Krog, Steven 84
Kulturhauptstadt 215
Kunsthaus 215
Kwenda, Forward 152

L

Laban, Rudolph von 96
Labanotation 97
Labanotation system 96
Landmarks 102, 116, 118, 125, 126
Laneway 155
Lang, Pe 265

Language addressed to the eyes and to the ears 33
Lantern 61
Larynx 171
Lascaux 16, 253
Launceston, Australia 231
Launceston School of Contemporary Music 16, 244
Leitner, Bernhard 13, 54, 62-63, 70, 263-264
Level 96
Le Corbusier 23-25, 27, 32-33, 83, 221
Libeskind, Daniel 15, 172, 174
Ligeti, György 89, 91
Lighting designer 95
Light actions 95
Light and shade 121
Light and shadow 57
Light and space 53
Light brix wall 241
Lim, Liza 178, 179
Linearity of perception in music and space 14
Linear recording 67
Liner as instrument 181
List, Helmut 216
Listening to the silence of the site 64
Little secret garden 79
Living City 221
Los Angeles Symphony 178
Lulu Zhengyi 201
Luminous Veil project 184
Lungs 171
Lute 182, 183
Lutz, Jim 14, 169
Lynch, Kevin 14, 63, 84-85, 101, 104, 112, 122-123
  and *The Image of the City* 81
Lyre 254

M

MacBurnie, Ian 14, 147, 149, 151, 160
Macintosh, Charles Rennie 172
Macy, Christine 72
Madan, Emmanuel 265
Mahler, Gustav
  and *Symphony Nr. 2* 37
Mandarendare 152
Mandrou, Robert 82
Maple 181
Marble 197
Marclay, Christian 180
Marionette theater 130, 131
Martin, Elizabeth 16
Martinez, Daniel J. 148
Materials and finishes 170
Mathematical principles 35
Matisse, Henri 180
Mausner, Claudia 14, 106, 107
Mahvash, Kourosh 13

Mbira ostinato 152, 154-155, 158
McIntosh, Thomas 265
Measuring with ears 64
Medieval and Renaissance scales 237
Meier, Richard 15, 173, 174
Melody 87, 235
Melos 223
Memory 67
   as mental recording device 68
Memory of the listener 86
Mental phenomena 64
Messiaen, Olivier 23-24
Metal fare box 159
Metal plates 265
Metaphorical lyricism 184
Meter 87, 161
Method of design based on sound 53
Method of observation 54
Metric proportions of spaces 255
Mezzo forte 158
Mezzo piano 158
Micro-rhythm 155
Middle Eastern *oud* 152
Minow, Martin 106
Mobile pavilion 41
Modal jazz 237-238, 241
Modulor 23-24, 26, 28-29, 33
Moerenuma Park in Japan 120

Monastery of La Tourette 27, 29
   and undulating glass panes 24, 33
Mondrian, Piet 92
Monophony 134
Monotony 121
Motion and rhythm 95, 111
Mott, David 152
Mount Abora 145
Mount Desert Island 119
Movement, motile perception and rhythm 77
Movement-Writing 99
Movement-Writing Alphabet 99
Movement actions 95
Mozart's Requiem 184
Mozart, Wolfgang Amadeus 184
Multi-sensorial experience 125
Multi-sensorial holistic experience 84
Multi-sensory spatial experience 57
Multifaceted spatial polyphony 37
Multisensory, physical, ocular and subjective experiences 78
Murinsel 216

Music
- and linearity 149
- and political functions 196
- and sonic potential 145
- as harmony between heaven and earth 196

Music, architecture, and the dramatic arts 258

Musical glass panes 33

Musical language 22

Musical notation system 28-29

Musical texture 158

Musical voicings and motifs 88

Music and architecture
- and mathematical proportions 22
- as spatial arts 22

Music and Architecture Research Institute (M.A.R.I.) 12

Music and dance 86

Music Architecture Sound Sculpture (M.A.S.S.) 260

Music as a matrix of ideas 39

Music Miriam 8

Music Technology Group at the Pompeu Fabra University in Barcelona 265

Music without a notation 113

Mussorgsky, Modest 146

Myer, John R. 101, 104, 122-123

Mysterious 118

Mystical music 60

Mythological sounds 63

N

Nan Feng 204

Nasal 94

Natural sounds 66

Nature as musician 185

Near versus distant focus of attention 101

Negative approach to acoustic design 62

Neo-Pythagorean wave 23

Nine heavens 198

Nine states, *jiu zhou* 198

Ninth heaven 198

Noguchi, Isamu 120

Non-hemitonic pentatone scale 236

Non-polarized reflection of sound waves 41

Non-visual approach to design 54

Northeast Expressway in Boston 101

Notational language 89

Notation system 14

Novak, Marcos 16

Numerical codes for scoring 100

Nuper Rosarum Flores 254

O

Objectification of music 223
Objectivity
 and music 147
Objectivity and precision of
 visual data 58
Oboe 171
Observation 64
Observation stage 64
Observer-listener 92
Octave 158
Odors 116
Ökostadt 215
Omnidirectional microphone
 68
Ong, Walter J. 14, 82, 147
Open-source software 265
Open and graphic scores 77
Open composition 89-91
Open score 94
Opera 79
Orchestration 161
Orchestrational palette 151
Organic geometry of musical
 instruments 42
Orthogonal co-ordinate
 system 28
Osaka, Japan 146
*Österreichs heimliche
 Liebe* 215
Ostinato 154, 155
Oswald, Peter 219

P

Pace, duration and duration
 relationships 87
Pace of movement 124
Pacing and space 99
Paleolithic-age cave art 253
Paleolithic artists 253
Paleolithic rock paintings 16
Paleolithic stone-tool makers
 253
Palladio, Andrea 255
Pallasmaa, Juhani 53
Panpipes 185
Parades 66
Parc de la Villette in Paris
 120
Parti 64, 70
Participatory envirotecture
 104
Part of the body moving 96
Path-note distance 115
Path event diagram 105
Path experience 112
Patterns of light and shadow
 56
Paul, Bruno 172
Pecan flooring 11
Pedal-lyre 173
Perceived physical aspects
 of the locale 55
Perceptual horizon 58
Perceptual response to
 sound 59
Perceptual tools 62

Perceptual way of design
 57, 59, 64
Percussion 152, 170
Percussive sounds 253
Pernthaler, Markus 15, 216,
 226
Persian garden 56
Pervasive sense of coolness
 57
Pesci, Joe 264
Phenomenological realities
 35
Philips Pavilion 31-32, 38-
 39, 41
 and Metastasis 32
Physical discomfort 84
Physical phenomena 64
Piano curve 173
Pictures at an Exhibition 146
Piermarini, Giuseppe 258
Pitch 159
Pitch-bending techniques
 236
Pitch and pitch relationships
 87
Pitch pipes 199
Pitch set 158, 160-161
Pizzicato 154
Place 64
 as cultural tie to ground,
  territory, and identity
  55
Placelessness 60
Plan views, diagrams and
 perspectives 82
Plastic bricks 241

Pleonasm 33
Poème Electronique 32
Pointillist approach 32
Point recordings 67
Police cars 66
Polykleitos 253
Polymath 185
Polymetric intellectual
 challenge 155
Polyphonic melodies 258
Polyphony 134
Polyphony of concurrent
 experiences 78, 111
Polytemporal structure 36
Position symbols 99
Power plants 66
Pre-recorded soundscape
 159
Process of building 57
Process of design 58, 68
Profane 57
Programme and site 64
Progressive music genres
 176
Protective windscreen 159
Proto-virtual listening
 situation 44
Proximity 40
Prunus 'Kanzan' 127
Purple Haze 177
Pythagorean idea of
 numerical proportions
 33

Q

Qianlong Era 192
Qing Dynasty 192, 201
Qing Jiao 204
Queen 501 154-155, 160-161
Queen Street, Toronto 14
Queen Victorian Museum and Art Gallery 232

R

Rashleigh, Patrick 160
reactable 265
Reading of a site 56
Reconceptualization of functionalism 16
Reed 170
Reflected sound 61
Reflecting pools 56
Reinterpretation and experimentation 231
Reinvention, adaptation and resourcefulness 231
Reinvention, resourcefulness, and adaptation 16
Relativistic dynamic gradation 158
Representation 68
Resonance 5, 16
Resonating chamber 42
Reunification of a paradoxically complementary pair 161
Reverberation between music and architecture 16
Reverberation of sound 61
Revington, Dereck 184
Revving car and motorcycle engine 159
Rhythm 87, 99, 112, 114, 121-123, 133, 233, 235
Rhythmic sound 61
Rhythmic swoosh of a street car door 159
Rhythm and density 26
Rhythm and motion 83
Riff-based rhythms of fusion 242
Ripley, Colin 147
Roads, paths and streams 81
Roll of thunder 59
Romanticism 184
Rothko Chapel 146
RSVP Cycle 108
Rudolf Ibach Sohn 173
Ruled surfaces 30, 34, 41
Rural commune 6
Ryerson University 12, 146, 152

S

Sacred 57
Sage-King 15, 191, 193-196, 204, 207
  and architecture 194
  and *king outside* 194

and music 196
and *sage inside* 194
Sands, John 15
Santa Monica 177
Sartre, Jean-Paul 213, 214
Savage, Niall 181
Sawmills 66
Saxophone 152
Scale 64, 65
    as human body, measure of all things 55
Scents of flowers and fruits 57
Schafer, R. Murray 13, 54, 59, 60, 62-63, 68, 71, 151
    and *The Tuning of the World and World Soundscape Project* 62
Scherchen, Herman 41
Schimmel 174
Schoenberg, Arnold 260
School of Contemporary Music at the University of Tasmania 231
Schopenhauer, Arthur 232
Schulz, Bernd 263
Scientific paradigms 34
Score
    as a design tool 95
Scoring device 95
Scoring symbols 87
Scoring system 101, 104, 111-113, 135

Scoring technique 95
Scoring techniques in music 96
Scoring the landscape path experience 135
Scoring the spatial linear experience 111
Scott, M. H. Baillie 172
Sculptor 95
Seating topographies 42
Sectional or planar recording 67
Seeing and hearing 58
Semantic communication between composer and performer 92
Semper, Gottfried 219, 259
Sensations of touch 104
Sense of delight in architecture 58
Sense of touch 70
Sensorial media 83
Sensory-based design 62
Sensory awakening 53
Sensory Garden 11
Sensory stimuli 58
Sensual *Gesamtkunstwerk* 259
Sensual stimuli 125
Sensuous experience of sound 23
Sensuous impact of sound 40
Shadow 64
Shakespeare Garden in

Central Park, NY 120

Shakespeare Garden path 127, 130
Shifting harmonies 159
Shift from oral to written speech 82
Shift from sound to visual space 82
Shipyards 66
Shi Ji 196
Shout scale 236
Shun Emperor 204
Sight
  and isolation 148
Signals 63, 68
Silence 63, 64, 265, 267
Silent reading 90
Silent reading of a score 86, 87
Silent speech 67
Silophone 266
Silo #5 266
Singing Ringing Tree 185
Sinus tones 264
Sirens 66
Sitar concert 6
Site 55
  and its full perception 56
Site-specificity 62
skene 253
Skyline 126
Sled 66
Slopes 124
Smells 99, 104
Smells, sounds, feelings
  of enclosure and openness 82
Smierzchalski, Tom 149, 151, 154
Social dimension of art 262
Soft spruce 181
Solar clock 131
Solar panels 217
Solid hardwood 218
Sonic environments 159
Sonic rendering 147
Sonic translation 155
Sonorous environment for house music 11
Sound
  and incorporation 148
  and sensory associations 61
  and the creative process of design 53
  as generator for the visual arts 253
  as material 54
  as material and medium 68
  as medium 64
  as theme and material of design 63
  as unifying sense 148
Sound-altered environment 263
Sound-based design exercises 62
Sound/space experiment 263
soundaXis 146

Soundforge software 160
Sounding universe 64
Soundmarks 63, 68
Soundscape 63, 159, 160
Soundscape recording 67
Soundscape timbres 161
Sounds of awareness 66
Sounds of a site 55
Sounds of buildings 66
Sounds of movement 66
Sounds of people 65
Sounds of utopia 63
Sound actions 95
Sound and noise 263
Sound and space 35
Sound awareness 71
Sound classification systems 63
Sound collage 69
Sound diffusion 35
Sound of rain pelting against leaves 59
Sound of sirens 264
Sound of smoldering coals 32
Sound pollution 83
Sound reduction 62
Space 64
  as cultural consensus on the perceptive grid of references 55
Space-time 30, 93
Space-time systems 37
Spatial awareness and aural attention 40
Spatial design 95

Spatial distribution of sound sources 38
Spatial envelopes 41
Spatial experience of sound 255
Spatial linearity 86
Spatial sequences 78
Spatial sound instrument 69
Spatio-temporal arts 95
Spindle 182
Spiral gangway 42
Spiritual awakening 60
Spontaneity and movement 88
Spontaneity and randomness 237
Spontaneous and random nature of fusion 242
Sports events 66
Static visual depictions 77
Stave 87
Stave system 96
Sterken, Sven 13
Stick figure 99
Stimmung 261
Stockhausen, Karlheinz 14, 35, 88-89, 137, 146, 260
Stradivarius, Antonio 181
Street car 159
Stretto House 233, 234
String
  as minister 204
Stringed instruments 170, 179
String of pearls 219

Structure and mechanics 170
Subjectivity
 and asthetic choice 147
Successive perception of
 volumes and spaces 33
Suicide barrier 184
Sunny dome 145, 161
Sunrise 56
Sunset 56
Supra-sensory perceptual
 aspects 53
Supreme power of the
 emperor 198
Surround sound system 60
Suspension of time 86
Sutton, Valerie 96, 99
Sutton system 99
Swing style of jazz 237
Sympathetic resonance 252
Symphony 79
Synergistic relationship of
 music and architecture 171
Synthesis of rationalism and
 metaphysics 21
Syrinx 185
System of tonal
 measurement 15

T

Tape-recorder 67
Taxonomy of sounds 63
Tectonics of buildings

And musical instruments 169
Tempo 87, 161
Tempo, dynamics, touches,
 and atmosphere 89
Temporal theories of music 77
Tensegrity structures 241, 242
Tensile and compressive
 forces 182
Tetrachord 254
Theater of Performing Arts 180
Thermal Baths in Vals,
 Switzerland 16, 251
The *Great Gate of Kiev* 146
Thiel, Philip 14, 104-105, 111
Three-dimensional acoustic
 grid 38
Tianjin University 198
Timelessness 60
Timing 96
Titanium inlay 174
Tonkin Liu 184-185
Toronto
 and Beaches 149
 and Danforth-Coxwell 149, 158
 and Humber Park 149, 158
 and multicultural landscape 151
 and Parksdale 149
 and Queensway corridor 151

and Queen Street 149
Total sensory immersion 62
Touch-me Art
  and TOM Gallery 57
Trachea 171
Traffic 80
Train 66
Transport hierarchy 123
Trauma of loss of hearing 60
Trauma of loss of sight 60
Treib, Mark 84
Triumvirate
  of Euro-North American,
      Chinese, and African
      cultures 152
Tschumi, Bernard 120
Tuan, Yi-Fu 56, 60, 73
Tubular brass handrail 252

U
Unconscious 10
Unidirectional microphone 68
United Nation 215
University of Chicago 6
University of Florida 8, 11
Ur-impulse 219
Ural 184
Utter vulnerability 252

V
Vagueness 58
Valéry, Paul 21
  and *Eupalinos ou l'
architecte* 21

Valkenburgh's Mill Race Park 119
Vallon des Roches 253
Vals Thermal Baths 253
Van der Rohe, Mies
  and Crown Hall 261
Varga, Andras Balint 35
Variation in densities 33
Venart, Catherine 72
Venetian School 37
Véret, Jean-Louis 41
Vernallis, Carol 154
Vibration 70
Vibrato 236
Violin 181, 200
Violin case 181
Visual
  as antagonist 53
Visual and kinesthetic
    senses 81
Visual translation of sound 145
Vitruvius 214, 253, 254
Vocal tuning 252
Voice loudness 100
Voyeur 243
Vulnerability to sound 59

W
Wagner, Richard 259
Waller, Stephen J. 253
Walt Disney Concert Hall 178, 180

Wang, Yidan 149, 151, 154
Water 252
Water-control system 192
Webb, Craig 176
West-African music 234-236
West-African slaves 235
Western European music 235
Western guitar 154
Whirling dervishes
 and Sufism 60
Whistling of wind in tall grass 59
Wind chime 61
Winter solstice 197
Wittkower, Rudolf 254
Woodwind 170
Wreath 219
Wright, Frank Lloyd 15, 79, 119, 220, 222, 225
Writing
 as non-conventional method 68

X

Xenakis, Iannis 13, 22, 146, 260
 and *Arts/Sciences Alliages* 34
 and *City of Music* 23, 41
 and *Concret PH* 32, 40
 and *Hibiki Hana Ma* 39
 and *La Légende d' Eer* 41
 and *Le Sacrifice* 24, 25
 and *Metastasis* 27-29
 and *Metastasis* as sonic interpretation 31
 and *Musique Architecture* 22
 and *Nomos Gamma* 37
 and *Notes sur un geste Electronique* 38, 44
 and *Persephassa* 37
 and *Polytopes* 33
 and *Terretektorh* 36

Y

Yellow Emperor 204
Yi, Dai 192
Yonge Street 155
York University 151
Yoshida 61
Young, Roland 148
Yuanming, Tao 206, 207

Yue Ji 196

Z
Zhang
 and reduced length 198
Zhang, Yu 15, 191
Zhi, Han Shu Lu Li 199
Zimoun 265
Zither 184, 204
 with five strings 204
Zither Rhythm Studio 15, 191-192, 194-195, 197, 202, 205-207
 and garden architecture 195
 and waterfall 203
Zither without strings 206
Zumthor, Peter 16, 251, 260, 261

Books now available from Culicidae Press
http://www.culicidaepress.com

Our current bestseller is Miriam Zach's *For the Birds: Women Composers' Music History Speller, Volume 1*, the first book that teaches children and adults how to read music by combining twenty-five biographies of women composers throughout history with music notation examples and several quiz sections. This is the first of several volumes Zach is working on. The book is available as a softcover, 80 pages, 8.5 x 11.0 in., ISBN 1-4116-3355-5 through www.culicidaepress.com and www.lulu.com

David Otieno Akombo's new book *Music and Healing Across Cultures*, in which the author unfolds the mechanics of the relationship between music, healing, and the cosmos is available as a 6.0 x 9.0 in. paperback (ISBN 978-1-4116-8931-2) at www.lulu.com, the world's fastest-growing provider of print-on-demand books.

Opus 28, Emily – A House Organ by A. David Moore is available now as a 7.5 x 7.5 in. book that chronicles the commission, design, construction, and installation of a portable one-manual four-rank house organ by the premier pipe organ builder A. David Moore from Pomfret, Vermont.

Books now available from Culicidae Architectural Press
http://www.cularchpress.com

An updated reprint of Mikesch Muecke's dissertation from Princeton University, published through Culicidae Architectural Press as *Gottfried Semper in Zurich: An Intersection of Theory and Practice*, is available now through Lulu as a 6.0 x 9.0 in. paperback book with illustrations and an index. This book is also available through Amazon.com

Essays on Architecture and Other Topics by Mikesch Muecke is available through Lulu as a 6.0 x 9.0 in. paperback book (includes illustrations and index). The book contains twelve texts on a variety of topics that engage architecture, history, theory, philosophy, and popular culture. There are four thematic sections: Architecture & Mobility, Philosophy & Aesthetics, Case Studies, and History, Theory, and Practice in Gottfried Semper's Work. An extensive bibliography completes this book designed primarily for scholars.

Mikesch Muecke's *Personal Views/Persönliche Ansichten*, is a bi-lingual (English and German) book of evocative and poetic color photographs accompanied by short descriptions that link the visual narrative to ideas about site, landscape, family, economy, and culture—among others. The book is available as an 8.5 x 11.0 in. paperback (ISBN 1-4116-3262-1), and also as a downloadable eBook version at www.lulu.com

A pamphlet-style book (7.5 x 7.5 in. paperback) about a condominium kitchen renovation for a nonagenerian retiree in Florida. Available now at Lulu.com.

The book describes a design/build project by misumiwaDesign from 2003, transforming a 1970s kitchen to 21st-century standards for a disabled and retired music teacher. The book chronicles the decision-making process through design sketches, CAD drawings, demolition, construction, and final installation/in-use photographs, and a descriptive text.

Also available is the most recent publication by misumiwaDesign about the renovation of a bathroom suite in the same condominium that already saw the transformation of the kitchen mentioned on the left. This book includes full-color illustrations of design sketches and drawings as well as demolition, construction, and in-use photographs.

Forthcoming books from Culicidae Press

A book that teaches the reader how to draw precise freehand perspectives by architect and retired architecture professor (University of Florida) Harry Merritt will be available in the Summer of 2007.

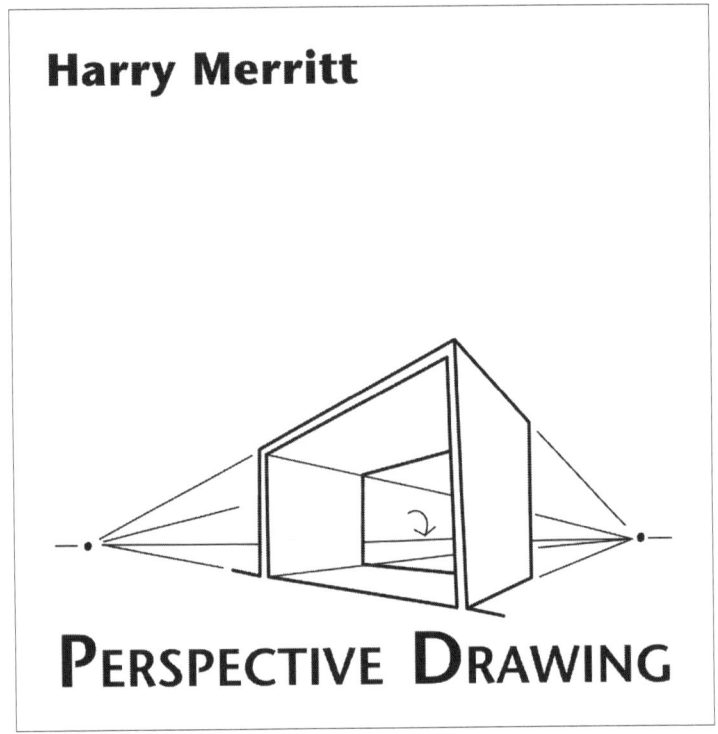

German/Italian author Stefanie Golisch' dark and humorous novel *Pyrmont*, about the mid-life crisis of a women who is encouraged after a nervous breakdown to visit a spa town for recuperation—followed by unintended consequences—will be available in the Summer of 2007. Originally published in German, this book will offer English-speaking readers for the first time a taste of Golisch' writing talent. For more information go to http://www.stefaniegolisch.net

Printed in Great Britain
by Amazon.co.uk, Ltd.,
Marston Gate.